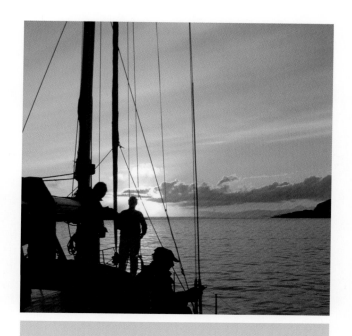

CRUISING SCOTLAND
The Clyde to Cape Wrath

CRUISING SCOTLAND
The Clyde to Cape Wrath

*A Companion to the
Clyde Cruising Club Sailing Directions*

Mike Balmforth & Edward Mason

Clyde Cruising Club Publications

First published in 2010 by:
Clyde Cruising Club Publications Ltd.
Suite 101 The Pentagon Centre
36 Washington Street
Glasgow G3 8AZ
Scotland
Tel: 0141 2212774
Email: hazel@clyde.org
www.clyde.org

ISBN 978-1-899786-00-8

Designed and typeset by Clyde Cruising Club Publications Ltd.
Printed by Centric Print Solutions Ltd. Milnthorpe, Cumbria, LA7 7LR
Bound by Hunter & Foulis Bookbinders, Scotland

CAUTION

This book has been written as a general guide and should not be used for navigation. Skippers requiring navigational information should consult the relevant volume of the Clyde Cruising Club Sailing Directions and current Admiralty charts, pilots and other hydrographic data.

Cover: *The anchorage on the southern side of the spit between Eilean Orasaidh and Lewis, Loch Mariveg, one of several in this sheltered lagoon.*

Frontispiece: *A yacht's crew enjoy the long northern twilight whilst anchored in Bagh Gleann nam Muc on the Jura side of Corryvreckan.*

Title pages: *A solitary Starlight 35 at anchor in the small inlet to the west of Rubh' Ardalanish, Ross of Mull.*

Opposite: *The anchorage behind Goat Island in Loch Craignish is very popular, giving good shelter and good holding.*

Contents

Foreword

BUCKINGHAM PALACE

I wish to congratulate the Flag Officers, committee and members of the Clyde Cruising Club on the occasion of the Centenary of the Club.

For many years the Club has been of great service to yachtsmen cruising the West Coast of Scotland through the publication of its widely known and respected 'Sailing Directions and Anchorages' which covers this magnificent cruising ground. These are waters for which I have always had a great love, ever since first seeing them as a child from the deck of HMY BRITANNIA, when sailing in BLOODHOUND and now sailing in BLUE DOUBLET, which never goes to sea without a full set of Clyde Cruising Club Directions onboard.

I can think of no better way of marking the Club's Centenary than publishing a book which celebrates this very special part of our coastline, and which you are privileged to be able to call your home waters and thanks to your regular publications, so many more people can also enjoy.

I wish the book every success and may the Club continue to prosper throughout its second century.

Anne

Opposite: *The peaks of Sgurr Dubh Mor and Sgurr Dubh Beag tower above a Moody 376 anchored in Loch na Cuilce, Skye. The traverse between the two is one of the classic scrambles in the Cuillin.*

Preface

I have been very much aware of the need for a book such as this since becoming involved with the Clyde Cruising Club Sailing Directions, as in our efforts to provide the navigator with clear, concise directions, hopefully condensed into a single page for each anchorage, it is often necessary to omit much of the interesting and useful additional information by which a cruise on the west coast of Scotland and the Hebrides is greatly enhanced. After all, who, when fast approaching an unfamiliar anchorage, wants to wade through pages of absorbing but extraneous detail recounting the deeds of the MacLeods or the whereabouts of the nearest good hotel, when something resembling a rock has appeared in what you thought was the fairway and the helmsman is pleading for instant instructions? Likewise, it has not been possible to illustrate the Sailing Directions in the manner that such a magnificent coastline deserves, and which the latest printing technology now allows. This book sets out to rectify the above omissions in a format designed for a more leisurely appreciation, once the anchor is securely down, of what might be in store for tomorrow.

Many books have been written about the west coast of Scotland. Some have dealt with special aspects of the area but only a few have been written with the sailor in mind. *The Whisky Run, A Cruising Man's Guide to the West Coast of Scotland and Hebridean Waters* by Jim Andrews, originally published as a series of articles in *Practical Boat Owner*, was an introduction to west coast cruising and was the inspiration for this new book. It was produced by the CCC well over thirty years ago and its text referred to the Club's Sailing Directions throughout.

I somehow came by a copy of it in the early 1970s, and after reading it rapidly, for it was only forty pages, I decided that I simply had to go and find out for myself why the west coast of Scotland drew people to it time and again. We chartered on the Clyde the following year and I, my family and my friends, have returned to the west coast every year since.

Now, on the occasion of the Club's centenary, it seems to be the right time for a new guide, a Companion to the Sailing Directions, to be published. If it encourages just a single family to do what we did, it will have achieved one of its aims. I also hope it will encourage a great many others to expand their cruising horizons within these unrivalled waters. For old hands who know the area well the photographs will help them to recall their own experiences, and the extracts from accounts written by our predecessors will enable them to see their place within the continuing tradition of sailing in one of the world's finest cruising grounds.

We are fortunate in having as a member of the Club Mike Balmforth, who is, amongst other things, a writer and yachting journalist. Mike has written the bulk of the text, and I am grateful to him for doing this so thoroughly, and also for agreeing with my editorial adjustments.

Opposite: One of a pair of idyllic anchorages on the east side of Pabay Mor, West Loch Roag, Lewis.

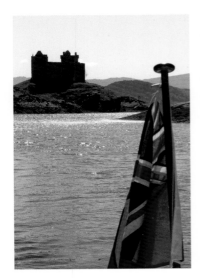

Mike observes: 'cruising Scotland's west coast was a boyhood ambition, which during a career in yachting publishing, and in other aspects of the leisure marine industry, I was fortunate to realise in good measure. Like Edward, I had long thought that a Cruising Companion for our home waters was well overdue and the meeting of minds that resulted in this book was fortunate indeed. It has been a pleasure to help it become a reality. Another important part of the catalyst has been the CCC's willingness to take an initiative that no commercial publisher had been prepared to take. I, too, hope that this book will either bring back good memories or inspire future exploration of our superb west coast. When doing the research I certainly recalled many happy times spent sailing in our ever-varying waters.'

My own role, apart from general editing, has been to make some contributions to the text, source all the photographs, and to do the design and layout work. Both of us have benefited greatly from the help and encouragement that we have received from Arthur Houston, who has also done much research and preliminary proof reading, ably assisted by Jimmy and Gillian Dinsmore. Iain Macleod kindly agreed to produce the Gaelic glossary, which he did promptly and efficiently and I thank him for this. I must also acknowledge the valuable professional help that we have received from Dr. James Deboo, a proof reader who fortunately also happens to sail on the west coast, and the unfailing support of our printer, Geoff Thould of Centric Print Solutions, who has given advice from the earliest stages of the project and to whom nothing but perfection is acceptable.

I would especially like to thank H.R.H. The Princess Royal, the Clyde Cruising Club's most recently elected Honorary Member, for kindly agreeing to write the Foreword to this book and I trust that it will earn a place on *Blue Doublet*'s bookshelf this coming season.

Well over half the photographs have been taken by Club members and their friends, and without their input we could never have afforded to illustrate the book so lavishly. I am indebted to all of them. Their names are listed in the photographic credits in the Appendix, but I will make special mention of John Anderson and Steve Goldthorp, who between them submitted the lion's share of the photographs, all of which were artistically and technically flawless. Whilst on the subject of photographs, I must admit that we have a preponderance of blue skies and seas that perhaps does not tell the whole story. In my defence, I would counter that it would be a poor editor or photographer who did not seek to portray their subject in the best light but, sadly, we all know that the sun does not shine incessantly.

However, I will leave the last word to Ronald Faux, writing in his excellent book *The West*: 'The West often requires a stoic spirit and a keen appreciation of shades of grey but such bad days are always relieved by times when the sun puts a bright sparkle on the Hebridean sea, when the breeze is steady, the tide is under the stern and sailing among the islands is a delight. In those conditions the islands are unforgettable and most enjoyably explored in a small cruising boat'.

Edward Mason
Editor, Clyde Cruising Club Sailing Directions.   March 2010

Introduction

Sailing Directions – A brief history

'Sailing directions to the west coast of Scotland have a unique flavour. "Keep the left side of the white farmhouse in line with the stone wall to clear the reef," is one. "When the last two letters on the wall of the distillery disappear behind the 14th century castle, it's safe to enter the bay," is another.'

I prefer Scotch off the rocks, Adrian Morgan, *The Independent,* 18th August 2002

Man must have been using similar methods of keeping off the Scottish rocks ever since he first floated off in his *currach* and no doubt he scratched helpful diagrams on the leather skin with which it was covered.

Little is known of how the Vikings managed to navigate long distances over open water using mainly the sun and only rudimentary instruments, possibly including the legendary 'sunstone'. However, having achieved a landfall they must have relied on silhouettes, transits and keeping a good lookout. Their manoeuvrable, shallow draft boats were well suited to inshore pilotage, their preferred method of voyaging, and they would have felt very much at home on the Scottish west coast with its many prominent shore marks. How their knowledge was recorded is not known, but much was probably passed on by word of mouth, the best way of ensuring that it did not fall into the wrong hands, though it is inconceivable that they would not have attempted to draw rough plans and diagrams on whatever came to hand.

The oldest surviving sailing directions for Scottish waters, or rutter (derived from router), were compiled in 1540, or possibly earlier, by Alexander Lindsay, acting on instructions from James V. The area covered in these directions extended from the Humber anti-clockwise around Scotland to the Solway Firth and was divided into four coastal sections. The information given in each section included tidal streams, times of high water, soundings, anchorages, distances, courses and dangers, following the common style of European sailing directions from the mid-14th century (and still followed today by the Admiralty Pilots). Lindsay's rutter was probably used by King James' fleet of 16 or 17 ships in 1540 when, after several postponements (once because of the impending birth of the future Mary, Queen of Scots) it sailed around Scotland.

In the 18th century more accurate instruments and a wider knowledge of the mathematics of surveying led to charts, as we would know them, being produced and, in the case of the Admiralty, it was the Hebrides that came first. This was a direct result of the Jacobite rising of 1745 when, in the aftermath of Culloden, the Royal Navy had to patrol the Minches for five months in an attempt to intercept either the Prince or the French warships that were sent to rescue him. They were unsuccessful on both counts, but it must have been the

complaints in the reports from our naval captains, hampered by a lack of reliable charts and local knowledge, that persuaded the Admiralty that something should be done. The result was that from 1748 to 1757 Captain Murdoch MacKenzie diligently surveyed the whole of the west coast of Scotland and the islands and produced a series of charts that were far ahead of anything else available at the time. Much later, in 1776, he followed this with his first Sailing Directions for the west coast: *A Nautical Description.*

The next major leap forward was when Captain Henry Otter carried out his surveys of the Outer Hebrides between 1846 and 1860 and produced his celebrated charts which some yachtsmen still refer to today. Many areas of the current metric charts are based on his data and he achieved a remarkable degree of accuracy, considering the equipment used and the conditions under which they were produced. They, and the first edition of the West Coast of Scotland Pilot, published in 1867 and which was largely based on his work, set the standard for the next hundred years.

The first amateur cruising yachtsmen of the Victorian era made use of the Admiralty's charts and Sailing Directions – indeed they had to, as there was little else – until Frank Cowper came along at the end of the century. He realised that the new breed of amateur cruising sailors, who sailed their boats themselves, without the help of professionals, needed something slightly less austere than the Admiralty tomes and set out in 1890 to produce the first of five volumes of his *Sailing Tours,* which would eventually cover all the British coast and much of the French channel coast as well. His last volume, *The Clyde to the Thames Round North* is quoted once or twice in this book and for those who would like to read more, all five volumes were reprinted in facsimile in 1985 and can still be found.

Opposite upper: *The anchorage in Loch na Cuilce looking out into Loch Scavaig.*

Opposite lower: *Loch nan Uamh looking south east from the anchorage in the Borrodale Islands. It was in this loch, in May 1746, that two ships of the Royal Navy engaged two French warships in what was, effectively, the last battle of the '45.*

Despite the prodigious amount of work that Cowper put into his books they were not universally acclaimed and C.C. Lynam, another pioneering amateur on the west coast who is also quoted in this book, criticised them heartily and publicly, resulting in the famous court case in which Cowper was awarded one penny damages. Possibly others agreed with Lynam, as when the Clyde Cruising Club was founded in 1909 one of its principal aims was 'to help the cruiser to a greater knowledge concerning the vital things of the cruising ground'.

This aim was duly realised by the inclusion of an instalment of the Sailing Directions and Anchorages forming an appendix to all four Club Journals produced before 1914. After the war they were published in book form in 1922 and continued in a very similar format but with ever-expanding content until the tenth edition of 1974. About this time Admiralty charts were being metricated and the area covered by the CCC Sailing Directions had been expanded to take in the north and north east coasts of Scotland and the Orkney and Shetland Islands, so the opportunity was taken to change to A4 format with a totally new layout and to publish them in six volumes. This format and the titles adopted then continue in use to this day.

However, in the mid 1980s, competition emerged in the form of *The Yachtsman's Pilots,* written by Martin Lawrence and published by Imray, Laurie, Norie and Wilson, who themselves were no strangers to Scottish waters, one of their founders, Robert Laurie, having published a chart of the Orkneys in 1794. These new books, using at first two colours and later full colour with many photographs, raised the standard yet again, a challenge to which the CCC responded once the advent of desktop publishing and digital printing allowed them to do likewise at reasonable cost.

No doubt the fast-moving technology of the publishing world will bring about further changes before long – the contents of some Sailing Directions are already available as a part of chart plotter packages – but until a reliable digital reader is produced at a reasonable price that can be sat on, dropped, trodden on and read in bright sunlight or pouring rain and with a battery that will last the season, the CCC will continue to produce Sailing Directions printed on paper!

Passage planning

The west coast of Scotland has a coastline approximately equal in length to that of the rest of Britain, so it is not surprising that it is regularly counted amongst the world's finest cruising grounds.

These deserved superlatives describe the very special features of the region, which could have been tailor-made for boating recreation. The Clyde is sheltered by the Mull of Kintyre, and the seas to the west are almost entirely sheltered from the Atlantic by the Outer Hebrides. The scenery – mountains and sea lochs in close proximity – is spectacular, and with deep water virtually everywhere, pilotage is mostly a matter of avoiding the odd unmarked rock!

Once away from the mainland, the Inner Hebrides is near wilderness – few villages, sparse or no population – meaning abundant wildlife everywhere, and a complete sense of escape from the rest of the world. You don't have to cross oceans to find solitude, it is widely available on Scotland's west coast.

Although we deal with some more detailed aspects of cruise planning in each of the main sections that follow, the general principles that should be in the back of every cruising sailor's mind are that Scotland's west coast distances are quite short, and sheltered anchorages are plentiful. What are not so plentiful, especially as one ventures north and west, are marinas and boatyards, so planning should be built around a degree of self-reliance, whether that be in respect of fuel, stores, crew or repairs.

It goes without saying that careful scrutiny of distances and tides, together with the best weather information that can be obtained, will be most likely to lead to successful passages and therefore a successful cruise. Working the tides, especially in the inner Sounds and Kyles, is not only important, it also gives a great sense of satisfaction after a swift sail.

However, many cruise programmes are predicated by destination, whether that be getting to Cape Wrath and further north, out to St Kilda, or just getting back to base when time is running out. In these situations there is always the risk of a day or two of adverse weather, so building some reserve time into the itinerary is prudent.

Free spirit cruising, or more accurately free wind cruising, is the alternative for the more relaxed holiday sailor. Take each day as it comes, sail with the wind behind you, and explore ashore when conditions do not promise a pleasant day at sea. Less derring-do, more Xanadu!

In practical terms, a pit stop will be needed once or twice a week for stores, so identifying these places will dictate the nodes in an otherwise loose itinerary. A good guide in this respect is the free publication *Welcome Anchorages*, which is available from marinas and marine companies all over Scotland, or by downloading from www.welcomeanchoregesscotland.com.

Weather

A comparison of the climate data in the Admiralty Pilots for The West Coast of Scotland and The English Channel puts this topic in perspective for many visitors. The mean daily maximum and minimum July temperatures are 11° to 16°C at Tiree and 14° to 18°C at Portland Bill. The mean August sea temperature is 3° lower than in the English Channel, the frequency of fog is less, and summer wind direction is more varied than the predominant south to west of southern waters in summer. There is a slightly greater occurrence of winds of Force 7, but no greater incidence of gales – one gale day per month in both cases.

The biggest difference is in cloud and rain. Although some of the immediate coastal areas are quite wet – indeed Ben Nevis, at the head of Loch Linnhe, receives Britain's highest rainfall – the island rainfall is in the 55–90mm monthly range from May to August. Portland's rainfall over the same months is 51–61mm. As a rule, the further west you sail, the drier the weather is likely to be, as the low lying islands do not produce clouds to the same extent. Indeed, the annual rainfall at Tiree, the furthest west of the Inner Hebrides, is just over 1,000 mm; at Oban, only 45 miles away, it is 50 per cent higher!

Most of the time the weather is variable. A wet and windy day will be followed by a fine nor'westerly, as the succession of lows and ridges march across the country. At other times, when low pressure is further south, the west coast enjoys successive days of easterly winds, with long days of sunshine.

But enough statistics! Those who already cruise the area know its vagaries, and those who first visit should try May and June, when the weather is often superb, although paradoxically offset by quite low temperatures when the weather is at its high pressure finest. In mid-June the sun sets for less than six hours, and in fine weather it does not really get dark, so that it is possible, when in the north west islands, to read in the cockpit at midnight by natural light!

Storm clouds over the moorings at Castlebay, Barra.

Communications

Communications, be they social, for business, or to obtain weather and safety information, have improved dramatically over the past decade, largely due to an excellent mobile phone network (provided one is using Vodafone or O2), the recent improvements in Navtex, and the installation of a better network of coastguard transmitters. On the other hand, 3G coverage for mobile devices is almost non-existent (2010) in the area, regardless of network.

Public broadcast reception is also generally good, both on VHF and long wave, and BBC Radio Scotland also transmits on medium wave. Irish long wave and VHF forecasts are particularly useful in southern parts.

The caveat is, however, that thanks to the topography there are areas where radio reception is poor, or non-existent.

Facilities

One of the attractions of cruising in Scotland is the combination of good facilities, such as marinas and boatyards, in some areas and the complete absence of them in others. The convenience of marinas and short term berthing facilities makes many practical aspects of cruising much easier, but being able to escape to a quiet anchorage just a short distance away is the charm and essence of the west coast.

The heartland of west coast cruising lies between Crinan and Tobermory, with the lochs of the mainland coast to the east, and the islands of Jura, Colonsay and Mull to the west. These, together with the smaller isles further west, like Iona, Staffa, the Treshnish Isles and a score of others, are a boating paradise of short passages, interesting pilotage, sheltered anchorages and almost totally unspoiled scenery and undisturbed wildlife.

Within this 40 mile circle, there are over a hundred anchorages, and more than a dozen centres with facilities. It has the scope for almost any kind of seagoing holiday, from a tour of fine waterside restaurants or 'interesting' golf courses, to playing 'island hop-scotch' away from the crowd. In the Clyde there is a greater availability of services and facilities, and conversely, as you sail north and west of Ardnamurchan and Skye they diminish to almost nothing.

The moorings in the bay at Tayvallich.

Anchoring

This subject could occupy a substantial book, as there have never been more types of anchor on the market, or more methods of using them advocated. Here, however, we are not telling you how to do it, or with what, but rather we highlight the challenges that might face the cruising sailor, and suggest how best to plan for them.

The first topic is type of seabed. Scotland's topography is just as varied underwater as above it, and every kind of seabed will be encountered. Good anchorages, like anywhere else, will have a mud or sand bottom, but many others will offer a greater challenge as you try to anchor on rock, loose shingle, or, in the ultimate challenge, kelp. Other more difficult scenarios include varying depths within an anchorage, and sometimes lack of swinging room. On the other hand, anchorages are seldom crowded, few have any current to complicate matters, and the tidal range is small.

For Scottish cruising you need the right gear, and to know how to use it. If you cannot enjoy anchoring in out-of-the-way places, much of the point of cruising in these waters will be lost. However, the Clyde Cruising Club Sailing Directions distil the experience of thousands of cruising sailors over a century, and provide exactly the information needed for any given anchorage.

The second topic is shelter and weather. Many anchorages are vulnerable to winds from certain direction, so having a good weather forecast is essential when selecting the best place for a peaceful night. In bad weather the surrounding land can also affect matters: anchorages near hills and mountains may seem sheltered, but once the wind gets up you can be assailed by gusts many times stronger than the general wind speed. The most extreme example of this is in Loch Scavaig on the south side of Skye, where the Cuillin mountains tower thousands of feet above the sea.

The third topic is selection of gear. This involves the usual compromise between weight and ease of handling. As a general rule, having heavier rather than lighter anchor and chain will give better holding and peace of mind, but above a certain weight a windlass is highly desirable. This is not a matter of being work-shy: it is a safety item that will enable you to re-anchor when you

don't feel like it, but know you should, and to enjoy more easily short stops en route. Finally, you should have a second anchor and rode on board, and also an anchor buoy and tripping line. You will then be equipped for most eventualities. Finally, what design of anchor should you buy? All we can say is: talk to as many fellow sailors and do as much research as possible before deciding.

Opposite: Yachts berthed against the wavescreen on the north side of the ferry pier at Scalasaig, Colonsay.

Travel to and within Scotland

Whether it is for crew changing, getting to a charter yacht, or planning to base your yacht in Scotland for a while, researching Scotland's travel infrastructure is important and the website www.travelinescotland.com will be found to be very helpful for planning journeys using all forms of public transport.

There are good air connections to both Glasgow and Prestwick airports and from Glasgow onward to Barra, Benbecula and Stornoway. From both airports travel to the Clyde coast or further north can either be by car, rail or bus, with good regular services from Glasgow to all the main ferry ports by the latter. All the marinas on the mainland Clyde coast are relatively close to rail stations, and rail coastal access points further north are at Oban, Fort William, Mallaig and Kyle of Lochalsh. These latter routes are classed among the 'great railway journeys of the world', and are a good introduction to Scotland's coastal and mountain scenery. Driving north to west central Scotland is an all-motorway experience, and although the roads to the west coast north of Glasgow are generally good, they can be slow during busy holiday periods.

A significant number of yachtsmen now base their craft in Scotland, often for several seasons, which sometimes stretch to many more! The attractions of cheaper berthing than in many other parts of Britain and Ireland, and arguably better sailing waters, has boosted this trend as more people discover the benefits.

Research into travel and berthing is easily done on the internet, and a good starting point is the *Sail Scotland* website, www.sailscotland.co.uk, or the *Sail Scotland* brochure, both of which offer much key information.

With the mountains of Rum in the background, an entrant in the 'Classic Malts Cruise' heads slowly north towards Skye, where the day will no doubt be rounded off with a glass of the local waters!

1 Firth of Clyde
and Approaches

The Firth of Clyde, one of the largest expanses of sheltered water in Europe, has been used for sailing and boating for centuries. Recreational sailing developed from the wealth created by shipbuilding and engineering around Glasgow, but although the Royal Northern Yacht Club was founded in 1824 and the Royal Clyde Yacht Club in 1856, cruising, such as it was in those days, was an activity for individuals and the Clyde Cruising Club did not come into being until the autumn of 1909.

The practice of yacht cruising began around the same time as the earliest clubs, as gentleman adventurers bought or chartered fishing or trading smacks in order to explore the coast and view their country from a different perspective. In a few cases preaching religion to the natives was the object, but that practice has unsurprisingly died out!

Jane, CCC, 1952.

The Clyde estuary's numerous islands, many small towns and sheltered anchorages offer an attractive and safe place to sail, but the Clyde is also important as a base for wider cruising activity. The remainder of Scotland's west coast is accessible through the Crinan Canal, as is the east coast and Scandinavia via the Forth & Clyde and Caledonian Canals. Ireland and the northern Irish Sea are approximately a day's sail away.

Sailing in the Firth of Clyde splits into four areas, enabling the sailor to find water that is suited to his boat, level of experience, the weather and crew ability. The east shore has the majority of the large marinas used for permanent berthing, good transport links and easy access from centres of population. The western areas generally offer destinations; places where sailors wish to visit, varying from secluded anchorages to harbours with pontoons and village amenities.

Coire Uisge, CCC, 2009.

Upstream the River Clyde and its sea lochs are well suited to powered craft and smaller sailing yachts, with the city of Glasgow again turning its face to the river and seeking to attract more activity on the water. Berthing facilities which now exist close to Glasgow city centre will enable a cruising yacht to visit for a few days, or more.

To the south is the North Channel and the seaways from Ireland, England and Wales. For many visiting cruising folk this is the gateway to Scottish cruising. With good havens on the mainland coast, and the grandeur of Ailsa Craig and Arran on the horizon, it is a splendid introduction to cruising in Scottish waters.

Cruising on the Clyde has many advantages over land-based touring, where, unless a ferry can be taken, long journeys around the heads of the lochs take up much of the time. On a yacht one can hope for a near-direct line. This a great source of satisfaction in itself and it soon becomes apparent why this region became so highly developed for industry and tourism long before road or rail travel was practicable.

Cruise planning in the Firth of Clyde

One of the delights of yacht cruising, like other types of expedition, is that the experience can be extended over much more than the allotted time by planning in advance, and then later by recording what has been seen and done. These may not be essential parts of the cruise, but they add greatly to its purpose, often to its success, and to the pleasure it brings in both anticipation and future reminiscence.

The Clyde offers a wide variety of sailing areas, ranging from long, narrow lochs extending north into the hills to the more open waters surrounding Arran in the south, with gentler passages around the Isle of Bute and the Cumbraes in between. Navigation is straightforward and hazards are well marked. Tidal streams are rarely significant and the shelter is such that in all but the most extreme weather conditions it is usually possible to get some sailing, an important consideration for weekend sailors.

For most people, the starting point will be one of the marinas on or near the Ayrshire shore: Kip, Largs, Ardrossan and Troon. The latter is especially well placed for owners from the south of England who can take advantage of cheap flights to nearby Prestwick airport. Rhu marina at the north of the Firth and Holy Loch marina over on the western shore offer useful alternatives and, for those who do not mind travelling a little further, Port Bannatyne marina on Bute and Portavadie in Loch Fyne allow immediate access to the best cruising areas. For cruise planning, access to convenient transport links, supermarkets and yacht service facilities make these marinas ideal for starting out on a charter holiday, or as a short term base whether it be for a month or a season.

Cruising opportunities within the Firth are boundless and planning a two week cruise with a different anchorage every night is no problem. Perhaps the best advice is to allow extra time over and above a basic itinerary in case of poor weather or spontaneous stopovers at attractive places, and diversions to others. There is nothing worse than to be driven by a timetable that turns a holiday into a logistics exercise!

Tarbert, Loch Fyne: Most people who have cruised the Clyde, even if only for a weekend, will have visited this idyllic fishing village which must rank as one of the most popular cruising destinations in Britain.

Approaches to the Firth of Clyde

Although the majority of yachts cruising the Clyde sail out of the marinas and anchorages in the upper reaches, this chapter will begin by describing the Firth as it would be experienced by a yacht approaching from the Irish Sea or further south. In adverse weather this can be an uncomfortable and protracted experience but by careful tidal planning and making use of the harbours and anchorages in and adjacent to the North Channel, it can be one of the most delightful delivery passages in the British Isles.

Of course many northbound yachts bypass the Clyde altogether in their haste to reach the more dramatic and remote west coast cruising grounds. A small number may approach from the north or west by rounding the Mull of Kintyre, which has its own weather and tidal hazards, but whatever the approach the attractions of the Clyde are well worth the effort expended in getting there.

The Solway Firth

Before entering the North Channel it is worth considering a short diversion into the Solway Firth, especially if the wind is set in the north. It has an interesting though little frequented coastline, as the majority of its ports and anchorages do not offer convenient on-passage stopping places when cruising directly to or from the Clyde. However, **East Tarbert Bay** is a useful stopover other than in easterly winds, to wait for the tide or weather for a passage northbound, or before heading eastwards into the Solway Firth. The Solway can best be enjoyed in a vessel that can take the ground but, given reasonably fair weather, deeper draught boats will usually find somewhere to lie.

From the west, Isle of Whithorn, Kirkcudbright and Kippford are the main sailing centres offering some facilities for passing yachts. **Isle of Whithorn** is

Isle of Whithorn is a popular harbour on the Solway coast. Yachts that can take the ground will obtain reasonable shelter within the harbour. Deep keel yachts have to anchor in the bay outside where they are very exposed to the south.

Little Ross Island, at the mouth of Kirkcudbright Bay, offers deep water anchorage in settled weather and is a good place to wait for the tide before entering the River Dee.

Above and opposite: The pontoons at Kirkcudbright provide secure deep water berthing, approachable by deep keeled vessels approximately 3½ hours either side of HW.

Solway smugglers

Although the inner parts of the Solway Firth are not easily navigable by yachts, the outer parts are, even if most of the rivers and harbours are tidal.

None of this deterred our predecessors, the smugglers of the Solway. The whole area was a hotbed of illegal importing of spirits, tobacco and tea, as fishermen, farmers and even clergymen helped the smugglers! The activity was aided by a largely unpopulated coastline, peppered with cliffs and caves, and the ease of making a landfall after a run up the Irish Sea for vessels carrying contraband from Europe.

All this nefarious activity was opposed by the government's Excisemen, using revenue cutters to intercept the smugglers' vessels, aided at times by the military.

This was a dangerous job, as the smugglers and their ships were generally armed, and they often faced the death penalty if caught. One of the 'gaugers', or excisemen, was Robert Burns, who from 1791 to his death in 1796, held the post in Dumfries.

Adjacent and opposite: Kippford on the River Urr offers mooring or anchorage only for vessels that can take the ground.

a sheltered bay (except from winds between south and east) with a drying quay and an attractive village. Some yachts are permanently moored in the lee of the quay and, although this part of the harbour dries, a visiting yacht can tie up if prepared to take the ground or alternatively anchor in the bay.

Isles of Fleet offers three anchorages amongst the small islands, but they are also exposed to the south. Yachts able to dry out unsupported can, of course, enter the Fleet estuary to seek refuge.

Little Ross Island is on the west shore of the approach to the Dee estuary, and offers an anchorage in Little Ross Sound, between the island and the mainland, and also in Ross Sound. Most of the anchorages are exposed to the south, but some shelter is possible in the lee of the island, off its north side: however, in these conditions a retreat to Kirkcudbright would be prudent.

Kirkcudbright, despite the shallow approaches of the Dee estuary, has good deep water berthing at pontoon berths in the town centre. It is a medium sized town, and offers the usual range of amenities.

Furthest east is **Kippford**, a busy boating and holiday centre, but one with challenging approaches and nowhere to lie afloat at low water. Despite this, it is a popular sailing centre, and has a yacht club, repair facilities and a chandlery.

The North Channel

The North Channel is covered fully in the CCC Sailing Directions for the Firth of Clyde, which also include information on the Solway and Cumbrian Coasts, the Isle of Man and some harbours and anchorages on the Antrim coast which, being usually on the weather shore, often provide better shelter than those on the Scottish side.

When passage planning for this leg, whether approaching from the south or the west, tidal streams and weather systems must be given close attention. Tides are strong throughout the North Channel and, in wind-over-tide situations, produce a nasty sea. As the Clyde is approached the tidal strength diminishes, and winds can become variable in the lee of Arran, but from this point the waters are progressively more sheltered.

Opposite: An aerial view of Portpatrick from the west, which illustrates the exposure of its entrance to the west and south west.

Portpatrick is a snug and historic harbour which has the virtue of being virtually on the rhumb line from the Irish Sea to the Clyde, but has the disadvantage of an exposed entrance which may be impassable in strong westerlies.

As its name suggests, this was for centuries the main ferry harbour linking Scotland with Donaghadee in eastern Ulster, but during the 19th century traffic began to transfer to Stranraer, and despite the railway arriving in Portpatrick in 1862, the town declined as a ferry port due to the increased size of ships, and the ongoing problem of the harbour entrance in poor weather.

Today, Portpatrick is a seaside holiday town with considerable charm. Apart from its appeal to the passing sailor as a stopping port, it has a good selection of pubs, restaurants, hotels, shops, 'the best holiday golf course in the South of Scotland', and a bus link to Stranraer. Should the worst come to the worst, there is an all-weather lifeboat too!

To the north of the town, and sharing the same vistas as the golfers, is the Southern Upland Way, which begins in Portpatrick and crosses Southern

Portpatrick: A view of the harbour and town from the south. The deepest water within the inner harbour is generally to be found on the East side where a single yacht can be seen berthed.

Opposite: Corsewall Point lighthouse with a Stranraer – Larne ferry in the background.

The *Craigantlet*

If you set off on the Southern Upland Way north of the harbour you will first come to Portpatrick Radio Station, a familiar name to all mariners. Two miles further north is Killintringan Lighthouse, below which lies the wreck of the *Craigantlet*, a small container ship which ran ashore in February 1982 during a storm.

The ship broke in two after grounding, and there is little left of her now except a bit of bow in the middle of the bay, the main hull section having been salvaged and broken up by the seas. No lives were lost.

Scotland. The first section of the walk leads north along the coast past Portpatrick Radio Station to Killantringan Lighthouse, suitable points of interest for any sailor. Killantringan Lighthouse, which was recently extinguished, was built in 1900 and was, like almost all Scottish lighthouses, designed by the famous Stevenson family, successive generations of whom, with the notable exception of writer Robert Louis, were engineers to the Northern Lighthouse Board.

The views across the North Channel are stunning and, if the weather is bad enough to keep you in port, you will experience it in glorious action all along this coastal path. The wreck of the *Craigantlet* is still visible in the bay south of the lighthouse.

Portpatrick is just a half day's sail across the North Channel from Bangor, less in a powerboat, so in good weather you may find it busy with day or weekend visitors. Find a space to berth, and then an exploration of the waterfront will reveal a small souvenir shop run by the RNLI adjacent to their lifeboat station, and facing it across the harbour, the Crown Hotel, a long term favourite with waterborne and other visitors.

Loch Ryan

The town and port of **Stranraer** lies at the head of Loch Ryan, affording complete shelter from the south and west, and also sheltered from the east by the ferry pier, and more recently a new breakwater. This transforms the old inner harbour into a leisure craft haven, and the installation of a pontoon system in 2008 completes the change, with permanent shore facilities planned.

Milleur Point Buoy marks the loch entrance, 7.5nm from Stranraer Harbour, although if a short passage break is all that is required, to wait for tide or weather to set fair, then the anchorage at Lady Bay, just over a mile into the loch, is sheltered from south west to west and clear of the ferrys' route, although subject to their wash.

Stranraer is the main town of the area, and has been the transit port for the Larne and Belfast ferries since the mid-19th century, when it took over from Portpatrick. Change continues as the service is due to relocate to a new facility at Cairnryan, leaving the way open for leisure boating developments at the harbour. Apart from transport links, this busy town offers a good range of shops and services.

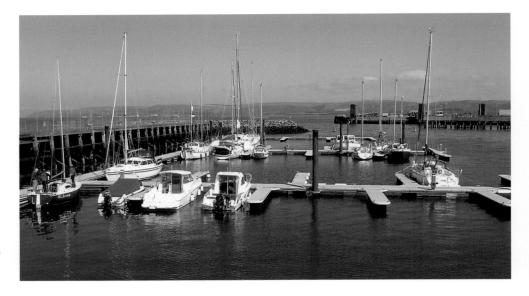

Stranraer: A recently constructed breakwater and the installation of pontoons has revolutionised Loch Ryan as a destination. Previously the nearest anchorage was in The Wig, almost 3 miles from the town.

The most important historic building is the Castle of St John, which was built early in the 16th century by the Adair family, who developed the town. The view from the tower is spectacular, and the castle's own museum complements Stranraer Museum, which deals in particular with the life of polar explorers Sir John Ross and his nephew James Clark Ross.

For active people, or to burn off the childrens' energy, the Ryan Centre – a leisure centre, cinema and theatre all rolled into one – has a 25m competition swimming pool and ancillary diversions, and is situated 1 km south of the harbour.

Ailsa Craig

Knicknamed 'Paddy's Milestone', Ailsa Craig (photograph on left) is a massive granite volcanic plug standing in the approaches to the Firth of Clyde, about 40 miles from both the Cumbraes and Belfast Lough, and 10 miles west of Girvan.

The rock, which rises to 340m (1,100ft) above sea level, is the third largest gannetry in the British Isles, and home to over thirty thousand pairs of these magnificent birds. Since the eradication of the brown rat from the island, colonies of herring gull, lesser and greater black-backed gull, kittiwake, guillemot, razorbill, fulmar and puffins have flourished.

Landing is only possible near the lighthouse, and details of the temporary anchorage are in the CCC Sailing Directions.

The island was also a source of the very fine grained granite used for the manufacture of curling stones, and the remains of the quarrying activity can still be seen.

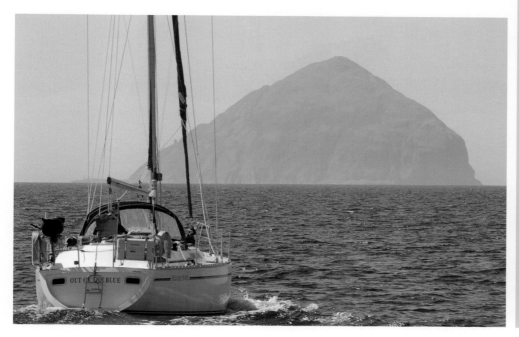

Entering the Firth of Clyde

Once clear of Loch Ryan and heading north, the tides rapidly become less commanding and the conical silhouette of **Ailsa Craig** ahead marks the entry point to the Firth itself. Beyond and to port, the Isle of Arran offers shelter and some good anchorages, while to starboard the Ayrshire coast has a number of harbours that formerly catered almost exclusively for commercial traffic but now offer good facilities for yachts.

The first to be encountered is **Girvan**, a small man-made harbour at a river mouth which was once home to an inshore fishing fleet, but today most commercial fishing boats now work out of nearby Troon. The entrance should be approached with caution in bad weather and not within 2 hours either side of LW, as depth may be less than that shown on the chart. The harbour is formed by the entrance to the Water of Girvan, protected by a South Pier and North Breakwater, which encloses an area where it is planned to create leisure berthing facilities. Berth either at the pontoon in the centre of the harbour, or at one of the quay walls.

The tiny drying harbour at **Maidens** is a few miles north of Girvan, but although a scheme to improve it is under way, at present it is only suitable for shallow draft and bilge keel craft, or small fin keel boats prepared to dry out alongside the breakwater. The main attractions of this tiny village are the nearby Turnberry Golf Course, the excellent small hotel and fish restaurant overlooking the harbour, and Culzean Castle, perched on the cliffs to the north.

Girvan: The yacht pontoon.

Maidens: A small drying harbour undergoing gradual improvement by local effort.

Troon Yacht Haven is often the first major port of call for inbound yachts and can supply every need, including the rare capacity to cater for very large superyachts.

The Ayrshire coast

Although **Ayr** is the county town, a commercial port, and was once a busy fishing port, its exposed entrance and lack of berths make it of little appeal to the cruising yachtsman and, despite the CCC Sailing Directions describing the approach and the limited available berthing facilities, most will opt for nearby Troon.

Troon Harbour, with its **Yacht Haven**, provides the southernmost of the Clyde marinas, offering a safe entrance in any weather, shelter within, modern fully serviced berthing and good transport connections by rail, air and bus.

The port was created in the early 19th century for the export of coal by the Duke of Portland who owned extensive mines in Ayrshire, and he built the first railway in Scotland, which carried steam locomotives, notably *The Duke* (built by Stephenson), nine years before the Stockton–Darlington line; thus it is believed to be the first steam hauled railway in the world. The port was advanced in many other ways, and was a centre of shipbuilding until a few years ago.

Troon is now a terminal for summer ferry services to Larne, which is home to the local fishing fleets and handles commercial cargoes. The inner basin is now the 350 berth Troon Yacht Haven and home to Troon Cruising Club.

Troon also has an excellent selection of hotels, pubs, cafés and restaurants, together with a variety of independent shops. There are also six top golf courses around the town including the famous Royal Troon, a venue for the British Open Championship.

Troon Yacht Haven is very popular as a staging and crew change port for inbound and outbound cruising yachts, thanks to its transport links. An increasing number of yachts are migrating north to be based there, due to the proximity of Prestwick Airport and the availability of budget flights from other parts of Britain and Europe.

The central Ayrshire area has many attractions a short taxi, bus or train ride away, including horse racing at Ayr, various Robert Burns centres, and good shopping in Ayr itself.

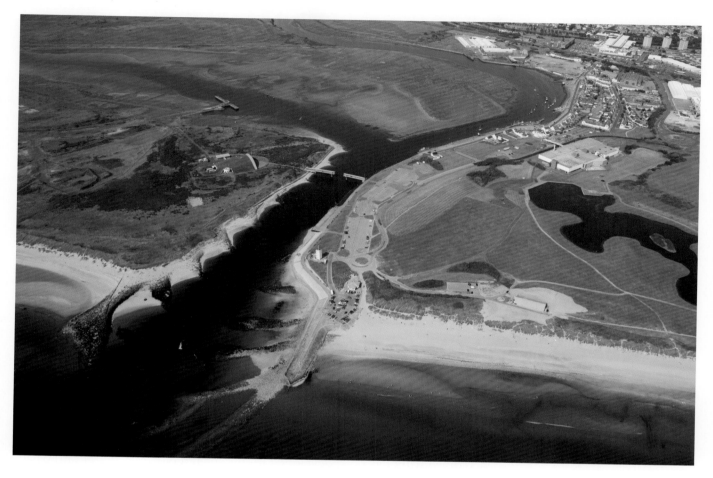

Irvine was an important port for Glasgow before the River Clyde was navigable above Greenock. Today it is hard to believe that in 1760 Irvine was the third most important port in Scotland, after Port Glasgow and Leith. Like other harbours to the south, the entrance is difficult, being shallow and exposed to the west, so must be approached with caution in all except settled weather.

The entrance to Irvine harbour can be difficult in onshore winds above Force 4.

Historically the industries of Irvine included shipbuilding, engine-making, iron-founding and chemical manufacturing along with explosives research and production at nearby Ardeer. Today, although it is a designated new town, the historic town centre is still attractive.

The regenerated harbourside incorporates the Scottish Maritime Museum and the Magnum Centre, Scotland's largest leisure centre, which together are features of interest to the visitor.

The moorings in Irvine Harbour.

Ardrossan developed during the 18th and 19th centuries as a coal and iron exporting port, but shipbuilding was also one of its important industries. In the early days local firms were involved in building wooden craft, used as fishing vessels or cargo boats, but due to competition from abroad, Ardrossan's shipbuilding industry almost ceased to exist after the 1950s. Passenger boat services to Arran started in 1834, to Ireland in 1884 and to the Isle of Man in 1892. Only the Arran service survives today.

Clyde Marina, Ardrossan from the north west.

Fife of Fairlie

Tributes have been paid by many to William Fife the third, the master designer of the classic yacht, in particular by the late Eric Tabarly who enthused over the artistry, balance and unmatched construction of Fife designs. Between 1899 and 1903 two America's Cup yachts for Sir Thomas Lipton, *Shamrock II* and *Shamrock III* were designed and built. From 1907 until the outbreak of the Great War William Fife designed nine of the magnificent 15 metres. Those which survive continue to be treasured by their owners. Thereafter in the 1920s and '30s many fine cruising yachts were built. Fife designed yachts are easily identified by the unique Chinese dragon scrollmark chosen by William Fife for the forward end of the cove line on the topsides.

Ardrossan town became a Burgh of Barony in 1846 with a Provost, magistrates and commissioners, and by 1886 the Ardrossan Harbour Company had been formed to deal with the huge increase in use of the harbour. The company built the Eglinton dock in 1892, along with the outer breakwater. Growth continued into the 20th century with new manufacturing industries, including the Shell-Mex refinery, Metallic Manufacturing and the Winton Foundry, but as these industries declined so did the harbour, until the establishment of the marina in 1997 transformed the Eglinton basin from an out of work commercial dock into a marina and boatyard, beginning a new chapter in Ardrossan's maritime history.

Clyde Marina has been developed in this sheltered deep water (4.5m) basin, and now provides over 250 pontoon berths with water, shorepower and security. The boatyard has a 50 ton hoist, and storage and repair facilities. The next phase of the marina development will be the creation of a new basin to the east of the existing entrance which will at least double its capacity.

Meanwhile, regeneration has steadily replaced the post-industrial waterfront with modern housing and amenity buildings, and a new bar and restaurant is located in the Old Power House overlooking the marina. Ardrossan needed to re-invent itself, a process that was well under way as this was written. There are good road and rail connections and it is 30 minutes to Glasgow and Prestwick airports.

The Upper Firth

Coming from the Ayrshire coast you enter the Upper Firth between Little Cumbrae and Farland Point. To starboard is Hunterston power station with extensive, though well-buoyed, shoals offshore. Immediately north of the Hunterston jetty is the small village of **Fairlie**, once renowned as the home of the William Fife yachtbuilding yard which is, alas, no more. However the Fairlie and Largs area is still a hive of marine industry and it has become a main centre of both sailing activity and the industry that supports it.

Largs Yacht Haven from the south west.

The entire stretch of water from the Cumbraes to the Gareloch provides a splendidly sheltered area for racing, day sailing, weekend cruising and all manner of watersports. It is no surprise that the majority of yacht clubs and marinas have grown up around it and that the Scottish National Watersports Centre has been established on the island of Great Cumbrae since 1992.

Largs Yacht Haven was created from a sandbank to become the largest marina in Scotland, and in addition to its comprehensive facilities and services it is also a marine business park, home to a range of specialist marine companies. Nearby **Fairlie Quay**, formerly a NATO facility, is planning to develop marina berths to add to its already extensive and popular boatyard facilities.

Largs is a large and prospering traditional Clyde holiday town with a wide range of attractions for visitors. It is a short walk along the coast from the Yacht Haven and offers all the usual services and shops as well as some excellent eating and drinking places. There are pleasant walks on the high ground overlooking the town if you need to work up a thirst or an appetite, a golf course near the marina and the attractions of Kelburn Country Park, also close to the marina.

The Battle of Largs

The Firth of Clyde does not always provide plain sailing. On 30th September 1263 part of King Haakon of Norway's fleet of longships was driven ashore at Largs where Scots loyal to Alexander III engaged and drove off the Norsemen.

Haakon died in Orkney on his journey back to Norway; the legacy of Largs being that his son Magnus, three years later, ceded sovereignty of the Western Isles to the Scottish Crown with the Treaty of Perth. The monument on the Largs shore, The Pencil, was erected in 1912 to commemorate this important battle in Scottish history.

'Fyne': A Fife designed 60' gaff cutter racing on the Clyde in the July 2008 Fife Regatta.

Little Cumbrae castle and the pier, from the south end of the anchorage.

On the west side of the Hunterston Channel lie the Cumbraes, two small islands guarding the entrance to the Upper Firth, the name Cumbray meaning shelter or refuge in Gaelic. The highest point of the outer island, **Little Cumbrae**, was once the site of a coal-fired lighthouse which was established in 1757 and later superseded in 1793 by the lighthouse on the western side of the island. This was the first lighthouse to be built by Robert Stevenson, the founder of the family dynasty of lighthouse engineers (see p.108). There is an anchorage on the east side, in the bay to the north of the castle, but landing was actively discouraged by the former owners. Recent changes in ownership and management have now improved the position and exploration of the island should be well worthwhile.

Millport is the only town on the island of Great Cumbrae and took its name from the grain mill at the top of Cardiff Street. It is well-served by shops and has all the traditional activities of a seaside town, including an internet café. There are many places to eat ranging from restaurants to fish and chip shops.

For exercise there is a golf course and many good walks. Millport Golf Club was founded in 1888 and is one of the oldest established on the Firth of Clyde. Visitors are welcome to the 18 hole course (tel. 01475 530306), which is just short of 6000 yards and commands panoramic views over the Firth taking in Ailsa Craig, the Isle of Bute, the Cowal Peninsula and Arran.

Millport pier and moorings, Great Cumbrae.

The island is excellent for cycling and bicycles may be hired easily. One can either circumnavigate the island on the 10 mile coastal route, or cut inland to enjoy fine views from the higher ground. The tearoom at Fintry Bay is a good place to take a break on the way round.

Visitors can see the smallest cathedral in the British Isles, which was built by Lord Glasgow in 1849 as a theological college, consisting of two college buildings, a chapter house, a hall and cloister as well as the church itself. It later became the Cathedral of the Isles. Nearby, the University Marine Biological Station has a small museum and aquarium.

Garrison House originally housed the crew of the revenue cutter *Royal George*, stationed at Millport to deal with smuggling, which was rife and well supported by islanders. Later it was the Barracks Captain's mansion, then the home of the Earl of Glasgow, and in 2009 was being renovated. There is a Country and Western Festival held there annually in late August.

Kip Marina, situated at the mouth of the River Kip, was the first to be developed in Scotland. Some of the aggregate dredged from the marina basin was used to build Inverkip Power Station, the chimney of which was one of the tallest structures in Britain. It has been a landmark since the early '70s but is shortly due to be demolished to make way for housing development.

The nearby village of Inverkip has grown rapidly over the past few years, and is now a dormitory for both Greenock and Glasgow, whilst around the marina another village of town houses has been built, giving the yacht harbour a suburban feel, with the nearby benefits of excellent rail and bus links, convenience stores and a long established small hotel.

Kip Marina offers virtually all aspects of service and maintenance, as well as new and brokerage boat sales. It is also the nearest south bank yacht harbour to Glasgow.

The Cathedral of the Isles: Designed by William Butterfield, the height of the tower (123 ft.) is over three times the length of the nave!

Kip Marina: The visitors' berths are the two long fingers to starboard on entering.

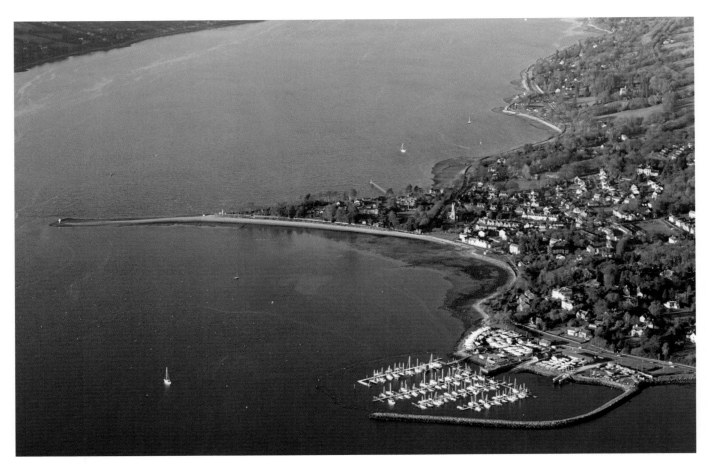

Rhu Marina from the south east looking up in to the Gareloch. The RNCYC clubhouse is in the centre of the picture at the base of Rhu Point. The marina is protected on its south and west sides by floating breakwaters which are hard to see on the photograph.

The Gareloch

This sheltered loch is a traditional centre of leisure sailing and a major naval port. In the approaches lie Helensburgh town and Sailing Club, Rhu Marina, and Scotland's senior yacht club, the Royal Northern and Clyde (RNCYC). Also within the loch are several boatyards.

The whole area is governed by the Queen's Harbour Master (QHM), and there are some regulations to be observed, all of which are published in the Clydeport Marine Leisure Guide, or are obtainable from the RN's information website: www.rnopsscotland.com. Guidance is also given in the CCC Sailing Directions.

The main yachting facility is Rhu Marina, which has both swinging moorings and pontoon berths. Apart from the RNCYC, there are several hostelries within walking distance and Helensburgh, the birthplace of John Logie Baird the inventor of television, is just over a mile away.

The RNCYC's clubhouse is a listed building in a beautiful setting on Rhu spit. The Club moorings are accessed from the Club jetty, north of the spit. Yachting visitors are welcome to use the Clubhouse, where bar lunches and suppers are available every day.

The River Clyde

The river is entered at the Tail of the Bank, due south of the entrance to the Gareloch and just off the Clydeport container terminal at Greenock. The channel is very well marked by buoys and beacons and is dredged to a minimum of 5m all the way to Glasgow. Until very recently the only reason for yachts to enter the river was to gain access to the boatyard at Dumbarton and the Forth & Clyde canal at Bowling Basin. However developments to the Glasgow waterfront, with the promise of more to come, have now led to a trip upriver being a serious option for cruising yachts, perhaps when weather conditions further down the Firth might not be too pleasant.

The River Leven enters the Clyde at the prominent Dumbarton Rock, with Sandpoint marina located a short way upstream. The main activity here is laying up yachts, but there are pontoon berths which can be used by visitors, and a chandlery in the boatyard. Entrance to the river is tide restricted.

The adjacent busy town of **Dumbarton** (Dun Breatann – Fortress of the Britons) is a short walk away, as are transport connections to Glasgow. The river area could only be described as post-industrial, the shipyards having now disappeared. However the shipbuilding heritage of the river can be recalled by a visit to the Denny Ship Model Experiment Tank. This can be combined with a visit to Dumbarton Castle, which is in the care of Historic Scotland. The castle stands on a volcanic plug, and from the 5th to the 11th centuries AD was the centre of the Briton's kingdom of Strathclyde, although the present structures mostly date from the 18th century, when it became a garrison rather than a strategic gateway.

Historic **Bowling** is the western terminus of the Forth & Clyde Canal, which links the Firths of Clyde and Forth. Through passage is available for yachts of less than 19.2m length, 6.0m beam, 1.8m water draft and 3.0m air draft. There are 38 locks to negotiate, and there are (DIY) demasting facilities at each end of the waterway. The 35 mile transit will normally take two or three days.

Bowling Basin and its immediate surroundings have been well developed by British Waterways, and the harbour now has new shore facilities, serviced pontoon berths, car parking, and convenient transport links. Close by, the village has several shops and pubs.

British Waterways publishes full details of Bowling Basin and the Forth & Clyde Canal in their Skipper's Guide, which can be obtained from the BW Scotland website, www.britishwaterways.co.uk/scotland/, or at the canal office.

Dennys of Dumbarton
William Denny was the most well known and prolific of the many yards in Dumbarton and, although they ceased trading in 1964, their Ship Model Experiment Tank can still be seen. This is a unique chance to step back into the world of the Victorian ship designer. Built in 1882, the Denny Tank was the first commercial ship model testing tank in the world and it retains many original features today – a water tank as long as a football pitch, clay moulding beds for casting wax model ship hulls and the original Victorian machinery used for shaping models. The Tank has been restored to working condition by the Scottish Maritime Museum and is still used for testing ship designs. (Castle Street, Dumbarton. G82 1QS. tel. 01389 763444)

Bowling Basin, at the entrance to the Forth & Clyde Canal.

The River Clyde looking westwards from the Erskine Bridge towards Dumbarton Rock.

Opposite upper: HMS Defender, the fifth 'Daring' Class destroyer, being launched from BAE Systems' yard at Govan in 2009.

Opposite lower: The Glasgow Tower and Science Centre mark the entrance to the Princes Dock where there are plans for a marina. Pontoons for visiting yachts can be seen in the centre of the picture.

The ongoing regeneration of **Glasgow's** waterfront from Clydebank upstream has made the city accessible to visiting cruising yachts, thanks to the provision of secure visitors' pontoons close to the city centre, as well as at Clydebank and Braehead. The policy of Glasgow City Council and Clydeport is to encourage leisure traffic, so improvements should continue.

From Bowling you pass under the Erskine Bridge, some 7 miles from the City, and then successively pass Clydebank, birthplace of the Cunard Queen liners and the Royal Yacht *Britannia*, Rothesay Dock (and its boatyard), the River Cart, Braehead Shopping Centre and thence to Glasgow Harbour. The new Transport Museum, the Glasgow Science Centre, the *Glenlee* and the Scottish Exhibition and Conference Centre are some of the riverside attractions around Glasgow Harbour. Berthing arrangements and river regulations change as redevelopment proceeds so it is important to obtain a copy of Clydeport's Marine Leisure Guide which will tell you all you need to know to plan this passage and to book a pontoon berth before you set off. It is available from marinas and other boating establishments or direct from Clydeport.

The *Glenlee*

The three masted barque *Glenlee*, built in 1896, is one of only five Clyde-built sailing ships still afloat in the world. During 20 years as a trading ship, with never more than 23 crew, she made four circumnavigations and rounded Cape Horn 16 times.

She was bought by the Spanish Navy in 1922 and served as a sail training ship until 1982. She was then left, without masts, to rot at a remote quay in Seville until bought by the Clyde Maritime Trust in 1992. She was towed 1,400 miles back to the Clyde for restoration, now completed at a cost of £3 million. The ship is open to the public every day between 10am and 4pm.

Loch Long and Loch Goil

Though it is only about twenty miles from the centre of Glasgow to the entrance to Loch Long, the contrast between the two is remarkable and to visit both in a day by yacht would be a rare experience. Dominated by the high mountains of the Cowal Peninsula to the west and penetrating some fifteen miles inland into the Loch Lomond and the Trossachs National Park, Loch Long, and its shorter branch Loch Goil, are the most spectacular part of the Clyde's fiord system and for sheer grandeur they can compete with many of the west coast sea lochs.

Unhappily for the yachtsman, the grandeur comes at a price: the high mountains to windward invariably play havoc with the wind. This is noticeable over much of the Upper Firth, which probably suffers more than its fair share of calms and baffling winds, as testified in the extract below, but in the lee of the higher mountains further north the effect can become even more dramatic.

Loch Long runs north from the mouth of the Holy Loch, and Loch Goil branches off to the north west. This area is part of the Queen's Harbour, and therefore subject to regulations, particularly off Coulport, where Britain's nuclear submarine fleet is serviced and armed. In practice this means keeping to the western shore to avoid the prohibited areas which are clearly shown on the chart.

Navigation within both lochs is straightforward as most of the dangers are marked or lie close inshore, except at their heads. The better anchorages are to be found within Loch Goil: **Swine's Hole** and **Carrick Castle** are the most favoured. Visitors' moorings can be found at Carrick Castle and also at **Lochgoilhead**. This is a pretty village with restaurants, bars and shops within five minutes walk from the moorings. The Drimsynie Leisure complex has a 9 hole golf course, a swimming pool and other attractions which may be available to non residents. There is excellent walking in the hills around the head of the loch, about which details are obtainable locally.

Arrochar at the head of Loch Long is less attractive and has fewer facilities for yachts but nevertheless has a good anchorage on the west shore which is ideally placed for serious walking and climbing in the 'Arrochar Alps'.

Opposite: *Looking across the head of Loch Goil to the village of Lochgoilhead.*

Carrick Castle: A clan Campbell stronghold since the 14th century, it is now a popular weekend destination for yachts, offering anchorages both north and south of the castle and a mooring for visitors.

A baffling breeze on the Clyde

'Soon on our left we saw Innellan, a watering-place much frequented by the people of Glasgow. Looking at this place through the glasses, I noticed that we did not seem to be passing it very rapidly, and remarked upon this fact to the skipper, who replied as cheerfully as usual, "Oh yes; we are in a dead calm; often happens." Well, there we stayed, without moving, although I several times rebuked the skipper rather strongly for wasting our time like that. At last it seemed to dawn on him that I was insulting his vessel, and then I thought it prudent to get up and stroll forward. Then I found the bosun, standing with his arms folded, leaning against the mast, and gazing dreamily into vacancy. He made some snarling remark about passengers being always in the way and obstructing him in his laborious duties; and it was with some difficulty that I convinced him that I was an officer of the ship. However, at last he said "Ay, ay sir," quite properly, and then we went below to play piquet till the calm should cease. We had just reached an interesting part of the game, when the skipper shouted, "All hands on deck—there's a black squall coming." It came, and I was just thinking of hoisting a signal of distress on my own responsibility, and firing a gun or two, when another dead calm arrived with surprising suddenness. That is the beauty of sailing on Scotch lochs, you get so much variety of wind, and it comes in all directions too, so that you are seldom quite sure which way you are going. That day, we were specially favoured with specimens of this variety, black squalls and dead calms succeeding one another with great regularity; at last, however, we reached Hunter's Quay, a charming little place at the entrance to Holy Loch. This is the yachting centre for the crack Clyde Club; they keep a splendid hotel, and a first-class sunset. The picture of Holy Loch was perfect: dark hills in the background, with the *Dragon* and other yachts lying in the smooth, reflecting water in front, and was alone well worth the journey to Scotland. The crew, however, had a soul above sunsets, and stayed in the cabin, sucking peppermints.'

The Log of the Blue Dragon, C.C. Lynam, 1907

Racing off Hunter's Quay in 1900 during a Royal Clyde Yacht Club regatta. The leaders, 'Brynehilde' and 'Caress', are off to a fine start with upper jibs hoisted and almost fully set.

The Royal Marine Hotel overlooks the pier and moorings at Hunter's Quay and has a long association with yachting, having been for many years the headquarters of the Royal Clyde Yacht Club.

The Holy Loch

The waters off **Hunter's Quay** were an important centre for early Clyde yachting, and home to the Royal Clyde Yacht Club until the 1960s. However, in sailing terms, Holy Loch is not what it was when the *Blue Dragon* anchored there in the late 19th century. At that time the Royal Clyde had a thousand members owning over four hundred yachts and as a result two boatyards prospered at **Sandbank** in Holy Loch – Robertson's and Morris & Lorimer's – and built many fine yachts over a century or so. Both eventually succumbed to competition from marinas and, ironically, the new Holy Loch Marina straddles both sites to provide a fine modern facility.

Dunoon has been a popular seaside resort since the mid 19th century, but it does not have any facilities for visiting yachts other than the fair weather anchorage in the West Bay. However, the town amenities at Dunoon, and berthing at **Holy Loch Marina,** combine to make this a popular place for permanent berthing, and to call at for short visits. The marina has on-site specialists in engine repairs and brokerage, as well as a café. The village has a shop, a pub, and a good taxi and bus service to Dunoon.

The Isle of Bute

Sailing south from the Holy Loch, or any of the Upper Firth marinas, and heading to Loch Fyne or beyond, a decision has to be made as to whether to go south of the Isle of Bute or take the inside passage through the Kyles. In distance there is not much to choose between them; the outer route around Garroch Head will give you steadier winds and less tide plus good views of Arran, but the Kyles are attractive and they have many sheltered anchorages.

However the former route does offer some stopping places, the first being **Kilchattan Bay.** The village here grew around the Kilchattan Tile Works, which used local clay to produce both tiles and bricks from 1845 to 1915. 1½ million tiles and ½ million bricks were produced each year, mostly shipped for export from the pier at Kilchattan Bay. With the coming of the Clyde steamer services it became a popular holiday place, when the imposing Victorian villas and tenements were built. Just 2 miles further south and around Rubh' an Eun lies the snug anchorage of **Glencallum Bay,** or Callum's Hole, ideal for a lunchtime stop but beware of the rocks which are described in the Directions.

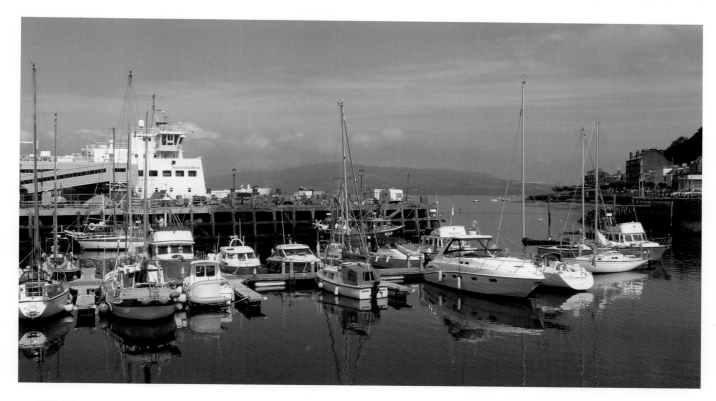

Whichever route is chosen, a visit to **Rothesay** will not take you far out of your way. Rothesay is best known as a popular Victorian seaside destination. For many years it was the headquarters of the Royal Northern Yacht Club and, more relevantly, was where the CCC held its inaugural meeting in 1909.

Rothesay Harbour: Pontoon berthing in the Outer Harbour. Since 2009, additional berthing has been provided in the inner harbour.

Bute has a rich history, as is evident from standing stones, cists and a vitrified fort in the south at Dunagoil Bay. Details of all these are on display at the Bute Museum in Stuart Street, together with information on early Christian sites dedicated to St Ninian and St Blane. Bute is the ancestral home of the Stuart kings of Scotland. Rothesay Castle was built 800 years ago by a hereditary High Steward of Scotland from which the surname Stewart, later Stuart, was derived. The castle withstood many onslaughts from Vikings and 13th century English but was retaken by Robert the Bruce. Oliver Cromwell's troops partially destroyed it in 1659 and finally the Duke of Argyll finished the job in 1685. The castle has been gradually and substantially restored over the last 120 years.

Mount Stuart, some 7 miles to the south of the town, is one of the finest Victorian Gothic mansions in the world. It is open to visitors all summer, and a regular bus service links it with Rothesay.

Rothesay Harbour is now fully re-developed as a marina for both resident and visiting craft, and is run by Bute Berthing Company, who also provide 35 visitors' moorings in the bay. The harbour is right in the town centre, where you will find a good selection of shops, pubs and restaurants.

The Victorian 'loos' at the harbour are worth a visit, if only to see the splendour that remarkable era would bestow on such a mundane facility. Bute is a beautiful island and well worth exploring. It has good bus and taxi services, and bicycles can be hired in Rothesay.

Port Bannatyne, in Kames Bay, a couple of miles to the north, has been a popular yacht mooring area ever since the steamer services first linked Bute with the mainland. The 100 berth Port Bannatyne Marina opened in 2009.

The founding of the Clyde Cruising Club

'The beginnings of the CCC were of the most informal and almost casual kind; and tradition rather than documentary evidence supplies its first chapter. The birthplace of the Club is, however, well enough known in the small Rothesay hotel officially and formally called the Argyll Arms, but more familiarly know to its habitues as The Gluepot, a scene (in days before the licensing laws exercised their restraining influence) of goings on that could with moderation be termed lively. Some six men meeting in The Gluepot were responsible for bringing the Club into existence.'

A History of the Royal Clyde Yacht Club, George Blake, 1956

The Clyde Puffer 'Eilean Eisdeal', originally 'VIC 72', continued in operation as the last of the true working "puffers" into the mid 1990s. Now renamed 'Vital Spark', she can often be seen alongside the pier at Inveraray.

Para Handy on Yachting

In 1905, not long before the founding of the CCC, Neil Munro under the pen name of Hugh Foulis, started publishing regular short stories in the Glasgow Evening News recounting the escapades of a fictitous Clyde puffer, the 'Vital Spark', skippered by Para Handy and her crew of three. They soon became immensely popular and the CCC appears to have prevailed upon Munro to write a special episode for their first Journal in 1910. It has been reprinted a time or two since but the Centenary seems to be a good opportunity to give this tale of the tribulations of yachting a further airing.

"If I wass a man wi' a pickle money by me there's no' a hobby I would sooner have than sailin' a bit yat for my own amusement," said Dougie, as the *Vital Spark* came puffing out of Rothesay Bay through the fleet of the C.C.C.

"Sailin' yats for yoursel' iss no an amusement; it's wan o' them contagious diseases," said Para Handy. "You're better to get bye wi't when you're young, and spend the rest o' your days in the bosom o' your femily listenin' to the mistress playin' the pianolio."

"It's a great sport," insisted Dougie, looking with envy at a young fellow out on the bobstay of a plunging little cutter trying to clear a ton or so of deep-sea vegetation from the flukes of her anchor.

"Chust that! And so's keeping white rabbits: but for a man tha's up in years a yat o' his own's a terrible affliction. It's the ruination o' many a happy home. A chentleman that hass it iss not much use to his wife and femily; he's away on the heavin' billow every Seterday afternoon wi' no address where they can send a telegraph to tell him that his warehoose iss on fire. It' worse than bein' a chenuine sailor on the Western Ocean tred, for a sailor will be always bringin' something home – a bottle of Florida Water, a parrot, or a pound or two o' sweet tobacco. A chentleman that hass a yat o' his own never takes anything home to his wife and femily, except a picture post-card o' the inns at Hunter's Quay, and a splash o' tar doon the front o' his week-end weskit."

"You wouldna see aal them chaps goin' roond in yats o' their own if there wassna some diversion in't," said the Mate.

"There's some people'll do anything: you'll even see them climin' mountains, and not a drop o' anything to be got on the top when they get there. Mountains iss good enough to look at, or for grazing sheep; if they were meant for men to climb on they would be flet. My idea of a pleesant sail iss a cabin ticket to Ardrishaig, and two or three cheery laads in the fore-saloon. Where iss the fun of yattin'? You'll take your week-end bag wi' your pynjamahs and a bottle of Fruit Saline in't, doon to Cardwell Bay on a Saturday and you'll likely find your *Jackeroo* hass dragged her moorin's and done fifty pounds o' damage to a boat belongin' to a Lloyd's surveyor. Before you get a dozen or two o' beer and some refreshments put on board, and have gaithered thegither two or three handy fellows that can haul a rope, it's three o'clock in the efternoon, and there's only a flan o' wind to take you doon the length o' Lunderston. There you are, my laad, and where, then, are you? A deid flat calm and nothing to do but open a tin of Australian meat and make the best you can o't wi' the wan knife and the two tumblers. Perhaps she's a weel-found ship and hass a Primus stove; then wan o' your friends will say. "I'll make an omelette, sunny boys; chust you hold on a meenute and you'll see a toppin' omelette!" The principal ingredients of a Primus omelette is a taste of paraffine oil; and it's no' an omelette anyway, it's either a piece of flannelette or a thing like an embrocation. 'Put oot your heid, Johnnie, and see if you see a sign o' wind,' says you to wan o' the laads. 'It iss blowin' an Irishman's hurricane – up and doon the mast,' says Johnnie; 'The next time I come oot for sport I'll take a parasol.' 'Then we'll anchor here and go to our beds,' says you; 'I like the way the sun's goin' doon, we're sure to have a nice 'bit breeze in the mornin'. So you sleep on a plank, and you waken every twenty meenutes wonderin' whether it's the foghorn at the Cloch or Johnnie snorin'. It's chenerally Johnnie. There's only enough o' wind next day to take you up the length o' Gourock and the beer iss done. That's the worst of beer, when it's feenished there's none left. You take the early train to Gleska on the Monday mornin' and go back wi' your face aal sun-burnt. 'Where have you been wi' that face of yours?' says the chentlemen in the Stock Exchange – where you make your money. 'Oh, chust for a bit of a trip on the *Jackeroo*', says you; it's a splendid healthy life. The crops iss looking beautiful oot in the Western Islands. Buy a yat,' says you; 'it's the sport of kings.' 'Where can I get wan?' says your frien', 'I'll sell you the *Jackeroo*,' says you; 'I'm thinkin' o' startin' a motor car – or a laundry'."

"Aal the same if I had time and money it's a yat I would have for my diversion," said Dougie. "It's a cleaner job to be a common sailor on a yat than the mate o' a coal-boat."

"Clean enough, I'll aloo, and that's the worst of it." said Para Handy. "You might ass weel be a chambermaid – up in the mornin' scourin' brass and scrubbin' decks, and goin' ashore wi' a bass of loafs, and a fancy can for sixpence worth o' milk and a dozen o' syphon soda. I've been there mysel, my laad; not much navigation!"

"Maybe no', but a suit or two o' clothes in the year and a pleesant occupation. Most o' the time in canvas sluppers."

"You're better the way you are," said Para Handy. "There's nothing bates the mercantile marine for making sailors. Brutains hardy sons! We could do withoot yats, but where would we be withoot oor coal-boats?"

Dougie went forward to coil a rope, and the Captain watched him with some uneasiness and curiosity. "Iss there anything wrong wi' Dougie – do you ken?" he asked Macphail, the engineer.

"Naething extra that I ken," replied Macphail with his usual cynicism.

"Do you think he's no' pleased wi' his job?" asked the Captain anxiously.

"Pleased wi't!" said Macphail, wiping his face with a fistful of waste. "The only men that's pleased wi' their jobs is bank directors. There's no' much gaiety about a sailor's life on the *Vital Spark*."

"I'm afraid," said Para Handy, "that we're goin' to lose him; he's taken an aawful fancy for the yats. And I would be sorry to see this ship withoot a man I could depend on like my old frien' Dougald Campbell."

"Yats!" exclaimed Macphail. "Ye needna frighten yoursel'; Dougie wouldna sail in a yat for a couple o' pounds a week; he kens quite weel that a yatsman has to wear a collar whiles, and hae all his faculties aboot him. No, there's nae chance of us shiftin' him oot o' the *Vital Spark* as lang's there's the heel o' a loaf left in her, and nae right place to wash your hands,"

"I'm gled to hear it," said the Captain, much relieved. "I got a start, I can tell you, when I thought I might lose Dougie. And I wass rubbin' it into him yonder aboot the poor life that they had in the yats. To hear me speakin' you would actually think it wass worse than linen-draping or bein' on the stage. 'Nothing in it but flet calms, tinned beef, and bottled beer,' I told him."

"Then there's whaur ye were wrang" said Macphail. "Naething to dae in a calm and plenty o' bottled beer would look like Paradise to Dougie."

"I woudna say but you're right." said Para Handy. "I'll have to shift his mind for him later on. But between you and me, myself, Macphail, I always think that dacent coal-boat sailors, when they die and go to heaven, should be put in chairge o' a handy size o' nice wee cruisin' yats wi' all expenses and no needcessity for puttin' them on the hard in winter."

The other 'Vital Spark': For many years the puffer 'Auld Reekie', formerly 'VIC 27' and now renamed 'Maggie', lay in Crinan Basin under the name of 'Vital Spark' which had been given to her for the 1995 television series. She is now (2009) on the slip at Crinan Boatyard where her restoration is underway.

A calm day for a CCC muster at Wreck Bay in the Kyles of Bute, seen here looking north from Bute up into Loch Riddon.

Kyles of Bute

The channels round the north of Bute are renowned for their dramatic fiord-like scenery, and are a favourite way for Clyde-based sailors to get from the inner to the western Firth, or beyond.

Not everyone, however, feels the need to go further than this cruising ground in miniature, where many secluded and sheltered anchorages nestle amid the hills and woods of Cowal.

The villages of Colintraive, Tignabruaich and Kames provide a touch of civilisation, in the form of hostelries, a few shops, a golf course and many pleasant walks.

Rightly regarded as the jewel in the Firth of Clyde, it is either home port or favoured destination for many sailors.

The Kyles of Bute

Separating the Isle of Bute from the Cowal peninsula, this narrow stretch of water forms almost three sides of a rectangle around the north end of Bute. This endows it with endless variety, both of scenery and wind, and no two passages through are ever the same. Because of this it is the favoured route for the majority of mainland-based yachts making for Tarbert, Loch Fyne and the Crinan Canal.

Heading north from Rothesay Sound the East Kyle branches off to the north east a mile beyond Kames Bay but before it is reached you are faced with the entrance to **Loch Striven.** Opinions vary on this loch: the CCC Directions describing it as 'beautiful and isolated' whereas others call it 'bleak and rather featureless'. Perhaps it all depends on the weather! What is not in doubt is that it can be subject to very fierce and erratic squalls and its shores are steep-to making anchoring difficult. However anchorage can be found at the head and off Glen Striven estate, where the road ends on the east shore, and lovers of solitude will, in fine weather, appreciate its remoteness.

Further up the **East Kyle** you arrive at **Colintraive**, a quiet village which like nearby Tighnabruaich has always been a popular place to lay a mooring, and still is for those who do not wish to be marina-based.

The Colintraive Hotel has been popular with yachtsmen for many years, indeed the first Clyde Cruising Club muster was held here in 1910, and it is still frequently used for such events. The current owners continue the tradition of offering food and drink in convivial surroundings that generally feature a log fire and the company of local people. The hotel provides six visitors' moorings for patrons which are very welcome. Both here and in the adjacent village shop you will find locally produced food of a high standard.

Beyond Colintraive you arrive at the **Burnt Isles** where the tidal streams can be strong and there is a choice of passages. However both are well buoyed and are easily negotiated provided the Sailing Directions are consulted. At the Burnt Isles there is a choice of two sheltered anchorages on the Bute shore and, over to the west, probably one of the best known and most attractive anchorages on the Clyde, **Caladh Harbour. Loch Riddon** beckons northwards, though most of the anchorages here are already filled with moorings and the depth prevents anchoring elsewhere

The Kyles of Bute Boatyard at Port Driseach has moorings, available for short or long term use, set amongst stunning surroundings.

Opposite: An aerial view of Caladh Harbour. Strictly speaking 'harbour' is redundant, 'caladh' itself meaning 'harbour' in Gaelic. However, the Admiralty chart refers to it as 'Caladh Harbour' so the CCC Sailing Directions do likewise.

A mile or so south west of Caladh the channel narrows at Rubha Ban and then merges into the **West Kyle** which gradually widens out and, beyond Kames, trends to the south east. The wind generally becomes a little less fickle at this point and, for those still under sail, things get to be a bit more straightforward.

Four villages, **Port Driseach**, **Tighnabruaich**, **Auchenlochan** and **Kames** lie on the north shore of the waterway linking the East and West Kyles, which has long been regarded as a boating paradise. Beautiful scenery, sheltered waters, and quiet anchorages, combined with a boatyard, permanent and visitors' moorings, a range of places to eat and drink, and excellent village shops, makes this stretch of water almost 'all things to all men'. Many weekend sailors spend their time happily pottering here, and it is a popular area for sailing rallies and musters as well as being the base for one of the oldest established sailing schools in the country. The hotels provide visitors' moorings for their clientele, and there is an inshore lifeboat station at Tighnabruaich.

There is, of course, no formality here, although like the rest of the Upper Firth of Clyde it is within Clydeport's jurisdiction. They require leisure sailors to navigate carefully in these confined waters and, in particular, motor vessels should keep their speed to a level that will not cause wash damage or injury to other water users.

Lower Loch Fyne

After rounding Ardlamont Point, which can be challenging in strong southerlies, you enter **Inchmarnock Water** which leads to Lower Loch Fyne. Although open compared with the Kyles, this area is still comparatively sheltered and with the dramatic silhouette of the Arran mountains to the south it must be one of the finest stretches of sailing water in Europe. CCC members have always known this and in the 1970s established their now well known Scottish Series at East Loch Tarbert, thereby enabling up to two hundred boats from all over the UK and elsewhere to enjoy four days of keen racing in this relatively tideless and hazard-free area.

Although exposed to the south and south west, there are two anchorages on its east side between Inchmarnock and Bute, one in **St. Ninian's Bay** close to two ruined chapels and some standing stones, and to the north, **Kilbride Bay** and **Ascog Bay** are occasional anchorages off wide sandy beaches.

The Scottish Series fleet racing in Inchmarnock Water against a backdrop of the Arran mountains.

Tarbert developed as a fishing village around a perfect natural harbour and is a popular destination for sailors at all times of the year and an ideal weekend destination for yachts cruising from the marinas of the Clyde. Yachts used to anchor or raft up alongside the fish pier but neither of these is necessary now as ample pontoon berthing is available on the north side of the harbour. Toilets and showers are provided and power and water points are located along the pontoon system. Reserved berthing may be arranged by giving advance notice.

Berthing fees are levied on a daily, weekly or monthly basis. To obtain details of these or other harbour information contact the Harbour Office (tel. 01880 820344) which is open 9am to 5.30pm Monday to Friday. There are half a dozen pubs and eating places around the harbour, together with good shops for provisions and other necessities, as well as arts and crafts galleries.

Tarbert's main historical feature is its castle, a fortified structure that was built in the 13th century. It was reinforced with the addition of an outer bailey and towers in the 1320s by Robert the Bruce to protect it against the Lords of the Isles. A towerhouse was added in the 16th century, still the most prominent part of the remains. Although the castle is a ruin, a recent grant has enabled some stabilisation and clearing work to be carried out, so that its ground plan can now be seen, making it well worth a visit. The Campbeltown to Lochgilphead bus calls at Tarbert, and there is a regular ferry to Portavadie on the Cowal peninsula.

Above: Tarbert still has an active fishing fleet seen here alongside the fish quay on the south side, with the castle above.

Above left: The 2006 Bell Lawrie Scottish Series fleet almost fills the entire harbour.

The Waverley used to be a regular visitor to Tarbert but now calls at Ardrishaig. Here she is seen steaming through the Kyles.

The Scottish Series

The Scottish Series has been the most important regatta in Scotland since it first took place in 1975. Apart from the first two years off Tobermory, the series has always been held at Tarbert, Loch Fyne, on the May Bank holiday weekend under the name of its main sponsors, Tomatin Distillers, McEwans brewers, Rover cars and Brewin Dolphin (previously Bell Lawrie) investment managers.

The series was initially only for cruiser racers rated under the International Offshore Rule (IOR) or local handicaps but over the years Channel Handicap and now IRC have replaced IOR and classes have been introduced for various level rating and one design classes (notably Sonatas for over 30 years) and sportboats.

An overnight feeder race was a fundamental feature of the series for 25 years but most of today's sailors do not seem to like sailing at night and the series now takes place over four days at Tarbert only. The other most obvious change since the early years is that very few crews now stay aboard the boats they are racing during the series and accommodation for miles around Tarbert is booked up months in advance. Top racing yachts from the East of Scotland, Ireland, Northern England, the South Coast and France visit the event every year but the Scottish Series still offers racing for sailors of all levels of experience. Details are available on www.clyde.org.

Opposite upper: An aerial view of East Loch Tarbert from the west. Since the photograph was taken the pontoons on the north side have been extended.

Opposite lower: A becalmed Scottish Series fleet struggles to make progress.

Stonefield Castle Hotel looking over the Barmore North Bay anchorage.

For those who might find Tarbert just a little too busy for their taste the two bays either side of **Barmore Island**, 1½ miles north of Tarbert, offer a quiet alternative. The wooded knoll of Barmore is actually more of a peninsula and good shelter is available in any wind direction. The north bay is deep and much anchor work will be avoided if advantage is taken of the patrons' moorings belonging to the Stonefield Castle Hotel, from where a magnificent panorama of Loch Fyne – and dinner – can be enjoyed from the dining room.

Alternatively the anchorages on the **east side of Loch Fyne** could be considered in offshore winds or settled weather. Although on the chart they all appear to be quite open to the prevailing wind it is surprising how often conditions will allow a quiet night to be spent there. There are at least five bays and all are well described and illustrated in the Directions.

The striking new onshore facilities building at Portavadie.

Portavadie Marina from the south east showing clearly the man-made lagoon into which the pontoons have been inserted

Recently however a further alternative has emerged in the shape of the new **Portavadie Marina**, a deep water lagoon protected by a breakwater and accessible at all states of the tide. The marina will accommodate vessels up to 70ft loa (notice required for larger vessels) with no restriction on draft. The basin, hewn from solid rock, was originally built by the UK government in the mid-1970s and was intended to be an oil rig construction site, but no rig builders ever used it.

The marina is convenient for access to nearby Tarbert, for sailing north to the Crinan Canal and Upper Loch Fyne, or south to Arran and southern Kintyre. The new marina building is perhaps one of the finest in Britain, and offers all the usual facilities in considerable style. The bar and restaurant are open from early to late, and the company is now developing holiday flats and lodges.

For a change of scene, Tighnabruaich and Kames villages are nearby, with shops, hotels and a 9 hole golf course. The ferry to Tarbert, across the loch, leaves from Portavadie every hour in summer.

Proceeding further up Loch Fyne towards Ardrishaig there are no more anchorages on the west side and only the possibility of **Kilfinan Bay**, a wide open indentation on the east shore, in settled weather. From here a walk of about a mile will bring you to the well known Kilfinan Hotel, where you can be assured of an excellent meal.

Strictly speaking **Ardrishaig** is not in Loch Fyne at all but in the much smaller and shallower Loch Gilp. So shallow is it, that the head dries out for 2 miles and the entrance is obstructed by shoals. However, they are all well marked and lit and approach to the **Crinan Canal** sea lock at night is quite feasible, as it often needs to be after a long passage from the Clyde or further afield.

Crinan Canal sealock: The waiting pontoon can just be seen outside the lock on the port hand.

There is safe berthing in the basin, close to the Canal Office, where provisions can be bought in the village and warps and fenders adjusted in preparation for the next eight miles on an even keel. With luck you may travel in the company of another yacht, in which case crews can help each other with the opening or shutting of sluices and lock gates.

Heading north through the canal is an enjoyable experience. Not only is there the anticipation of the challenging west coast ahead, but the calm water of the canal is a respite from the sea and the surrounding scenery is delightful. The passage should be savoured and the temptation to rush resisted.

Near the canal and at the head of the loch is **Lochgilphead**, administrative centre of Argyll and Bute. First laid out as a planned settlement in 1790, soon after the completion of the road from Inveraray to Campbeltown, it is an excellent shopping town with banks, a swimming pool, a golf course and a community hospital, most of which can be reached on foot from Oakfield Bridge on the canal. It is also a bus hub for travel to Oban, Campbeltown and Glasgow and a good place for a crew change.

The basin at Ardrishaig: A good place to have a breather before the rigours of the canal.

The Crinan Canal

The Crinan Canal Company was formed in May 1793 and the route and dimensions were decided by engineer John Rennie. Inadequate finances retarded completion of the waterway, which opened, unfinished, in 1801. Flood damage in 1805 necessitated the cutting of a new line, the canal was reopened to navigation in 1806, and finally declared complete in August 1809. More flood damage occurred in 1811 and the canal was closed for a year. Two years later Thomas Telford reported the canal to be in a 'very imperfect condition', and he supervised repairs estimated at £18,251 between 1816 and 1817. The canal was again reopened to traffic in November 1817.

The hardness of the local rock and softness of peat moss contributed to the difficulties of construction, in particular along the south shore of Loch Crinan where blasting operations left rocky projections which sank eleven steamers between 1885 and 1921!

The Oystercatcher, Otter Ferry

Otter Ferry

Nothing to do with otters unfortunately, despite the elegant otter depicted on the Forestry Commission sign! The name is derived from the Gaelic *oitir* meaning sandbank or spit. The ferry used to run from the pier in the photograph across the narrows to West Otter Ferry, about half a mile north east of Port Ann, where a ruined quay can still be seen. The ferry ceased operating in 1948.

Inveraray: A lone yacht shares the bay with the 'Arctic Penguin'. Built as a lightship in 1910, she is now in the care of the Inverarary Maritime Museum.

Upper Loch Fyne

The approach to Upper Loch Fyne is through The Narrows formed by a long shingle spit extending westwards from Otter Ferry. The approaches are well marked by buoys and the spit itself by a substantial beacon. Take care however, as it has been recently reported that the spit is extending south westwards from the beacon and it should be given a berth of at least 250 metres.

Just before entering the narrows there is an occasional anchorage in Glac Mor, between two islands. Like most of those in Loch Fyne it is very exposed to the south but in the right weather you will be rewarded with magnificent views of Arran while you eat your lunch.

Otter Ferry is on the east shore of Loch Fyne, just north of Otter Spit. It is an anchorage sheltered from southerly winds, but otherwise best visited in fair weather. The Oystercatcher pub and restaurant is located beside the pier, overlooking seven visitors' moorings and a landing pontoon. It is the social centre of this tiny clachan and is owned by a keen sailor, so this little corner of Loch Fyne is becoming increasingly popular, and not only for the locally brewed Fyne Ales on sale!

Loch Fyne, interestingly, is longer than Loch Long, the trip to its northern point being just over 20 miles. This is no problem for a quick powerboat, but it will take more time in a sailing yacht. The mystery is why so few yachts are to be seen. For somewhere so beautiful, within a day's sail of one of the biggest concentrations of boat moorings in the country, it is inexplicable. The only answer must be either that the counter attractions of the rest of the Clyde area are too strong or that skippers are wary of a potential long beat home.

There are a few small ports of call along the way: **Loch Gair** is a sheltered spot, with various permanent moorings. It has rather difficult and muddy shore access but there is a small hotel to visit once you get ashore. Further north on the west side are the villages of **Minard** and **Furnace**, the tourist honeypot of **Inveraray**, and the Loch Fyne Oyster Bar at the very head of the loch. The reward for reaching here is a visitors' mooring – there are none anywhere else on this shore.

The east shore does have some fair weather anchorages, **Lachlan Bay** (Inver Cottage Restaurant) being one, and visitors' moorings at **Strachur** (The Creggans Inn), so in quiet weather they will be useful stopping points.

As well as at least half a dozen very good eating places, and the potential of a visit to the renowned Crarae Gardens near Minard – anchor north or south of Crarae Point – Upper Loch Fyne offers magnificent scenery, generally sheltered waters, and straightforward navigation.

Approaching Dunderave Castle near the head of Loch Fyne.

Inveraray

Built in 1744 by the 3rd Duke of Argyll to replace the original village which inconveniently marred the view from his new castle, Inveraray is the oldest planned town in Scotland. Amongst Inveraray's many interesting attractions, and not to be missed for good food and refreshment, is The George which has been owned by the Clark family since 1860.

***Below left:** In addition to moorings the Loch Fyne Oyster Bar has other rewards for those who penetrate to the very head of the loch.*

***Below:** Lachlan Bay with the old castle on the point beyond. Most of the bay dries so check soundings carefully before anchoring.*

The Isle of Arran seen from near North Glen Sannox, an occasional anchorage off a small sandy bay.

Isle of Arran

Having explored Loch Fyne, a yacht cruising the Clyde for a week might consider a circumnavigation of the Isle of Arran before returning back to a mainland port. Whether to go clockwise or not depends on the weather and timing but it must be remembered that Arran has only two reasonably secure anchorages, Lochranza and Lamlash, and none on the west side, although the east shore of Kintyre does provide some alternatives.

Approaching from the north the dramatic silhouette of the Arran peaks is impressive and the narrow cleft sheltering **Lochranza** is a natural first stop. The loch was formed by glaciation when Arran was an icecap and sea level was a great deal lower. The ice carved a U-shaped valley with a terminal moraine which is now the spit at the northern entrance, and another on which stands the castle. Unfortunately, this type of glacial action also produces scooped-out areas, which is why the middle of the loch is 15m deep and the sides shelve steeply. This can be confirmed by generations of yachtsmen who have struggled with their anchors whilst dragging rapidly out of the loch. So don't be fooled into thinking that Loch Ranza is sheltered in strong southerly winds: they whistle down off the mountains in alarming gusts.

Despite the above drawbacks, Loch Ranza is a favourite anchorage for many Clyde-based boats and it is well placed as a weekend destination. A dozen visitors' moorings now lessen the need to anchor and a recently installed dinghy landing and short stay pontoon just south of the pier facilitates taking on stores and water.

Ashore, the 13th and 16th century castle situated on the spit is well worth a visit and, for boats that can take the ground, the spit provides perfect shelter. Up the glen beyond the castle is the recently opened distillery which has a shop and a café. A caravan site, where showers and a laundrette may be available, and a golf course are about ten minutes walk from the pontoon. A bus service connects with other villages, including Brodick on the east coast, and a vehicle ferry to Skipness on Kintyre runs from the pier.

Lochranza Castle and the moorings.

Sailing in a clockwise direction around the island takes you past occasional anchorages at Sannox and Corrie before you arrive at **Brodick**. Although not a natural harbour, Brodick is the principal ferry port for Arran and has accordingly developed into one of the main settlements, and a popular holiday destination. There are visitors' moorings in the bay and ample room for anchoring, but dinghy landing and shore facilities for sailors are virtually non-existent. Although the basics are available – visitor centre, shops and pubs – the surroundings are a greater attraction and the view of Goat Fell from the bay is striking. Brodick Castle and Gardens, the Arran Heritage Museum and walks around the bay or into Glen Rosa are all attractive ways to enjoy the area and for the energetic, the summit of Goat Fell beckons: at 875m (2,866ft) it is a serious but rewarding climb from sea level.

Brodick Castle

This National Trust for Scotland property has a 600 year history, a fabulous collection of valuable artefacts, and stunning views over Brodick Bay to the Ayrshire Coast. The Park extends from seashore to mountain top with over ten miles of waymarked trails and abundant wildlife. The Castle Gardens comprise a formal walled garden and woodland walks, and Brodick Castle holds three national collections of rhododendron which flower in almost every month of the year.

Holy Island seen from the Lamlash moorings. The island is now owned by an order of Buddhist monks.

Lamlash Harbour, being almost completely landlocked, is a large expanse of naturally sheltered water which has protected vessels since Viking times. King Haakon anchored here before his defeat at the Battle of Largs in 1263 and more recently it was a naval base in both world wars. It has now become the main yachting and dinghy sailing centre for Arran and the pretty village of Lamlash is the home of the island's sailing club which operates many moorings in the north of the harbour, 20 of which are reserved for visitors. Ashore there is a pier and slipway for landing, several shops, restaurants and a chandlery.

The shelter is provided by Holy Island, off which good anchorage can be found. Named after St. Molias, a little known Celtic saint, the island is a very special and quiet place and the present owners, a Tibetan Buddhist order, are maintaining this tradition. Landing on the island is well worth while and is encouraged providing the Buddhist's rules are followed, which include no alcohol or smoking.

The south end of the harbour is mainly taken up by fish farming, though very good shelter from south westerly gales can be found here. In the north part of the harbour a no-take zone for both commercial and recreational fishing has been established.

The lighthouse on Holy Island at the southern entrance to Lamlash Harbour.

Above: Carradale Harbour, a busy fishing village half way down the Kilbrannan Sound.

Above right: Saddell Bay, an occasional anchorage 4 miles south of Carradale, with Arran beyond.

The Mull of Kintyre

Kilbrannan Sound, dividing the Mull of Kintyre from Arran, is invariably taken in one unbroken passage, either from a wish to catch a tide round the Mull or to get home after a long cruise. This is a pity because there are a few pleasant bays to anchor off and it is worth calling at the fishing port of Carradale.

Carradale is a busy fishing village and its small harbour can be crowded. It is the largest settlement between Tarbert and Campbeltown, due mainly to the fishing but also holidaying, as it was once served by steamer services from Glasgow, and well-to-do families built houses for summer residence.

The village has two hotels, a shop with a bakery and Post Office and a golf course. Just outside the village is the Carradale Network Centre, a heritage centre which tells the local story, focusing on fishing, farming, forestry and tourism.

There are waymarked walks in Carradale Forest, one of which leads to the top of Cnoc nan Gabhar (230m, 750ft), from where you can see north to Ben Cruachan, east to Arran, and south to Ailsa Craig. **Carradale Bay**, with its fine beach, and **Torrisdale Bay** are both around Carradale Point and are good anchorages in appropriate conditions.

Campbeltown Loch and harbour were once home to a major whisky industry, a substantial fishing fleet, a nearby air base at Macrihanish and a busy shipyard. Today the pace of life is much less frantic, with leisure activities playing a more important role, although the surviving whisky industry is in good shape.

Campbeltown, once known as the Whisky Capital of Scotland on account of its twenty or so distilleries, has a sheltered harbour and pontoon facilities which make it a popular stopping place when en route round the Mull, or to or from Ireland. The harbour is close to the town centre, which has the usual range of small town amenities and facilities. Other diversions are the Campbeltown Heritage Centre, the museum and library, and for the more active a swimming pool with sauna, gym and a bistro.

A visit to the Tourist Information Centre will also reveal details of distillery tours, the whisky shop, and the two nearby golf courses.

Full details for rounding the **Mull of Kintyre** are given in Part 2 of the CCC Sailing Directions, Kintyre to Ardnamurchan. As with other notorious passages, such as Corryvreckan, make it in fair weather at neaps and you will wonder what all the fuss was about. Get it wrong, and you will know! Timing is everything, as is being reasonably confident in the medium term weather forecast. As it says in the Directions, 'It is a long way back to the Canal if conditions turn out to be unsuitable when approaching the Mull.'

The Mull of Kintyre light faces due west and, when heading westwards, is obscured until round Deas Point.

Sanda Island anchorage with the 'Byron Darnton' tavern on the extreme left.

Sanda Island's anchorage is a convenient place to wait for the tide when rounding the Mull of Kintyre, made all the more pleasant by recent developments on the island. For years the only inhabitants were the lighthouse keepers at the Ship Rock, but although they are long gone, the island's current owner has renovated many of the buildings for holiday letting, and opened the Byron Darnton Tavern (named after the Liberty ship which sank close to the Sanda Lighthouse in 1946), a remarkable act of faith on an island with no permanent population.

The pub, apart from the usual selection of drinks, has a good choice of freshly home cooked food and also an internet connection. The island has walks and trails which take in the ruined St Ninian Chapel, the Ship Lighthouse, and the bird observatory, as well as an orienteering course. Views to Ailsa Craig, Arran, the Mull of Kintyre and the Ulster coast are spectacular.

How not to Round the Mull

'Tide calculations are more than usually necessary to get round the Mull of Cantyre successfully. To miss one's connection so to speak, and have to mark time for six hours in an Atlantic swell, is a risk not to be run lightly nor unadvisedly. Jack's mental arithmetic is always carried on aloud, punctuated with "that's right, isn't it ?" to any one who appears to be listening. I, who never have an idea whether it's right or not, take the risk of saying "yes," but with a convincing hesitation as of a slower mind arriving at the same conclusion. With this amount of help from me, the Skipper decided that we must start about 8am, and would have ample time to catch our tide connection off the lighthouse, and short of disaster reach Campbeltown in time for dinner...

I must have put in a thoughtful "yes" or so too many, for something certainly went wrong with those calculations, and the tide behaved as it proverbially does, and did not wait for us. The train analogy is misleading. When you miss a train, you may at least remain in situ till another turns up; but if you miss a tide, the wrong one insists on carrying you some way back with it. This delay, even with a strengthening wind, meant it was about 9 o'clock when we reached Sanda, the south east corner of Cantyre. Our dinner was already but a dream, for it is a good twelve miles farther to Campbeltown, so we decided to anchor near the lighthouse. To us there seemed to be an anchor marked on our chart, but now I think it must have been the footprint of a currant from the cake we ate while consulting it, for there certainly is no anchorage in the actual sea. We ran into the little bay with a great air of knowing what we were doing, and anchored, as it seemed to me, far too near the shore. I was in an agony of anxiety, and the lighthouse keepers evidently shared my feelings, for they began shouting and gesticulating wildly. Jack said they were semaphoring, and had he been quietly ashore I daresay he would have understood it; but his pre-occupation with *Skeletta* and her inadequate crew made concentration impossible, so these epileptic wavings remained unintelligible, except as a general indication that all was not well, which indeed we already suspected. As no rest was to be had there, our hard-worked "crew" had to get up anchor again with comments appropriate to the job, and out we rushed in the gathering storm and darkness round the corner and up the coast.'

Skeletta and the White Knight, Isobel Jamieson, 1925

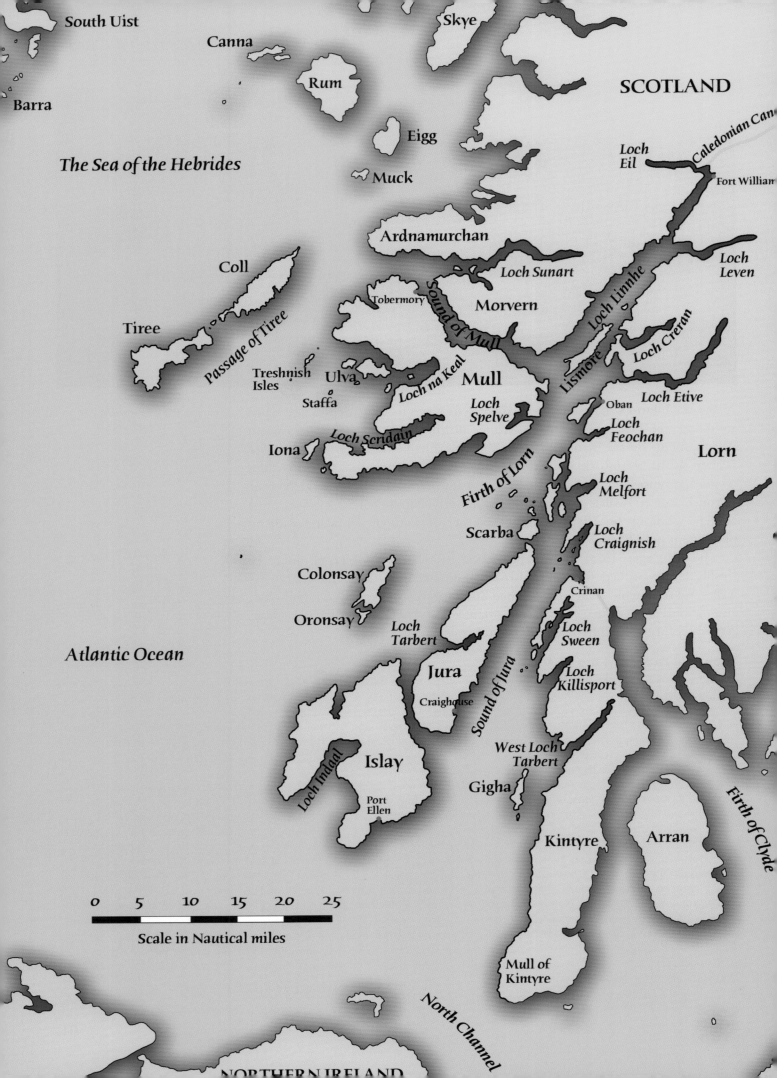

South Uist

Canna

Skye

Barra

Rum

SCOTLAND

The Sea of the Hebrides

Eigg

Muck

Loch
Eil

Caledonian Canal

Fort William

Ardnamurchan

Loch Leven

Loch Sunart

Coll

Morvern

Loch
Leven

Tobermory

Sound of Mull

Loch Linnhe

Tiree

Passage of Tiree

Loch Creran

Lismore

Treshnish
Isles

Ulva

Loch na Keal

Mull

Loch Etive

Oban

Staffa

Loch
Spelve

Loch
Feochan

Lorn

Loch Scridain

Iona

Firth of Lorn

Loch
Melfort

Scarba

Loch
Craignish

Colonsay

Crinan

Oronsay

Loch
Tarbert

Loch
Sween

Atlantic Ocean

Jura

Sound of Jura

Loch
Killisport

Craighouse

West Loch
Tarbert

Islay

Loch Indaal

Gigha

Port
Ellen

Kintyre

Arran

Firth of Clyde

Mull of
Kintyre

0   5   10   15   20   25

Scale in Nautical miles

North Channel

NORTHERN IRELAND

2 Kintyre to Ardnamurchan

The stretch of coast from the Mull of Kintyre to Ardnamurchan Point is the heartland of Scottish cruising and for decades has been the focus of ambition for all cruising novices. In days gone by it was a serious challenge; cruising in engineless yachts, or ones with unreliable power units, was difficult amongst the tides and variable winds of the Inner Isles, not to mention for the transit of the Crinan Canal.

Fortunately the way had been blazed for centuries by coastal traders, warships and fishermen who threaded their way among the islands, which was easier than trekking over moorland tracks amongst possibly hostile natives! These have been the west Highland's highways since man first arrived many millennia ago, for even remote St Kilda had been home to humans for more than 4,000 years. The Scotti crossed the North Channel from Ulster to Kintyre to found the kingdom of Dalriada in late Roman times, displacing or absorbing the native Picts.

The rest, one might say, is history!

Increasing coastal commerce led to the Crinan Canal being built over 200 years ago, created to open up the west coast and improve access to the Western Isles. It offered a safer route from the Firth of Clyde to the west coast, avoiding the often difficult sail around the Mull of Kintyre and cutting over a hundred miles off the journey. The canal opened fully in 1809.

However busy it was in the days before road transport, its commercial success was never in doubt: it never made a penny profit! Today it is maintained by British Waterways as part of Scotland's historic infrastructure and is a wonderful asset for recreational sailors.

Sound of Jura: A gaff ketch motorsails slowly north past Lowlandman's Bay on a misty September morning.

Seals basking in the evening sun may be a yacht's only companions in the Plod Sgeirean anchorage of the Ardmore Islands, Islay.

The canal's very existence opened up the west coast for Clyde-based yachts in the late 19th century and today this coast is a major area of marine activity, not just for yachts but also for divers, wildlife watchers, RIB (rigid inflatable boat) users, and in places a landing space for seaplanes.

In contrast to the challenges encountered by our forebears, the modern yacht is able to deal efficiently and comfortably with the watery phenomena of the southern Hebrides, which attract ever increasing numbers of cruising yachtsmen in their own boats or sailing on bareboat and skippered charter yachts. They come to explore and enjoy the solitude and wildlife, for Scotland's west coast is one of the last wildernesses in western Europe.

The evidence of the past is one of the great attractions of this area and a cruise can easily be devoted to visiting palaeolithic, early Christian, Viking and later places of interest. For those more interested in the present, the wildlife and scenic quality of this coast and islands is unsurpassed.

The area does offer amenities and attractions, some of which are described here, but much of the interest is in remote places and a lot of satisfaction comes from exploring uninhabited islands, unspoiled landscapes, and finding remote anchorages to share with no one else but perhaps a seal or an otter.

The Classic Malts Cruise

If an excuse was needed to cruise the west coast of Scotland, though of course none ever is, it would have to be to seek out those special distilleries which are located on the coast, often in the most idyllic anchorages. The Classic Malts Cruise does just this.

Started in early 1994 by United Distillers (now Diageo) in association with the Clyde Cruising Club, the purpose was to celebrate 200 years of Oban Distillery with a cruise in company. This involved the Talisker and Lagavulin Distilleries, being the seaward ones of the Classic Malts range which also embraced Dalwhinnie, Cragganmore and Glenkinchie.

What started with a handful of boats gradually grew to over 200 at the millennium, when a major sunflower raft was put together at Talisker in Loch Harport to celebrate the occasion. Both Diageo and the Clyde Cruising Club agreed that there was a lot of organisation for the event and handed it over to a management company who have run it most successfully on a slightly scaled down basis since 2001. Many with yachts have been attracted from other ports, with a good number from abroad. The event has a relaxed atmosphere about it and due to the location of the distilleries covers varied areas of the West Coast from Skye southwards to Islay.

Passage planning

The contents of this section are arranged to suit the cruising yacht arriving either from the north Irish coast by crossing the North Channel, rounding the Mull of Kintyre or passing through the Crinan Canal from the Clyde. In general, it follows the geographical sequence of the Clyde Cruising Club's Sailing Directions for Kintyre to Ardnamurchan. Information to help you form a strategy for dealing with the North Channel, Sound of Jura and Sound of Islay tides can be found in the CCC Sailing Directions.

First destinations range from Gigha or the southern havens of Islay or Jura, to the option of pressing on northward through the Sound of Islay to Colonsay or the Ross of Mull or alternatively continuing up the Sound of Jura to Tayvallich, Crinan or Ardfern.

Taking the former option, Port Ellen and Craighouse have facilities to offer, as does Ardminish Bay at Gigha, whilst stopping at Lagavulin, the Ardmore Islands or one of Gigha's other bays is a more remote alternative, a precursor to the many wilderness anchorages awaiting in the 'Tangle o' the Isles'. Both the Sound of Islay and the Sound of Jura are overlooked by the magnificent Paps of Jura, an uplifting scene to welcome you to the bosom of Scottish cruising.

The Kildalton High Cross. This is within walking distance of either the Ardmore Islands or Port Mor anchorages. Approach from the latter, over made up roads or tracks, is certainly easier going.

Islay

Islay is famous for its whisky, not surprisingly, as there are seven distilleries on the island, producing some of the more distinctive Scottish malt whiskies. Bruichladdich, Bowmore, Laphroaig, Lagavulin, Caol Ila, Bunnahabhain and Ardbeg are the established brands and well known all over the world. The new Kilchoman and re-opened Port Charlotte are small-scale distilleries, set up in the mid 2000s, which released their first products very recently. Islay of course has other attractions, including interesting bird populations at certain times of the year, great scenery and 3,200 friendly people.

Historically, Islay was the stronghold of the Lords of the Isles and was mentioned by and probably visited by Saint Columba, for Iona is not far to the north. The best known archeological remains are the bronze age Cultoon Stone Circle and the Kildalton High Cross, the latter is considered to be the finest ringed Celtic cross in Scotland. It dates from around AD800, and is not far from the Ardmore Islands. Also well known are the mediaeval settlements at Finlaggan, the headquarters of the Lordship of the Isles since before the overthrow of the Vikings in the 13th century until its decline in the late 15th century. The current Lord of the Isles is Prince Charles.

Special events which may be of interest to music lovers are the Festival of Malt and Music in May, the Cantelina Chamber Music Festival in early July and the Jazz Festival in September.

As well as Port Ellen, there are many attractive anchorages. **Portnahaven**, at the south western tip of the Rhinns of Islay is a former fishing village and home to one of the the first wave powered generating devices to be trialled around Scotland.

You can visit some of the distilleries by sea as there are anchorages, with varying degrees of shelter, at or near to **Caol Ila**, **Bunnahabhain**, **Lagavulin**, **Ardbeg** and **Port Charlotte**, all of which welcome visitors during the summer.

The drying harbour at Portnahaven. Yachts anchor out in the sound towards Orsay.

Round the Islands to Tobermory - *passage planning hints from the past*

'Long ago at CCC socials there was a spicy tale told of the adventurous voyage of a yacht and its crew from Rothesay to Colintraive. But how many of our members nowadays really do consider they have 'gone cruising' by following the recognised bottle chase route to Tobermory and back by the Canal and the Sound of Mull? Well, you may ask, what would you suggest otherwise? 'We want to get there quickly, to let us get as far north as possible in the limited time available'. Fair enough, if there's not an added unspoken reservation 'subject to the engine behaving and the weather being suitable for Ardnamurchan'.

The direct route to Tobermory through the Canal from, say, Fairlie is about 80 miles. It is over 150 miles going round the Mull of Cantyre and thence either through the Sounds of Islay and Iona and the West of Mull or alternatively carrying on up the Sound of Jura and continuing by the usual route up the Sound of Mull. But there is a third way, as a compromise, which offers definite attractions, i.e. through the Canal, south by the Sound of Jura then north by the Sound of Islay and west of Mull which works out at roughly 135 miles.

Contemplating Jura's unique silhouette on a calm day in the Sound.

Before considering this compromise route what is there to be said for going round the Mull? It is a long, time consuming passage, it probably means a lot of slogging into winds from S. to W. in open water much of the way and timing of the rounding is very important. Many years ago in *Wahine* we left Campbeltown rather late and proved the wisdom of 'battening down all hatches' after passing Sanda. When we did get round and could let out our sheets, we found we'd missed the tide. Sailing merrily past Machrihanish we couldn't get rid of the place for four hours, even with the help of the engine. Of course, we should have gone about for a bit, away from the worst of the opposing tide but that idea didn't seem attractive at the time. No, while there may be lovely views of Arran peaks etc. on the way and Campbeltown can give some shelter and refreshment, the Mull of Cantyre route is definitely for the tough, even if on some days 'a rowing boat could go round'. This phrase in the 'Directions' has always fascinated me.

So let's consider the route via the Canal, Sound of Jura, Sound of Islay and West of Mull. It's a mere 27 miles with a helpful ebb tide down the Sound of Jura to McArthur's Head and there are many attractions on the way. If it is a reasonable day, the bareness of Jura with its unique Paps can be very impressive while the more wooded prospect on the mainland side is a pleasant contrast. Most of the anchorages on the Jura side are not places to linger at for comfort. It might be of interest though to call at Ardlussa. There is a stone in the graveyard which reads 'Mary MacCrain, died 1956, aged 128, descendent of Gillour MacCrain.' Gillour MacCrain himself is buried on the west side of the old S.W. gate of Kilcarnadil churchyard, but with no stone to mark his grave. He is said on good authority to have 'kept 180 Christmasses in his own house'. Have a look into the lagoon in Eilean More in the MacCormaig Isles. It is one of the places the puffers make for in dirty wintry weather. The ruined chapel is well maintained by the Ministry of Works but you'll be too late to find the illicit still which it latterly housed. Before crossing over

The old stone jetty at Craighouse.

towards the Sound of Islay it is worth while taking a day to inspect Loch Swen, Tayvallich and the Fairy Isles. Form your own judgement as to whether Loch Swen beats Loch Sunart for sheer natural beauty. Tayvallich is as good an anchorage as you'll get anywhere. Although it's on the mainland it has many 'island' characteristics. Get away down the loch again on the ebb tide but instead of heading straight for McArthur Head, you'll find the fine new hotel at Craighouse in the Small Isles is well worth a visit – all home comforts there! If entering by the passage N. of Goat Island, keep fairly close to the island when inside as the water soon becomes deceptively too shallow further in. When anchoring near the new pier, choose a sandy patch if possible as seaweed has caused many a yacht to drag here. It's only a short sail to McArthur Head and the S. end of the Sound of Islay. Prevailing westerly winds have been favourable so far and one now goes about to get equal advantage on the other tack which you may well hold for the whole of the remaining 70 odd miles to Tobermory. The flood tide helps to speed the yacht up the Sound, a lovely place on a fine day, past Port Askaig and the gleaming white buildings of the distillery. Emerging at the N. end of the Sound of Islay, what then? Whatever course is followed, the Atlantic has to be faced. Nevertheless, one has plenty of sea room and after all there is no back wash such as one has to contend with when passing Easdale and Seil Island on the usual passage to Puilladobhrain. For sheer isolation and good fishing the inner recesses of West Loch Tarbert on Jura are worth a visit.

One can also toy with the idea of making for Coirebhreacain. If the idea becomes anything more than an idea, you will certainly earn some points in one of the new competitions and surely at least a round of drinks at Crinan Hotel. The tide will help you from a long way out but it would be just as well to time the critical passage at the overfalls pretty exactly to keep the butterflies in the tummy to a minimum!

The pier and anchorage at Scalasaig, Colonsay.

The most obvious next port of call though on our islands cruise is Scalasaig on Colonsay. There is still quite good swinging room on the south side of the new pier. Anchoring on *Siona* last year we found it already encrusted by barnacles and weed so here again it is as well to try to pick a sandy patch when dropping the C.Q.R. A strong E or NE wind could obviously be a menace as there is nowhere very handy to run to. Although, like Millport, the inner harbour dries out, there is sufficient depth at L.W. for the average cruising yacht to enter and tie up securely. Unfortunately this would be a tricky operation in a high wind with a big swell and when these conditions prevail, it will possibly be too late. The Scalasaig Hotel may not be so modern in its furnishings as the Craighouse Hotel but the welcome, food and service are all first class, no broiler chickens here. How much more tasty are the old-fashioned kind, with all the trimmings!

After leaving Colonsay, one has to make a decision whether to play safe and head for Loch Spelve on the east coast of Mull or perhaps to Cuan and the calms of Melfort. If possible, though, get the satisfaction from carrying on north, keeping clear of these nasty Torranan Rocks covering quite an area off the Ross of Mull, on the direct course to the Sound of Iona. The inside passage is probably the better with the stone beacon surmounted by a cross as a good mark. But here again, plenty of sea room is always an advantage although the westerly course needed to keep well clear of the rocks may be rather uncomfortable! So why not do the thing properly and round Dubh Artach while you're at it? By doing so you are sure to pick up valuable competition points and you'll have a clear course for the 13 miles to the Sound of Iona. The really intrepid mariners will of course decide that having viewed Dubh Artach they must also visit Skerryvore only 9 miles SW of Tiree. That unmarked rock about midway between the two will have to be kept in mind if heading for Tiree. These two visits will almost certainly need use of the chart table and laying off compass courses but we're rather spoiled on the West Coast in that respect and a little bit of such work is good for us all. The thrill of a good landfall when it comes, never palls. Even if one does go too far west it is only necessary to veer east of north and Scotland won't be all that far away!

Skerryvore lighthouse.

Here we are then, heading for either the Sound or Iona or for Tiree. Now, Iona is very historic and all that but I never did like the anchorages in the Sound overmuch. Give me Loch Lathaich every time. The puffers and trawlers know the best places when the horrid wind is about to swing round all points of the compass. One can get one's creature comforts attended to also very nicely at Bunessan nearby.

The next island to try to capture is of course Staffa. From practical experience it is possible at times to anchor and land in order to explore the famous Cave but a canny eye should be kept on the yacht while ashore. A little further on lies Gometra Harbour. The entrance is really quite easy but it can be terrifying to see the waves crashing on rocks and reefs all round the approaches and particularly at the entrance.

Next to be considered are the Treshnish Isles. The Dutchman's Cap is visible from a long way round. I've never made the anchorage but imagine it is worth a point or two. Clearing these islands we're on the look out for Caliach Point and after rounding it feel almost as if we were entering Tobermory Harbour. What a difference from approaching it from the east against the prevailing westerlies!

Fingal's Cave, Staffa.

If you've covered the ground I've covered in this article I feel sure you'll be able to win one of the new competitions. After pulling yourself together at Tobermory, you can make a quick passage to Crinan by the usual route and rest on your laurels, if time presses. Alternatively, you can explore Loch Sunart, Loch Linnhe, Loch Melfort etc., etc., on the way back. Being now bold enough, you will disdain the usual anchorages and try out new ones, gaining a sizeable number of additional points which will ensure you topping the points.'

Clyde Cruising Club Journal, 1968

Port Ellen's new marina development has made it a serious alternative to Gigha for yachts arriving from, or leaving for, Northern Ireland or the Mull of Kintyre.

Port Ellen is the main town of the island and its harbour has recently been greatly improved by the installation of 20 pontoon berths, making it an increasingly popular port of call for yachts. There is no harbourmaster as such but dues are collected by volunteers who visit daily on behalf of the charity who run the marina from April to September. Water and electricity are laid on to all berths and diesel can be bought from a bowser that will come to the harbourside by arrangement. Showers, toilets and a laundry are located a short walk away. Port Ellen has several pubs as well as a good butcher, a variety of small shops, a garage, post office and an information centre.

Scheduled air and ferry services operate from the island, with taxi and cycle hire based in Port Ellen for those wishing to get further afield and enjoy the many diversions that Islay has to offer. These include whisky tasting (of course), golf, bird and wildlife watching, archeology and history, walking and cycling.

Just a few miles north of Port Ellen lies **Lagavulin**, renowned for its distillery which produces the distinctive, peaty malt whisky for which it is known worldwide. Entry to the small bay demands great care as you squeeze between the perches below Dunyvaig Castle, a 13th century ruin perched on a rock to starboard, but the Sailing Directions include a very large scale plan clearly showing the recommended course.

Once in, there are two visitors' moorings provided by the distillery and space also for anchoring, although the soundings are minimal. However, the small tidal range (only 0.6m at springs) in this part of the world makes things easier, and bear in mind that during the Classic Malts Cruise in July, the bay has had over 20 boats crammed into it. The distillery is open for tours on weekdays and landing is easy at the substantial jetty, where puffers were once loaded.

The distillery buildings at Lagavulin.

The south east of Islay is an islet and rock strewn corner, but although strict attention must be paid to pilotage, visiting the small anchorages near **Ardbeg** and in the Ardmore Islands is both peaceful and rewarding. The **Ardmore Islands** have a special attraction for, apart from the large colony of inquisitive seals, one can lie in good shelter, even in south easterly winds, and have excellent views over the low islets to Gigha and Kintyre.

Just around Ardmore Point the small bays of **Port Mor**, **Glas Uig** and **Aros Bay** give good shelter from the south west. The former is the best for visiting the Kildalton Cross and Glas Uig was reputedly a hiding place for a First World War German U-boat, although once you have shoehorned your yacht in, this story seems barely credible.

Ardbeg's recently restored distillery is just a short distance from Lagavulin and has moorings, a visitor centre and a restaurant.

Gigha

Gigha has been a favourite port of call for cruising yachtsmen for as long as anyone can remember. **Ardminish Bay**, the main haven of the island, has a dozen visitors' moorings and space around their periphery to anchor on sand. The approach to the bay has a buoyed reef to the south and a potentially dangerous unbuoyed one to the north, easy to avoid by consulting the CCC Sailing Directions. The bay is shallow as the shore is approached but, as the tidal range is less than one metre, anchoring calculations are very straightforward. In fact the whole of the **Sound of Gigha** is shallow and rocky though thanks to the comparatively recent buoyage it is much easier to navigate than in the past when it had a daunting reputation. Even so, care is required.

Ardminish Bay, Gigha. The wide sweep of this popular bay is usually well filled with yachts throughout the season, making good use of the visitors' moorings.

Opposite upper: *Looking across the Sound of Jura towards Islay from the viewpoint above the Achamore House gardens.*

West Tarbert Bay, Gigha. Either this bay or the one to the north of the spit will give good protection in winds from most directions, but especially from easterlies when Ardminish can be uncomfortable.

Achamore House gardens have recently undergone a programme of improvement and a new Orchid house has been built.

Once ashore, using the unique landing stage which stands as a testimony to the small range of tide in the Sound of Jura, the Boathouse café/bar now has facilities for visiting sailors, offering toilets, showers and washing machines. Up the hill is the village shop, which sells just about everything from fuel and gas to groceries and has bicycles for hire. Yachts using the visitors' moorings are invited to contribute to the Gigha Heritage Trust.

Apart from Ardminish Bay, Gigha has several other fine bays which, according to choice, afford shelter from almost any wind direction. This low lying island generally has dry and sunny weather and fertile land, and the Achamore House gardens are noted for their rhododendron collection which thrives in the moderate oceanic climate, protected from the wind by the surrounding woodlands. A 69m (225ft) climb to the top of the modest hill behind the hotel is rewarded with a fine panorama.

The residents bought their island from the Holt Leisure Group in 2002 and the community has prospered since. The Gigha Hotel is owned by the island trust and has a cheerful bar and dining room specialising in locally produced fare such as Isle of Gigha cheese. A nine hole golf course, a ferry service to the Kintyre peninsula and a grass airstrip contribute to the amenities. Gigha is a popular stopping place for light aircraft and microlights.

Sound of Jura – the Kintyre shore

Heading north from Gigha, **West Loch Tarbert** is the first loch to be encountered on the eastern side of the Sound. Penetrating about seven miles inland, its well-wooded shores offer good shelter although wash from the frequent ferry and fishing boat traffic can be troublesome. It is not entirely free from rocks and shallows and care needs to be taken with navigation. Most hazards are well marked and lit for the benefit of the commercial users. Apart from water at the pier at the head of the loch there are no facilities for yachts but all can be found at Tarbert, Loch Fyne, a 1½ mile walk across the isthmus.

Loch Caolisport (Loch Killisport) is not often visited by yachts as it is wide open to the prevailing winds and swell. The chart gives little indication of its attractions, though they are well worth sampling in settled weather or offshore winds. The several sandy beaches are amongst the most accessible on the Kintyre shore and they will be much appreciated by younger members of the crew.

Opposite lower: *Tayvallich anchorage seen from the south.*

Opposite: *Tayvallich in the early autumn with many of the moorings already vacated. On the other side of the isthmus is Carsaig Bay and Carsaig Island with the Sound of Jura beyond.*

Eilean Mor, MacCormaig Islands. The anchorage is only big enough to hold two or three yachts and a line ashore to prevent swinging is useful.

Celtic stone carving

Most of the chapels that can be visited in Argyll and the Islands are, or have been, simple structures but within them or in the nearby graveyard are many fine examples of carved stone crosses and gravemarkers. The earliest crosses date from the 8th century and the best examples can be seen at Iona, Oronsay and Kildalton. The intricate, interlaced decoration owes much to its Irish origins though it was further developed by the Iona masons.

This tradition lapsed somewhat during the period of Norse rule but flowered again in the 14th and 15th centuries when several schools of stonecarving emerged, the Loch Sween area being one. The majority of crosses and gravemarkers that can be seen today date from this period, as do those in Keills Chapel illustrated above.

The small group of islands known as the **MacCormaig Isles** is scattered across the approaches to Loch Sween. Mostly little more than rocks swept by the strong tidal streams of the Sound of Jura, the exception is **Eilean Mor** (Big Island) which has a small anchorage at the head of a natural gut, as well as the ruins of a chapel, attributed to St Cormac, and two Celtic crosses. The early Christians certainly liked to retreat to remote and desolate places and Eilean Mor is one of them. Perhaps it was this remoteness that led to the ruined chapel being used as an illicit still in times past – a good hiding place, it would seem.

The whole of **Loch Sween**, especially the upper reaches around the **Fairy Isles**, is a fascinating and picturesque collection of nooks and crannies well worth exploring either by yacht or dinghy. Entry to the loch can be tricky and needs care due to the sunken rocks and tidal streams off the entrance but the Sailing Directions cover it all in full detail.

Being one of the best natural anchorages in this area, **Tayvallich** has been used since before Viking times and, until relatively recently, as a safe haven for trading ships and fishing boats. It is now popular with yachtsmen and a great number of boats and yachts moor there. There are three marked visitors' moorings and a somewhat restricted area where visiting yachts can anchor within the inner bay, although there is more room to anchor outside but note the caution in the Sailing Directions. Tayvallich has a landing pontoon and a coffee shop with toilets and a shower for visitors. There is also an excellent restaurant in the north west corner of the bay.

Just north of the entrance to Loch Sween, and separated from it by the Island of Danna, lies **Loch na Cille** (Loch Keills). It is not a sheltered anchorage but again, like Loch Caolisport, it is worth exploring in the right conditions, especially as it gives easy access to the chapel at Keills which houses a fine collection of mediaeval carved stones.

Other anchorages on the Kintyre shore north of Loch Sween are much used as lunch stops by yachts based in Lochs Melfort, Shuna, Craignish and Crinan. The small bays of **Sailean na h'Airde**, **Carsaig**, and **Sailean Mor** and the Sound behind **Carsaig Island** are seldom busy and are surprisingly well sheltered in the appropriate wind direction. Indeed, between these and their opposite numbers on the Jura shore, the northern part of the Sound of Jura is a much more hospitable place than might be thought from a glance at the chart.

Tides on the West Coast of Scotland

As the tidal wave rolls around the earth it is obstructed by land masses and, when confronted with the British Isles, the flooding tide is deflected north into the Arctic. Amongst Scotland's west coast islands this means the flood tide flows north from the Sound of Jura, north west through the Sound of Islay and the Gulf of Corryvreckan and also north and west inside Skye. The situation is less clear in the Sound of Harris where the north flowing flood on both sides of the Outer Isles produces an indeterminate and weak tidal pattern.

The tidal flow between Islay, Kintyre and Rathlin is strong as the flood is feeding into the Irish Sea and up the Sound of Jura. Paradoxically, it is also a focus of the tidal waves (an amphidrome), which means there is virtually no rise and fall in this area, a boon for anchoring yachtsmen.

Craighouse. The old jetty is on the extreme right of the picture and is convenient for the shop, hotel and distillery. The moorings are off the picture to the right.

Drum an Dunan anchorage, a mile or two north of Craighouse, gives better holding than Loch na Mile if all the visitor moorings are taken.

Tides in the Sounds of Jura and Luing

Constantly in the back of every skipper's mind is the tidal regime of the Sound of Jura. Using this route north from the North Channel to the Firth of Lorn needs careful planning, for the strength of the current increases steadily as you sail north. South of Loch Sween, where the Sound is wide, the tide is merely strong, whilst further north, as the Sound of Luing is approached, it is commanding, reducing progress to almost nil when it is adverse.

For this reason, planning to have the tide with you is vital, for this conveyor belt can take you from south to north at twice your normal passage speed, which is in itself a source of great satisfaction to any navigator. If you get it wrong the only way to make any progress is to hug the shore, paying close attention to the chart of course!

If this is a first visit to Scottish waters, then it is a baptism by fire. The experience will be useful, however, as there are many places around the coast which have similarly strong tidal regimes.

Jura

The white rounded peaks of the Jura skyline are unmistakable and, rising to almost 880 metres (2,900ft), they dominate the area and are a mecca for climbers and hill walkers. The island provides two main areas of interest to the sailor: the village of Craighouse, the 'capital' of Jura in the south and the spectacular Loch Tarbert to the west.

Craighouse is by far the largest settlement on Jura and is located on the east coast by a large bay, Loch na Mile, protected by a group of islands known as the Small Isles. In theory this should allow anchoring in several places but thick kelp and swell encourage most boats to use one of the many visitors' moorings that are provided off the village itself.

The Jura malt whisky distillery, with its visitor centre and shop, is the main attraction in the village and tours can be arranged. Across the road from the distillery is the Jura Hotel, which offers showers for sailors and is a good place to have a meal, as is Antlers Bistro, a new (2009) restaurant, heritage and craft centre. All these, and the village stores, are within a stone's throw of the old stone jetty, which has now been augmented by a pontoon for dinghy landing and is from where the new fast RIB ferry service to Tayvallich operates.

Sailing north from Craighouse there are several quiet anchorages that can be used in settled weather at **Lowlandman's Bay**, **Lagg Bay**, **Tarbert Bay** and **Lussa Bay**, but none of these is sheltered from all wind directions and many are plagued by kelp. The best is probably **Drum an Dunan**, immediately to the south of Lowlandman's Bay, where good holding in sand and protection from most winds can be found.

On the west coast of Jura there are very few anchorages apart from those to be found within, and in the approaches to, **Loch Tarbert.** This fascinating loch lies just north of the Sound of Islay (see below). It is remote, uninhabited, and offers interesting pilotage opportunities with several wilderness anchorages. Despite the challenges, or perhaps because of them, the loch is quite popular with cruising yachts but there is so much space that crowding is never an issue and you are just as likely to have the place to yourself.

The loch penetrates almost the whole way through to Jura's east coast and if you tackle the Cumhann Beg (the entrance to the innermost part) a new world of narrow channels and sheltered pools is revealed. This secret place was resurveyed in great detail in 2006 by CCC member Randal Coe and his colleague Jon Hallam and, as a result of their efforts, making the passage through to the Top Pool is now much safer. The restoration of the many shore marks by the Tarbert Estate has also made recognition of the leading lines easier.

It is worth bearing in mind that, paradoxically, negotiating intricate channels can be much easier against the tide than with it. This is because the yacht's ground speed is lower, reducing the impact of inadvertent grounding and also making changes of course quicker, as the tide will rapidly push a vessel on to a new line without much forward progress being made towards an obstruction. In the opposite situation one sometimes feels helpless as the current speeds your boat towards real or imagined hazards.

Loch Tarbert, Jura. The raised beach south of Cumhann Mor can be reached by dinghy from the anchorage to the north.

Raised beaches

Raised beaches were formed during successive glacial periods which began 80,000 years ago, of which the most recent ended about 15,000 years ago. During these periods the sea level fell as ice sheets locked up the world's fresh water. As the ice melted the land which had been sinking under the weight rose thus resulting in extensive unvegetated shingle beaches well above the current coastline. Those on the west coast of Jura are some of the best examples.

Cumhann Beg looking west showing the narrows and intricate channels that lead to the innermost part of Loch Tarbert.

Opposite upper: *Oronsay. Sheep graze the machair bordering one of the anchorages in Caolas Mor. This is the most convenient point to land if visiting Oronsay Priory.*

Opposite lower: *Colonsay. The ferry pier and yacht berth with the old drying harbour on the extreme right.*

Sound of Islay and over to Colonsay

The Sound of Islay is the natural route from the North Channel to Colonsay, Iona, the west side of Mull and the Small Isles but, again, a commanding tide makes careful planning essential for it runs swiftly, particularly in the narrow parts of the Sound. As 5–6 knots will be experienced, it is better to have it with you! If you decide to wait rather than plug an adverse tide, then the Sailing Directions offer information on temporary anchorages at both the south and north ends of the Sound.

Colonsay and its southern neighbour **Oronsay** are a short sail from the Sound of Islay, and around half a day from Crinan. They are both interesting and will reward a little exploration. Colonsay has some of the finest sandy beaches in the Inner Hebrides and enjoyable walks on the only road or cross country.

The main harbour and ferry terminal is at **Scalasaig** but there is limited space for anchoring and the alongside berth at the pier is only long enough for two yachts, more if rafted. Whether alongside or anchored swell is likely to be present in all except settled weather. This could be avoided by using the small harbour, but this dries. The hotel is at the top of the hill and there is also a shop with a Post Office and a café with a bakery. The airstrip on the west coast of the island has scheduled services from Oban Airport. Colonsay Community Development Company runs the island's only petrol pump and has undertaken a feasibility study into the possibility of improving the harbour and surrounding area. A tank for marine diesel at the island's harbour is planned.

South from the main harbour at Scalasaig there are fine anchorages in Caolas Mor, on the south eastern side of **Oronsay**, from where access to **Oronsay Priory** is possible. This is a 'must visit' for anyone interested in the early history of Scotland. Situated just one mile away from the anchorage across the machair, it was an Augustinian monastic community, founded in the 14th century, and was dedicated to St. Columba. The priory is well preserved and you can see the church, cloisters, refectory, many interesting grave slabs and a Celtic cross. Ornithologists will know that Oronsay and southern Colonsay is a Special Protection Area, with a population of the rare chough and of breeding corncrakes. As in many west coast islands, the chances of hearing the unmistakable call of a corncrake on Colonsay and Oronsay are better than anywhere on the mainland.

At the north east tip of Colonsay there is a beautiful sandy bay, **Balnahard Bay**, sheltered from south west to north west winds. **Kiloran Bay**, a magnificent beach on the west coast, is sheltered from southerly winds, but open to the prevalent swell from the west.

Kiloran Bay, Colonsay. Only rarely will you get a chance to anchor here. When you do, take it!

Scarba Sound

'But the sea is not for ever raging in the Sound of Scarba. I crossed it in a toy of a yawl with a single boatman at six on a July morning, when the sky was without a cloud and the air without a breeze. The water would have been smooth if it could. It was, indeed, glassy, but it was a torrent of melting and boiling glass streaming and whirling in all sorts of evolutes and involutes of curves, and running forward all the time like a millstream, whirlpools, curves, and all. The poor little wherry went up and down, and sideways, and forwards, and backwards, and round about, and I thought it fortunate I did not go to the bottom. Yet after thus quadrilling it for twenty miles to get over a space of two we landed on Lunga, no one well knew how.'

Letter to Sir Walter Scott
Dr. John MacCulloch
c1815

Northwards from Crinan

The traditional cruising route to the Isles, typified by the Clyde Cruising Club's Tobermory Race, starts at Crinan with the negotiation of the Dorus Mor. This tidal gate and Cuan Sound are rites of passage for all newcomers to cruising. The Sound of Luing is a slightly easier undertaking, but the awesome Gulf of Corryvreckan is a menace in the west.

Dr. MacCulloch's letters from the Highlands to Sir Walter Scott recount many aspects of travel by sea on Scotland's West Coast and he described the tides north and west of Crinan thus: 'the tides are intricate enough, indeed, almost everywhere amongst the islands, but they are no-where so complicated and puzzling as in this little labyrinthine archipelago.'

The tides are not the only challenge. This 'little labyrinthine archipelago' incorporates a large number of unmarked rocks, necessitating close attention being paid to bearings and transits and of course a keen eye on the chart. These observations, however, should not put anyone off cruising north from Crinan. It is a beautiful area, a lot of fun to sail in and an unforgettable stage in any cruise in the Western Isles.

Most cruising sailors will have heard of the Dorus Mor (Big Door), the Gulf of Corryvreckan (Speckled Cauldron), the Little Corryvreckan (The Grey Dogs), the Sound of Luing and Cuan Sound. They are all relatively narrow channels with one thing in common – a powerful tidal stream. Each is fully described in the Sailing Directions, Kintyre to Ardnamurchan.

The **Dorus Mor** is the first tidal gate encountered when sailing north from Crinan, or when rounding Craignish Point. It runs at around 8 knots at springs and, as in most of these places, the stream features eddies, small whirlpools, areas of choppy waves and even overfalls in certain wind and wave conditions. Generally, however, an easy transit of this strait is mainly a matter of timing, although if you are caught out it is possible for a yacht with a powerful auxiliary to push through against the tide by keeping close to Craignish Point. It takes time, though!

The **Gulf of Corryvreckan** has a fearsome reputation and not without reason. Perhaps because of this, it is a major attraction for the cruising sailor, as well as the land based tourists who take boat trips to see the phenomenon.

Corryvreckan, showing the standing wave caused by the pinnacle off the Scarba shore, with Eilean Mor and Jura beyond.

Opposite upper: The Dorus Mor, Scarba Sound and the Sound of Luing seen on a morning similar to that experienced by Dr. MacCulloch.

Opposite lower: 'Where it all begins', Crinan Basin and sea lock, the starting point of countless west coast cruises.

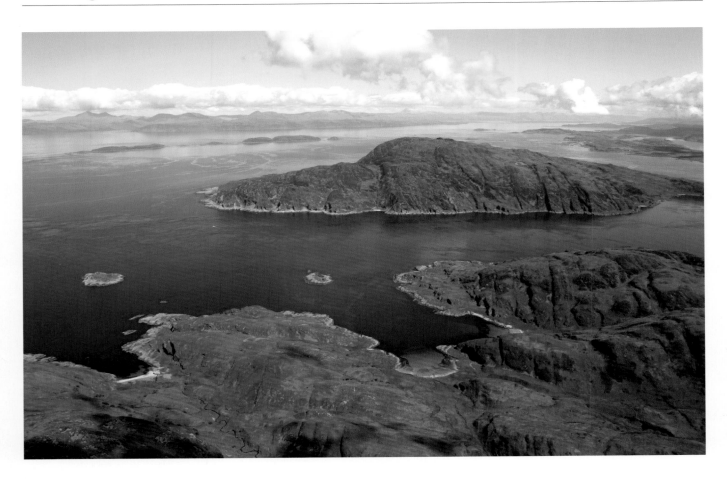

The Gulf of Corryvreckan from the south, in a placid mood. The twin anchorages in Bagh Gleann nam Muc are on the south side of the strait.

The diagram demonstrates why there is considerable disturbance on the surface, especially on the flood when the water is moving from right to left. Anyone wanting a close view of this, from the safety of an armchair, is advised to visit www.whirlpool-scotland.co.uk from where a DVD can be obtained.

In strong westerly weather and particularly when there is a pronounced swell from the Atlantic, the spring flood rushing westward through the narrow gap between Jura and Scarba produces awesome overfalls and standing waves and generates a major disturbance over a shallow ledge near the Scarba shore. It has been reported, although the authors have no intention of attempting to verify this personally, that in extreme conditions overfalls up to 8 metres high can occur – a serious threat to any vessel.

Logically, conditions are very different on the ebb, as the water is 'running away' from the seas and the western approach to the Gulf is relatively calm, except over the ledge off Scarba, which can produce turbulence at any time. Any larger waves will be formed where the stream meets seas generated by a strong southerly wind in the Sound of Jura, but are minor by comparison.

In quiet weather conditions yachts use the Gulf regularly as a route to and from the west side of Jura, Colonsay and the Ross of Mull, and also to anchor in **Bagh Gleann nam Muc**, which means the 'bay of the pig' (sea pig or porpoise), an isolated and sheltered anchorage tucked into the north coast of Jura. Here you will see wild goats and red deer on the hills above you, with the possibility of seeing golden or sea eagles as well.

The shores of both Jura and Scarba are clean so, if you get the tide wrong, it is possible to motor against the stream by keeping very close to the steep-to shore although little or no progress will be made. Needless to say, keeping a close eye on the depth sounder is to be advised but this writer has yet to find shallow water, except where shown on the chart, even when keeping the proverbial 'biscuit toss' from the shore!

The tide rushes downhill through the tiny gap of **Little Corryvreckan** between the north end of Scarba and the island of Lunga, resembling the rapids of a river in spate more than a sea passage. The passage is split by a group of small islets in mid-channel, which can be passed on either side, but nonetheless constitute the main hazard. Due to the narrowness of the gap, it should always be negotiated under power and generally it will only be possible with a fair tide. The western approach to this channel is relatively sheltered so overfalls are less frequent and less severe than at the 'big' Corryvreckan. This channel is the yachting equivalent of white water rafting and is just as exciting but should be tackled with great care.

An important point is to maintain good boat speed and therefore rudder authority, for although you will seem to be going fast enough with a stream velocity of up to 8 knots, it is essential to be able to manoeuvre and anticipate course changes.

Cullipool looks directly across the Firth of Lorn to the mountains of Mull beyond.

By comparison with the above, the **Sound of Luing** is more like a stately river to the north. Yes, the tide is strong but it resembles a conveyor belt rather than a dangerous maelstrom. Being a main seaway, its hazards are marked by buoys, beacons and Fladda Light on the island of the same name. There are useful anchorages on either shore where one can stop for lunch or to await the turn of tide. In particular **Cullipool** on Luing, a former slate mining village where whitewashed houses huddle together on the brink of the Firth of Lorn, is worth a visit. Adventurers with stout hearts and keels might care to explore the islets immediately to the south of Cullipool where complete shelter may be found in an area known as **'Back o' The Pond'**.

The Back o' The Pond offers more shelter than some marinas, although access is not so straightforward!

Passing the Cleit Rock in Cuan Sound. The perch is left of centre.

What can happen if you get too close to Rubha Breac, the point opposite The Cleit.

Opposite: *The slip and pontoons at Ardfern Yacht Centre which is set in splendid surroundings.*

Yachts about to enter the basin at Crinan from the sea lock.

Passing Fladda is a landmark on any passage, as it marks the transition from the tide girt channels to the south to the relatively open and less tidal waters of the Firth of Lorn.

Cuan Sound is the last of the gateways leading north to the Firth of Lorn. Like the others, it is held in some awe by cruising sailors, possibly a hangover from the days of engineless cruising but also because it is not without its hidden dangers – dangers that are regularly re-discovered by the incautious!

Following the detailed directions in the Sailing Directions is essential, for the combination of hidden rocks and a strong tide of up to 7 knots can easily catch one out. The chief dangers are around the north end of Torsa Island and at the infamous Cleit Rock, which is marked by a perch erected by the CCC. There are several quiet anchorages in the area south of the Cleit Rock, and pilotage in the Sound itself, between Luing and Seil, is quite straightforward.

The passage through is not much more than a mile, so it only takes a few minutes to transit – minutes that require a high level of concentration by the navigator and helmsman!

Loch Crinan and Loch Craignish

For many cruising sailors, **Crinan** is where it all begins! Many hundreds of yachts use the Crinan Canal each year to access the west coast and there is nothing quite like the sense of anticipation as the lock gates open to allow you, like a greyhound from a trap, to emerge to savour the many delights beyond.

The British Waterways' Skipper's Guide will tell you all you need to know about the canal and the sea lock offices also carry a good range of other tourist information. In bad weather you can lock into Crinan Basin for complete shelter, in more clement conditions use a boatyard mooring in Crinan harbour or just anchor off the hotel. Shower and laundry facilities are available at **Crinan Boatyard**, as are the full range of services from repairs to moorings, fuel to chandlery, undercover winter storage and more.

The whole Kilmartin Glen area, and the Crinan Moss, although perhaps too extensive to explore on foot, has a wealth of history covering many thousands of years from palaeolithic to near-modern times. Kilmartin village, about 5 miles from Crinan, sits at the heart of Kilmartin Glen and there are at least 150 prehistoric sites and 200 other ancient monuments within six miles of it. These include burial cairns, rock carvings and standing stones, as well as the remains of the Dalriadan fortress and capital of the kingdom at Dunadd.

There is an infrequent minibus service to Crinan but a Lochgilphead-based taxi will take you there and will also connect you with the west coast bus services.

Loch Craignish is an attractive island-studded loch reaching north from Crinan into the Argyll hills. It offers a number of anchorages and although its west side is preferred for permanent moorings, the channel east of the long islands has some pleasant and peaceful anchorages, all with good holding in stiff mud. The one east of **Goat Island** is probably the best (see photograph p.7) and is a popular place for cruising musters.

Ardfern village is the main population centre and has an excellent food shop and several eating places. There are walks down and over the peninsula, bikes can be hired in the village and you can go horse riding too. **Ardfern Yacht Centre** has pontoon berths and swinging moorings for resident craft and for visitors. Shore facilities include all those that are to be expected at a first class marina and it also has a chandlery with an excellent selection of books and charts. Slipping facilities can handle up to 20 tons and the yard has a workshop with a wide range of trades and skills.

Ardfern Yacht Centre has recently added further pontoons and a pontoon breakwater.

Loch Shuna and Loch Melfort

These waters, sheltered by the island of Luing to the west and largely free of strong tides, are not surprisingly the home of many yachts and form a safe day-sailing area as well as being ideally suited to dinghy sailing. However, they do contain many unmarked reefs and isolated rocks which give excellent pilotage practice for the inexperienced. There are marinas and moorings in several locations around their shores and the boat population probably exceeds four hundred.

Despite the number of moorings and some fish farms there are plenty of quiet anchorages to be found, particularly around the island of **Shuna**, on the west side of **Shuna Sound**, on the north shore of Loch Melfort, and in Seil Sound. These are all fully described in the Sailing Directions. One of the best known anchorages is **Ardinamir**, a sheltered lagoon between Luing and Torsa islands which has been a favourite with cruising folk for decades, if not centuries! It has a shallow and narrow entrance with a rock bar that requires a careful approach and once inside anchoring is best done clear of the tidal stream which can make yachts in the pool lie at various angles in the course of the tidal cycle. The effect can be left to the imagination.

On the east side of Loch Shuna **Craobh Marina** has been formed by linking three islands with breakwaters to provide a sheltered haven. The work began over twenty years ago, and after several ownership changes the marina is now complete.

The shore facilities are good and include the usual washrooms, laundry and chandlery and you can stock up in the small village store. Just a stone's throw from the pontoons is the Lord of the Isles, a pub and restaurant. Boatyard services include a 30 ton boat hoist and mobile crane, a covered workshop,

Craobh Marina, protected by its artificial breakwaters, provides 100% pontoon berthing - a rarity on the West Coast.

Irene MacLachlan

Irene MacLachlan was born on Luing in 1910, the only child of parents who were tenants of the farm at Ardinamir. Educated at home by her mother, she was extremely well-read, articulate and with a rare sense of humour. Her principal pastime during the summer months was to sit at her window (or on a chair outside the door) and note the passing yacht traffic. Certainly in the old days, she could recognise most of them and any who went past the entrance to Ardinamir Bay without coming in were roundly berated! For those who did come in to anchor it was obligatory to go to pay one's respects to Irene and sign her Visitors' Book. The whole ship's company had to sign in with details of date and yacht's name, in full – 'No dots now'! There were eventually nine volumes of these books which are now held by the CCC.

No one who has seen it could ever forget, after a hard sail, the sight of Irene standing on the shore on a dreich July evening in full length oilskin and sou'wester, gesticulating wildly and imploring the entering yacht (these were pre-perch days) to 'Keep over, keep over' to the gravel patch on the port hand in a voice which could probably be heard in Loch Melfort. Should someone be too faint hearted to do so and have the misfortune to run aground she would leap into her huge heavy boat with equally huge heavy oars and help the unfortunate to deeper water and a secure anchorage.

Her only full time companion was her cat, McKelvie, who was not always as welcoming as his mistress, particularly if you sat in his chair not realising that he was already esconced well hidden by the cushions. Of particular anathema to her in the 1980s and 90s were the Oban Times ('they didn't even print our Tattie Supper') and Margaret Thatcher!

Her final years were mainly spent in the Eader Glinn Retirement Home where visitors could not help but contrast the view from her window of a council housing estate with that from her little farm house at Ardinamir. She died peacefully aged 87, secure one hopes in the knowledge of what pleasure and interest she had given to the sailing fraternity who came to call in their hundreds each year. She was an Honorary Member of the Clyde Cruising Club and of the Royal Highland and Royal Ulster Yacht Clubs.

The anchorage at Ardinamir looking south east. The entrance channel is just off the picture to the left.

marine engineers and boat repair, with rigging, sail and electronics repairs available from local firms. Gas and fuel are both available.

Heading north from Shuna Sound takes you first past the east entrance to Cuan Sound, the most direct route to the Firth of Lorn, and then into **Seil Sound** which soon narrows and becomes too shallow for all but dinghies and very small craft. However, before this point you will pass **Balvicar Bay** where there are many moorings and the **Balvicar Boatyard** which offers full repair and storage facilities. Anchoring space is limited but it is possible south of Eilean Tornal. There is a small shop and Post Office in Balvicar village.

Ardinamir. As the Directions say: 'There is... only 1.0m depth N of the dr. 1.5 rock, so access is not possible for most yachts near LWS'.

Melfort gunpowder works

A century ago there were four gunpowder works in Argyll: at Glen Lean (Holy Loch), Millhouse (Tighnabruaich), Furnace (Loch Fyne) and Melfort.

The Melfort works, situated east of Melfort House, were opened by Harrison Ainslie & Co Ltd in 1853 and only operated until 1874, during which period the lives of six men were lost. Locations in Argyll were selected because they were remote, with good supplies of labour and, initially, charcoal.

The Melfort gunpowder factory had its own pier, where supplies of saltpetre, sulphur and charcoal were brought by sea and the finished product shipped away. A tramway connected the pier with the works.

Upper right: *The old Melfort gunpowder pier in Fearnach Bay, now developed as holiday cottages.*

Fearnach Bay, Loch Melfort. Kilmelford Yacht Haven is beyond.

Opening off Loch Shuna to the north east, **Loch Melfort** has similar qualities to Loch Shuna and also high hills to the north which offer excellent walking and magnificent views over the whole area. In Fearnach Bay, towards the head of the loch, **Melfort Pier and Harbour** can be found. This is an attractive development of holiday cottages built around the old gunpowder pier. There are many moorings that can be hired and a new waterside restaurant has resulted in two good eating places, both within easy walking distance of the pier. The second, the Shower of Herring, is in the timeshare complex built on the old gunpowder works.

At the head of the loch, in **Loch na Cille**, **Kilmelford Yacht Haven** has been established for many years. This boatyard and associated service company is situated on the south side of the loch and therefore closer to Kilmelford village. Although it is not a marina, yachts which venture to the head of the loch will 'always be found a spare mooring' or a spot at the pontoon. The yard offers a full range of yacht yard services including winter storage and repairs. Kilmelford village is less than a mile away and has a good village shop.

Firth of Lorn

Having spent time exploring the sheltered lochs to the south of Fladda, sooner or later it will be time to strike out into the Firth of Lorn, a fine stretch of open water where the majority of hazards are either visible or buoyed and a welcome change from the channels and unmarked sunken rocks previously encountered. Here the Atlantic swell can begin to be felt and even in quiet weather the five miles between Fladda and Insh Island can be unexpectedly bumpy. In strong southwesterlies, with wind against tide, it can be most unpleasant.

The Firth is an important crossroads and, if heading north, it is here that a decision will have to be made as whether to sail west-about round the outside of Mull or take the more direct route up the Sound. If the wind is not too contrary, the weather fair and stores are not needed in Tobermory, there is no better way to approach the waters north of Ardnamurchan than from the west of Mull. The prevailing westerlies may influence the decision, so you choose the Sound, consoling yourself with the thought that they might blow you back on your return. Whichever route is chosen bear in mind that, with the exception of crossing the Minch, the 25 miles from the Ross of Mull to Fladda is the longest passage without a secure anchorage to hand that the west coast has to offer.

However before launching out into the Firth of Lorn there are several anchorages in the immediate vicinity of Fladda that can be used as jumping off points.

The Garvellachs (p.88). The anchorage at Eileach an Naoimh. The reputed grave of St. Columba's mother, Eithne, is in the foreground.

The anchorage at Garbh Eileach is much smaller than the more popular one at Eileach an Naoimh.

Beehive cell on Eileach an Naoimh

The **Garvellach Islands** (Eileach an Naoimh and Garbh Eileach, photos p.87) and the Black Isles are popular destinations in fair weather. The most noteworthy of these is **Eileach an Naoimh**, the southerly Garvellach island, where there is a partly sheltered anchorage and an early Christian settlement to visit.

This settlement is possibly the oldest Christian site in western Scotland as it pre-dates the establishment by Columba of Iona Abbey. It was established by Irish monks, some think St Brendan the Navigator, in AD542. There is much to be seen, including the partly restored ruins of two chapels, several beehive cells and a graveyard with three crosses and a grave. Legend has it that St Columba's mother Eithne is buried on this island.

The northern Garvellach island, **Garbh Eileach**, has a small anchorage off a cottage on the shore which is sheltered from the west but not the south. Both islands are formed of strongly tilted rock, making for south and east facing terraces and sheer cliffs to the west.

The Black Isles form an anchorage that gives more shelter than is apparent from the chart, for although the passage between the islands to the west is navigable in a dinghy at high water, it is narrow and shallow enough to break the seas from that direction except in the worst conditions. A favourite lunch stop for local yachts and a good overnight anchorage in settled weather, the pool between Eilean Dubh Mor (Big Black Isle) and Eilean Dubh Beg (Little Black Isle) is well sheltered from all directions except from the north east. Caves, quite common in this area, can be found along the south shore of Eilean Dubh Mor but there is no evidence of human habitation on either island apart from the youngsters who occasionally camp here while attending the activity centre based on the island of Rubha Fiola nearby.

The Black Isles, looking south east from Eilean Dubh Beg over the anchorage. The drying spit is just off the picture to the right.

Looking north from Croggan over a calm and deserted Loch Spelve.

Loch Spelve on Mull provides the only really secure anchorage on the entire northern shore of the Firth of Lorn. Its entrance is due west of the south end of Kerrera and about 7 miles south of the entrance to the Sound of Mull. Until recently, entering was quite a challenge but the establishment of a perch on the rock at the apex of the bend has done much to reduce the hazard, although strong tidal streams of 3–4 knots at springs can make access a frustratingly slow process if they are not anticipated.

The loch is a popular spot for club musters and rallies, as there is plenty of space, good shelter and good holding in its north west corner. Most of the time, however, this large loch is empty of all but the many salmon and mussel farms which have proliferated in recent years.

Alternative anchorages are on either side of the south end of the loch, and off Croggan, a small and remote clachan (village) with a ruined pier on the south side of the loch entrance. Wherever you choose to stop in Loch Spelve will be remote and unspoiled, with views of the sturdy mountains of Mull and plenty of scope for rough walking ashore.

A not-so-deserted Loch Spelve is host to a Clyde Cruising Club muster.

Before crossing back to the other side of the Firth, those who like to go where few have gone before may care to investigate **Loch Don**. Aptly described by Martin Lawrence as 'a curious place of shoals and drying banks, rather like a river from the east coast of England set down among mountains', the unmarked channel will provide a challenge to yachtsmen who are happy to navigate by depth sounder rather than the marks and transits more familiar to west coast sailors.

Only an aerial view can reveal the extent of the honeycombing that the slate industry has inflicted on Easdale and the adjacent islands.

Seil

This relatively large island forms the north side of Cuan Sound and is itself joined to the mainland by 'The Bridge over the Atlantic', an impressive single arch, generally but mistakenly attributed to Telford, which spans Seil Sound at its northern end. Off the south east corner of Seil lies **Easdale**, which with sixty souls is the smallest permanently inhabited island of the Inner Hebrides. A visit ashore is rewarding for this island, together with Luing, Seil and the nearby island of Belnahua, are famous for their disused slate workings.

You may find a single visitors' mooring just north of the old pier in **Easdale Sound** which is suitable for smaller yachts in settled weather. Use it at your own risk and pay at the village shop on Seil as it belongs to Eilean Eisdeal, the island's community trust.

The island's history of slate working is well-explained in its excellent small museum and makes sense of a walk around the abandoned slate quarries. Climbing the little 37m (122ft) central hill to enjoy views of the Sound of Luing and Firth of Lorn, and possibly doing some passage planning, completes the exploration, except perhaps for a visit to the pub, restaurant and shop.

The sheltered pools created by the slate mining and the abundance of flat stones left everywhere has led to Easdale becoming the venue for the World Stone Skimming Championships each September. Visitors can have a free go any other time!

Belnahua is another hollow shell, as its centre was mined for slate until the sea flooded the workings early in the 20th century, sending the population of around 200 back to settlements 'ashore'. The reef to the north is as long as the island itself and landing is not easy, as there is no real anchorage and little shelter. Once ashore there are the ruined houses of the slate workers, remains of abandoned machinery and of course the central pool which once was the slate mine.

Ruined cottages on the slate mining island of Belnahua

The slate industry in Lorn

The slate industry in Lorn when viewed from today is a remarkable story. Reference to 'Easdale Slate' is made as early as 1554 but it wasn't until the mid-18th century that the quarries were worked commercially. In 1745 the then Earl of Breadalbane established the Marble and Slate Company of Netherlorn, buying in the existing fledgling firms working individual quarries. In that year more than a million slates had been manufactured and by the end of the century this had risen to 5 million. The main quarries were on Easdale Island, Balvicar (Seil), Belnahua (offshore at Fladda) and on Eilean-a-Beich, a small island of some two acres which lay between Easdale Island and Seil. It is said that up to 9 million slates were removed annually from this last quarry until the islet virtually ceased to exist and in fact became joined on to Seil by the dumping of waste material. This is what is now commonly referred to as Easdale Village. Most of the 'quarries' should more properly have been called 'mines' as they were excavated as much as 250 feet below sea level. Consequently they were all flooded in November 1881 when a disastrous tidal surge swept across the islands, breaching the thin buttress walls in many places. Although never the same again, the quarries were worked more or less successfully for a further 30 years under individual ownerships by dint of temporary sea walls and heavy pumping until production finally ceased in 1911. McLintock gives a record of ships entering Easdale in 1825: '245 steamers, 254 ships, 5 garriots, 15 schooners and 7 brigs'. In its heyday, and before the coming of the railway to the latter, it is astonishing to realise that Easdale had a larger population, and greater industry, than the fishing village of Oban.

This row of former miner's cottages is typical of those that are to be found in the villages around the mining district of Lorn.

To the north, Seil disintegrates into a scatter of small islets amongst which is hidden one of the best known of all Scottish anchorages, **Puilladobhrain** (Otter Pool). Once again Eric Hiscock, with his world girdling experience, provides a succinct appraisal of Puilladobhrain: '.... and when the sky cleared next morning we realised that Acairseid Mhor and Wizard Pool are only the second and third most perfect anchorages in the world.'

Puilladobhrain, indeed, has it all. Perfect shelter, good holding, splendid views of mountain and sunset to the west and a cosy pub half a mile over the hill – the perfect distance to work up a thirst! Having said all that the approaches to the pool require careful pilotage, and because of its unique qualities, not least being on the main north–south cruising routeway, it can be very crowded in the height of the season.

A perfect summer morning in the popular anchorage of Puilladobhrain.

Loch Feochan snakes into the distance though the narrowest and shallowest part cannot be fully seen in this view. Barrnacarry Bay lies to starboard before entering the loch and is a useful anchorage if awaiting the tide.

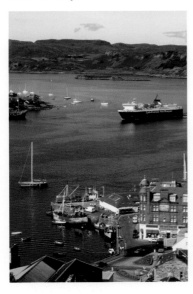

The north pier at Oban with a ferry approaching the Calmac pier to the south of it. The visitors' moorings in Cardingmill Bay can be seen to the left of the ferry.

Just 2 miles north of Puilladobhrain, **Loch Feochan** opens up to starboard. Its main claim to fame is its difficult entrance, which is shallow, tortuous and features a brisk tide running at up to 5 knots. The entrance is buoyed by the local boatyard to make things simpler and safer. The Sailing Directions recommend making the inward passage on the last quarter of the flood when the tide run is less swift and the depths greater.

Once inside, the Loch is a tranquil and sheltered stretch of water where a number of yachts are based on permanent moorings. There are facilities for visitors at the boatyard, **Ardoran Marine**, but no other services close by.

Oban Bay and Kerrera

Approached from the south through the attractive Kerrera Sound where most of the best anchorages are now occupied by moorings, **Oban** is the principal town and port in this part of the coast. It goes without saying that such a communications centre and tourist resort can provide most things the traveller by land or sea should need.

Paradoxically, though, Oban has never invested in facilities for day-to-day yachting traffic by providing berthing. However, visitors' moorings and an excellent new landing pontoon were completed in 2009 and there is also a plan to install a small transit marina in the bay between the North and South Piers. Anchoring is possible though not easy as the soundings are deep and there are many private moorings.

The fifteen visitors' moorings have now been concentrated in **Cardingmill Bay,** just off the new pontoon, and from here into the town centre is just over 1km (½ mile), although the more distant supermarkets are best visited by taxi. Oban Distillery is worth a visit.

Oban Bay from the west with Ben Cruachan in the background

Seaplane passengers on the pontoon at Oban Marina.

Oban has a rail and bus links with Glasgow and also a daily seaplane service from Glasgow in summer which lands in the bay and uses the Oban Marina launch service to ferry passengers ashore.

For those who seek the best shelter or need to leave their boat for longer periods **Oban Marina,** on the **Isle of Kerrera**, is ideal. The owners have upgraded its berths, facilities and boatyard equipment as part of their programme of expansion and development. The marina runs a free ferry service to the town's North Pier and also has full boatyard and repair services to offer customers. The Waypoint Bar and Grill is located here.

The marina is popular and very busy during the season at events including the Classic Malts Cruise and West Highland Yachting Week. The latter is held during the first week in August each year and attracts several hundred visiting yachts.

Further afield, visitors can enjoy wildlife watching, particularly by walking to the south end of the island via a series of secluded bays, cliffs and caves whilst enjoying outstanding views to Mull and the Argyll islands.

Looking north over the pontoons of Oban Marina towards the Lynn of Lorn. Hutcheson's monument is on the headland.

Loch Etive

A short sail from Oban brings you to Dunstaffnage which lies just outside the entrance to Loch Etive, whose entrance is guarded by the notorious Falls of Lora. This shelf of rock, which extends more than halfway across the channel under Connel Bridge, is a serious obstacle, as is the bridge which has just 15m clearance. The determined adventurer whose boat will fit will find comprehensive information on the tides and the various anchorages within the loch in the Sailing Directions.

Dunstaffnage Bay has long been a popular place to moor and anchoring space is now severely limited. However the majority of yachts are likely to want to use the facilities provided by **Dunstaffnage Marina** which has been developed during the last 20 years or so. The marina can now accommodate 150 boats on pontoon berths with power and water and has winter storage areas ashore. The hoist capacity is 18 tons and new workshop facilities cater for most servicing and maintenance requirements. The Wide Mouthed Frog is the social centre of the marina and is a seafood restaurant with a family bistro and a friendly bar.

The Lynn of Lorn

The Lynn of Lorn lies between the island of Lismore and the mainland and is the shortest route from Oban to Loch Linnhe and the Caledonian Canal beyond. It is also well-used by locally based boats for day sailing and although few of the anchorages within it give good all round shelter they are ideal for short stays and lunch stops, with the security of a marina berth or mooring only a few miles away.

In settled weather the sandy beaches of **Airds Bay**, **Camas Nathais** and **Tralee Bay** (Ardmucknish Bay) can be attractive temporary anchorages, the latter also allowing access on foot to the only sailmaker on the west coast north of Crinan! The small and rarely visited group of islands at the south west entrance to the Lynn of Lorn, known as **The Creags**, can provide anchorages sheltered from most wind directions if they are chosen and entered with care. Further north the isolated **Eilean Dubh** will also repay exploration. **Port Appin** is a delightful village with a carefree holiday atmosphere and is well served by both the Pier House and Airds hotels. The former has ten visitors' moorings for the use of its patrons and the views across Loch Linnhe are magnificent.

Opposite upper: Dunstaffnage Bay and Marina looking towards the Sound of Mull. Dunstaffnage Castle is on the end of the promontory and in the middle is the headquarters of SAMS, the Scottish Association for Marine Science.

Opposite lower: Looking east over Dunstaffnage Marina towards Connel and Loch Etive. The white water of the Falls of Lora can just be seen under the bridge.

The Artificial Reef

Marked on the chart, north of Eilean Dubh, is a rectangular blue area described as 'Artificial Reef'. This is the extent of the Loch Linnhe artificial reef which was constructed in 2006 for research purposes by SAMS (see above). It is one of the largest experimental reefs in Europe and 6300 tonnes of concrete blocks were used in its construction as 37 separate reef units. The ordinary yachtsman might be forgiven for thinking that there were quite enough reefs already but this one has been designed to facilitate research into many disciplines and is already proving very useful. It is safe to sail over it but do not anchor on it!

An occasional anchorage off the shingle spit joining Eilean na Cloiche and Eilean Dubh in the Creags.

Scottish Sea Life Centre

Situated on the south shore of Loch Creran the Centre is a spectacular aquarium and a rescue facility for grey and common seal pups. Canadian otters are also seen diving and swimming in a specially constructed sea water creek. Telephone 01631720386 for opening hours.

A feature of the Loch Creran Marine Special area of Conservation are the Serpulid Reefs which have been built by a rare type of marine worm and are very easily damaged. Accordingly anchoring is only permitted in designated areas within the loch.

The entrance to **Loch Creran** also lies at the north end of the Lynn of Lorn, just over a mile south of Port Appin, though both points of Airds Bay need to be given a very wide berth if approaching it from the north. This entrance is a much less fierce affair than that of Loch Etive although it is a little tortuous and the tide can run at up to 3–4 knots at springs. However it is well marked and lit. The loch is becoming popular for moorings which are situated both inside the entrance at South Shian and further within the loch at Barcaldine. Here **Barcaldine Marine** have recently developed a new yachting centre and, unusually for the west coast, they can provide a large amount of undercover winter storage, enough for around a hundred craft. Cruising yacht facilities include 50 swinging moorings, a short-stay pontoon and the usual toilets and showers.

Loch Creran is a Marine Special Area of Conservation, due to its unique Serpulid Reef Beds, and anchoring is prohibited in much of the loch. A prominent notice at the loch entrance reminds the navigator of this restriction.

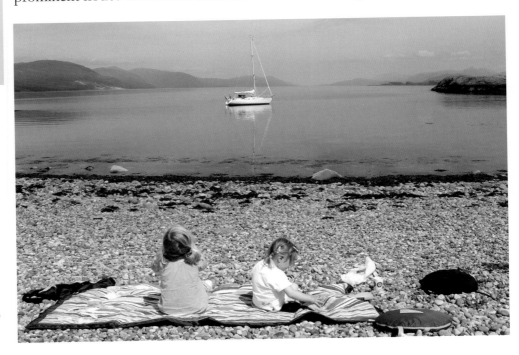

Two small girls enjoy the extensive view of Loch Linnhe from the shingle beach on Berneray Island whilst tucking in to their picnic.

Loch Linnhe

Northern Scotland is riven from north east to south west by the Great Glen Fault, the most dominant natural feature of the Highland landscape. It has long been a natural route from the North Sea and Moray Firth to the seaways of the inner Hebrides and the Atlantic, part of which is Loch Linnhe, which stretches from north of Oban to Fort William, in the shadow of Ben Nevis, Britain's highest mountain at 1,344 metres (4,409ft) above sea level.

For cruising yachtsmen the loch is best known as the route to the Caledonian Canal 30 miles north of Oban. However it does provide an attractive cruising area in its own right, suitable perhaps for a long weekend if sailing out of any of the Lorn marinas. Its southern end is approached either through the Lynn of Morvern, or the Lynn of Lorn, past the island of Lismore which separates them.

The lower part of Loch Linnhe runs from north of Lismore to Corran Narrows and is a broad open loch with the entrance to Loch Leven off to the east near the narrows. The upper part runs from the narrows to Fort William, and it is progressively overshadowed by the mountains on either side.

Eilean Balnagowan offers a useful passage anchorage in Loch Linnhe, approximately halfway between Corran Narrows and Port Appin.

Lismore is an attractive, fertile island of great character which thrives despite its relative isolation. It is good for for walking and cycling and there is a bicycle hire business, a store, a café and a Heritage Museum. It was once the seat of the Bishops of Argyll with a Cathedral church dating from the 13th century, partly surviving in the present Church of Saint Moluag, a contemporary of Saint Columba, who founded a monastery around AD565. You can also see an Iron Age Broch, a ruined Norse stronghold and several ruined castles. One of these, Achadun Castle, overlooks three pleasant anchorages near **Bernera Island** at the south west end of Lismore where, in one of the three, shelter can be obtained from most wind directions. The remaining anchorages around Lismore tend to be of a temporary, fair weather nature although **Port Ramsay** in the north gives excellent shelter from all directions except north, allied with good holding. The approach is complicated by many sunken rocks although a new white house has greatly improved the recognition of the principal leading line.

Opposite Port Ramsay, on the western shore of the **Lynn of Morvern**, is Glensanda superquarry which will eventually remove the entire granite mountain of Meall na Easaiche. The aggregate is transported along a mile of conveyor belts in tunnels to a jetty, where it is loaded directly into bulk carriers. The landscape disruption is controversial but from the passing sailor's point of view the main intrusion is the occasional passage of very large ships through the Sound of Mull.

Port Ramsay, a good anchorage at the north end of Lismore. The entrance to Loch a' Choire can be seen on the far side of Loch Linnhe.

Loch a' Choire, often bypassed because of its deep anchorage and potential squalls, now offers security and refreshment in the form of the Boathouse Restaurant which has laid six visitors' moorings.

Dallens Bay. The pontoon and moorings belonging to Linnhe Marine, a small and friendly marina situated in delightful surroundings.

Opposite: *Port an Dun (Bishop's Bay) at Ballachulish seen from the shore and above.*

Just a mile or so further north from Glensanda, **Loch a' Choire** opens up. This and Shuna Sound (see below) are just about the only natural anchorages that lower Loch Linnhe has to offer. Enclosed by high mountains on all sides it is a dramatic anchorage; 'dramatic' also describes the squalls that are generated in unsettled weather. To add to the problems, the shores shelve abruptly and soundings are deep but this drawback has been overcome by the provision of moorings for patrons of the newly established restaurant in the old Boathouse, (tel. 01967 411232) making the loch a worthwhile destination.

On the other side of Loch Linnhe, opposite Loch a'Choire, lies Shuna Island, separated from the mainland by the narrow **Shuna Sound**. **Dallens Bay**, approached from the south by a buoyed channel, is at the southern end of the Sound. Here **Linnhe Marine** welcomes visitors and have established 50 moorings and a pontoon for taking on stores, water and diesel and from which the yard ferry service will take you to and from your boat. Ashore, showers and toilets are available. There is a restaurant nearby.

Loch Leven

Before reaching the top of lower Loch Linnhe at Corran Narrows a turn to starboard will bring you in to Ballachulish Bay and the bridge at the narrows leading to Loch Leven. Shortly after the bridge, which has a clearance of 16m, is a large bay on the port hand, **Port an Dun**, known locally as Bishop's Bay, which is mainly taken up with moorings though space to anchor might be found. Better accommodation should be found further up at **Ballachulish** (West Harbour). This handy small harbour is the base of charter firm Lochaber Watersports, and is two miles from Ballachulish Bridge on the southern shore before Glencoe Islands. Berths are available, depending on demand from their own boats, and if you berth there you get free use of the swimming pool and sauna at the adjacent Isles of Glencoe Hotel. Your mooring fee is refunded against the cost of dinner.

Glencoe's excellent new Visitor Centre is 3km to the east, and provides all the information one might want about the Glen and its spectacular landscape, natural history, cultural heritage and diverse wildlife. The towering, brooding hills are a constant reminder of the tragic Glencoe Massacre which is chronicled at the centre.

Alongside at Corpach with Ben Nevis in the background; a yacht pauses before her passage up Neptune's staircase.

Neptune's Staircase is an impressive flight of eight locks, the longest in Britain. Passage through takes about 1½ hours and a lengthy wait may also be necessary while other boats finish locking through.

Opposite: *Ben Nevis dwarfs two working boats leaving the Caledonian Canal at Corpach and heading south.*

Caledonian Canal

Corpach and its locks and basin are situated at the south western end of the Caledonian Canal. Its main traffic today is leisure craft, including many visiting yachts from Scandinavia. Widely considered to be a masterpiece of canal engineering, the waterway joins Fort William with Inverness and is sixty miles long. Twenty two miles are man-made and the rest are natural lochs: Loch Lochy, Loch Oich, Loch Ness and Loch Dochfour.

Corpach is approached via Upper Loch Linnhe and Corran Narrows, where there is a significant tidal stream (up to 5 knots springs) that must be allowed for. There is a temporary anchorage just north of Corran Point but a much better place to await either the ebb through the narrows or the opening of the sea lock, as there is no waiting pontoon, is in **Camus nan Gall**, just over a mile south of Corpach. The canal basin usually accommodates yachts in transit east or west but does not have any long-stay berths. Corpach village has a few shops and amenities but main supplies will be found in Fort William. The adjacent railway runs a steam-hauled excursion train in summer from Fort William to Mallaig.

Within the canal operating hours, the sea lock can be entered four hours either side of HW. More information and a Skipper's Guide can be obtained from www.scottishcanals.co.uk or by contacting the Canal Office at Inverness on 01463 725500.

Building the canal

The Caledonian Canal was built between 1803 and 1822, partly to facilitate safer ship movements from east to west by offering an alternative to the hazardous Pentland Firth and partly as a work scheme for the impoverished Highlands, which was still suffering the aftermath of the Jacobite Wars and the consequences of the Highland Clearances.

The route was surveyed by James Watt in 1773, but nothing happened until the 1803 Act of Parliament, as a result of which that other famous Scottish engineer, Thomas Telford, was asked to be chief designer.

As the canal was intended to carry the ships of the time, the locks were the largest ever built but, by the time the canal was finished in 1822, they were too small for the new generation of iron steamships. Also, as the Napoleonic Wars were over, the navy had little use of the waterway either. The Caledonian Canal had cost almost £1m and faced a future of under-use for much had changed in the 20 years it took to build it.

The Sea Road to the Isles

The **Sound of Mull** runs south east to north west which tends to result in winds that blow along it, almost irrespective of the true direction. This, of course, means it is often against the hapless sailor who has to beat to windward when he had anticipated a fair wind! The tidal flow is also a factor when planning the passage of the Sound, ranging from ¾–1½ knots depending on location, reaching 3 knots at Duart Point and Lady Isle at its southern end. However your passage plan is more often than not dictated by the stronger streams south of Fladda and those in the Sound of Mull have to be taken as you find them though it pays to get it right at Duart if nowhere else.

Although sometimes referred to as a 'marine motorway' or 'milk run' the Sound is in fact a very pleasant waterway between the mountains of Mull and Morvern; there is always something of interest to see and, like the Kyles of Bute, no two passages are ever quite the same. There are tempting calling places en route, Loch Aline and Salen being the favourites and the Sailing Directions list another eight anchorages suitable for a brief stop to await the tide, or a longer stop in settled weather.

Loch Aline, about a third of the way up the Sound, is in a delightful setting. The two main anchorages are in the south east corner of the loch and at its head. The former is now fairly well filled with moorings and the anchorage on the opposite shore, south west of the beacon marking Sgeiran nan Ron, is an attractive alternative. Any of the Loch Aline anchorages will give access to woodland and coastal walks but possibly the best run ashore is at **Ardtornish** at the head of the loch to see the woodland gardens.

The village of Lochaline has a hotel, a restaurant and a snack bar. The dive centre offers shower facilities and a café to visiting sailors. The food store also sells diesel and petrol. Since the silica mine closed there have been ambitions to install a pontoon just north of the village, but it will probably be some years in the future before these are realised.

Salen, halfway up the Sound, offers a quieter alternative to Loch Aline with good protection from westerlies though care must be taken to avoid the Antelope Rock which is no longer buoyed.

Of the other anchorages in the Sound, **Ardtornish Bay** is worth a mention. It is only too easy to slip into here and drop the anchor when an anticipated fast reach turns into a boisterous beat and Tobermory begins to seem a long way off. The total calm afforded by the high escarpment to the north is a welcome transformation.

Opposite upper: The Sound of Mull stretches north west beyond Lismore Light and Duart Point. The strength of the tidal stream here can clearly be seen around Lady's Rock on the left of the picture.

The ferry terminal at Lochaline looking towards the head of the loch.

Ardtornish Bay anchorage gives good shelter from northerly winds.

Opposite lower: The West Highland Week fleet passing Lismore light.

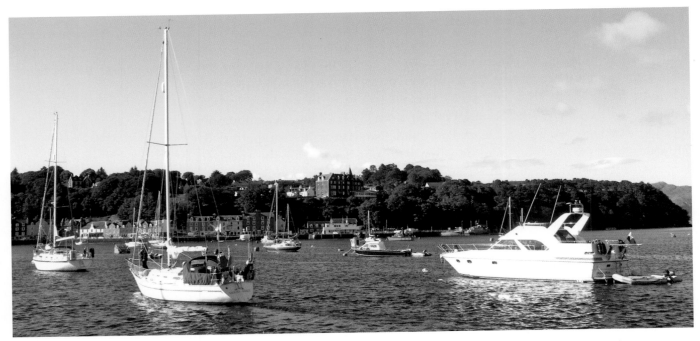

Tobermory. The view from the moorings. In high season you will have to arrive early to secure one.

Opposite upper: *Tobermory seen from the south with Ardnamurchan beyond and Rum in the far distance. The new harbour building has since been erected on part of the car park at the head of the pontoons on the left of the picture.*

Taigh Solais, the new harbour facilities and office building opened in 2009.

Opposite lower: *Tobermory fishing pier with the iconic painted buildings behind.*

Tobermory

Tobermory is everyone's idea of a traditional fishing village, which is not surprising as it was built as such by the British Fisheries Society in 1788 as part of their drive to encourage herring fisheries in the Highlands. The Society built the sea wall and reclaimed the land behind and the prolific engineer, Thomas Telford, designed the pier. The varied shoreside buildings, comparatively recently painted in striking colours, combine to produce the picturesque waterfront by which it is known worldwide.

Tobermory offers almost everything the cruising yachtsman could possibly want. A well-stocked supermarket, hardware store, banks, chandlery and chart agent will provide all that has been forgotten or overlooked before the yacht heads out to the west or north. For those who intend to stay a little longer, there is a wide range of hotels, restaurants and bars and a very good array of shoreside facilities including a distillery and a brewery.

The new harbour building overlooking the extensive serviced pontoons has state of the art showers, toilet, laundry and a visitor centre. The Tobermory Harbour Association runs the moorings and pontoons and is a community owned company which reinvests all profits to provide better facilities. The moorings are well organised and space has been allocated close to the shore for those who wish to anchor.

This port is so picturesque, interesting and lively that for some cruising sailors it is the 'port of lost cruises'!

The Tobermory Galleon

In August 1588 the English fleet, after their successful series of running engagements with the Spanish Armada in the English Channel, completed their rout of the ships off the Kent coast assisted by a strong southerly gale. Unable to sail to windward the Spanish galleons were driven north. One of them, believed to be the *Florenzia*, in the course of making her way westwards around Scotland took shelter in the bay of Tobermory. While there she blew up and sank in 20 metres. Rumours have persisted that she was carrying gold and silver treasure. Many salvage attempts, the first in 1665 and continuing at intervals until comparatively recently, have produced some gold coins, bronze cannons and cannon balls, along with pieces of plate and other artefacts, but none of the reputed treasure.

Loch Sunart seen from the Tobermory direction. Both the Stirks can be seen above water on the left of the picture and the more southerly one, which covers, has to be guarded against.

Loch Sunart

Loch Sunart, a very attractive loch and well worth visiting, is a popular diversion from the well worn route to the isles and is often used as a sheltered cruising refuge in periods of unsettled weather. Extending some 17 miles inland it certainly allows plenty of scope for exploration and it is well endowed with good anchorages and interesting diversions. However it is not hazard free and it demands careful pilotage in places.

Before entering Loch Sunart, the anchorage at **Kilchoan** on the south shore of the Ardnamurchan peninsular provides a quieter alternative to the fleshpots of Tobermory and the anchorage is better sheltered in north easterly weather when Tobermory can become less comfortable. Visitors' moorings are available.

Loch Drumbuie on its south shore is easy of access, offers a selection of anchorages for varying wind directions and is a popular place when Tobermory becomes too crowded or the swell begins to set in. **Sailean Mor** on the north side of Oronsay is snug alternative to Drumbuie but with limited depth and swinging room, whilst **Loch Teacuis** is something of a challenge to dedicated rock-hoppers due to its two shallow and rock strewn entrances either side of the island of Carna, where the tide runs at around 2½ knots and an even shallower second narrows leading to the inner loch. Lovers of complete solitude should find it here.

Salen Bay lies a little over 5 nautical miles east of Loch Sunart's entrance, past Glenborrodale Castle, Mingary Castle ruins, Ben Hiant and the Sunart oakwoods and is a popular sheltered stopping point offering a number of

Below right: A ruined croft on Oronsay with the anchorage in Sailean Mor beyond.

Below: Yachts anchored in Loch Drumbuie on a day that could not be more different than that described by Ronald Faux.

facilities. The Jetty has mooring buoys for hire and customers' vessels may berth alongside to take on water. Marine diesel at competitive prices is also available. Ashore, the Salen Hotel will provide sustenance for the hungry sailor either in the dining room, or more informally in the sun room.

Not many yachts make it up to the head of Loch Sunart at **Strontian**, where care is needed to avoid the extensive shoals off the mouth of the river, but those that do can avail themselves of a mooring provided by Kilcamb Lodge and their crews can enjoy a meal at this well-recommended hotel.

Salen, Loch Sunart from the south. The jetty is on the west side of the bay and the rocks in the middle are now marked by a buoy.

Loch Sunart

'It is usually assumed that sailing from Tobermory means heading north around Ardnamurchan or round to the superb western edge of Mull. The seeker after quiet corners need voyage no further than the sheltered waters of Loch Sunart. The wind was still bellowing from the south-west, the skies were overcast and the glass lingering around bottom C when we left Tobermory Bay. With a well-reefed main and the smallest jib we set a course for the haughty rib of Maclean's Nose on Ardnamurchan, which was just visible.

Hebe held course with rain-drenched sails, gurgling purposefully along. The thickening weather wiped away Maclean's Nose and reduced the wash to a dim grey line. It was the west at its worst. Suddenly the buoy marking the New Rocks appeared to port. We were not blessed with a log but there was nothing else the forlorn-looking marker could have been, so we set a course slightly north of east which would clear both the Red Rocks and Big Stirk and soon Auliston Head appeared in the gloom. The south-west wind gave a few more derisory blasts before Hebe slid into the lee of the coast, still going at top speed towards a dead end in the angle of the coast.

The sailing instructions described Loch Drumbuy as a perfectly sheltered anchorage but the entrance is not perfectly apparent on such a day. "It's there all right. I mean it can't be a Clyde Cruising Club wheeze, can it?" Trevor said. The dark rocks of the coast closed in forbiddingly. The shore was clear now, hard-shouldered and decorated with stretches of drenched moss. Hebe sailed into a narrow gap no more than half a cable wide between the Morvern shore and the island of Oronsay. The channel was deep but the instructions warned of a rock off the south point with 3ft. over it. The narrows formed a key to a perfect anchorage, quite unspoilt and with no sign of civilisation about it. The usual anchorage is in the south-west corner but a large raft of jolly sailing folk, the jingle of bottles and the appearance on his flying bridge of a man in immaculate white ducks, encouraged us to slip behind a rock on the opposite side of the loch where we were protected from everything.

Trevor was below, tearing the entrails from a couple of mackerel, warming up a sponge pudding and bringing the Bull's Blood up to body temperature by putting the bottle into a pan of boiling water. The rain beat down on the flat surface of the loch, water hung like jewellery along the branches of trees and on the high hillside opposite a number of burns had burst into silvery torrents. A heron watching Hebe from the bank when a lump of entrails flew from the hatch and over the side, launched himself in lumbering, reptilian flight to the opposite shore. There was a waft of warmth from below, the rich whiff of grilled mackerel and the bite of wine brought almost to boiling point (it is virtually impossible to destroy the qualities of Bull's Blood). I was dry inside my oilskins, the circulation was returning with a sting to my face and the rain could not destroy the impression of a fine day's sail.'

The West, Ronald Faux, 1982.

Inside the Ardalanish anchorage.

Right: The rockbound shoreline of Rubh' Ardalanish is hardly inviting, but once the small gut at the base of its west side is entered all becomes snug and secure when the anchor bites into the sandy bottom.

David Balfour's Bay & the Stevensons

Before the Stevenson family's lighthouses, life afloat was a hazardous business on the rock-strewn and tide-riven west coast: the only beneficiaries being the people of the islands who enjoyed the spoils of the boats which had foundered.

Dubh Artach lighthouse was just one of the many great lights designed and constructed around the British coast and abroad by no fewer than eight members of the Stevenson family between 1790 and 1940, from the very first and possibly the most hazardous undertaking on the Bell Rock in 1811 to the equally impressive feats of engineering at Muckle Flugga, Ardnamurchan and Skerryvore.

In 1870 Robert Louis Stevenson, aged 20, visited the Island of Earraid, the shore settlement for the workers building, to his father Tom's and Uncle David's design, the lighthouse on Dubh Artach. More interested in what he saw around him on the Ross of Mull than in the great engineering works offshore he stored away his experiences, later to emerge as the vivid tale in *Kidnapped* of the brig *Covenant's* wrecking on the Torran Rocks and David Balfour being washed up on what is now known as Balfour's Bay on Earraid pictured in the adjacent photograph.

Ross of Mull & Iona

It will be remembered from the section dealing with the Firth of Lorn that the passage west along the Ross of Mull is 25 miles without the option of a secure anchorage. However, this is only partially true as immediately west of **Rubh' Ardalanish** there is a splendidly remote anchorage in a small sandy gut which, although not recommended in strong winds from south to west, usually affords a decent amount of shelter in most conditions. From here westwards the geology changes and so does the pilotage, which requires great care as you pass inside the Torran Rocks in the approach to the Sound of Iona.

Before entering the Sound you will pass **Tinker's Hole**, on the island of Erraid. This is another celebrated west coast anchorage and it is a real haven, where the worst of weather can be ridden out, thanks to clean holding on sand and in *extremis*, mooring rings in the rock wall in the north east corner.

From Tinker's Hole to Iona is but a short step, usually via the channel between Eilean Dubh and Eilean nam Muc. This channel may seem narrow the first time you use it but if you consider that MacBrayne's 270ft *King George V* routinely swept through this narrow channel on its round-Mull voyages, the average yacht will not have a problem, particularly as this steamer service ceased decades ago!

No cruise is complete without visiting **Iona** for, despite its poor anchorage and tricky Sound, it is thought by many to be the most important place in Scottish history. The anchorage is just south of the ferry jetty but beware the submarine cables that link Iona to Mull which lie exactly where one might otherwise drop anchor. An alternative is the bay of **Port na Fraing** at the north west tip of Iona, close by some sandy beaches yet still within easy walking distance of the Abbey.

This delightful island is worth exploring beyond the famous Abbey. It has a rocky coast interspersed with sandy beaches and its low hills give a splendid panorama of Tiree and Coll to the west and Mull to the east. The views have attracted artists as well as religious recluses and the scenes painted by Peploe and Cadell are among the most evocative produced by these two members of the group, who came to be known as 'The Scottish Colourists'. Once you have seen the vibrant colours of the sea and sand in the Sound of Iona you will understand from where they got their inspiration.

Fionnphort, just opposite, is the best place in the area for stores although Iona also has several shops. You can anchor off the ferry jetty, again avoiding the cables. Like Iona, it is thronging with tourists all day but, again like Iona, peace descends with the departure of the last coach and that is the time to board the dinghy and land on Iona.

Bull Hole, a few cables north of Fionnphort, is somewhat encumbered by moorings but it is a wonderful place to view the sun setting to the north west. **Bunessan** in Loch na Lathaich on the north side of the Ross of Mull, offers good shelter when the anchorages in the Sound of Iona are uncomfortable.

'Welcome to Iona'. Yachtsmen can take some comfort from the fact that one expense they will not have to face is the fare for a boat trip to Staffa!

The Ross of Mull from the south with the Sound of Iona to the west. Tinker's Hole is just below the centre of the picture and David Balfour's Bay, named on the chart as Traigh Gheal, on the extreme right.

Iona Abbey, not only a unique building but a useful sea mark. The tower is one of the leading marks from the south and it also denotes the shallowest part of the Sound when it is abeam.

Iona

Perhaps the most visited and written about of all the islands, Iona is considered one of the principal foundations for Christianity in Scotland, its early monks the creators of the wonderfully illuminated Book of Kells and now home to the thriving Iona Community.
Iona impresses everyone in different ways:

• From the moment you enter the Sound of Iona, and particularly on a sunny day when the water colour changes dramatically to a pale azure reflecting the white sandy bottom, you know this is a special place – different from anywhere else on the West Coast – or, indeed, in the world.

• The take-your-breath-away drama of an Iona sunset seen from the top of Eilean Nam Ban, inside which is Bull Hole.

• How easy it is to step off the well-worn tourist/pilgrim track to the Abbey and experience absolute solitude.

• Whether one has faith or not, how close Iona feels to the 6th century and Columba's time.

• The survival of this place as a living community against all the odds: the fragility of Columba's original mission; Viking raids in the 8th and 9th centuries; misuse of Abbey revenues in the 14th century necessitating a rebuild around 1450; abandonment by the monks after the Reformation and gradual erosion by the weather thereafter.

Cragaig Bay, Ulva. The rash of islets looks daunting on the approach but once the cottage is identified access is surprisingly straightforward.

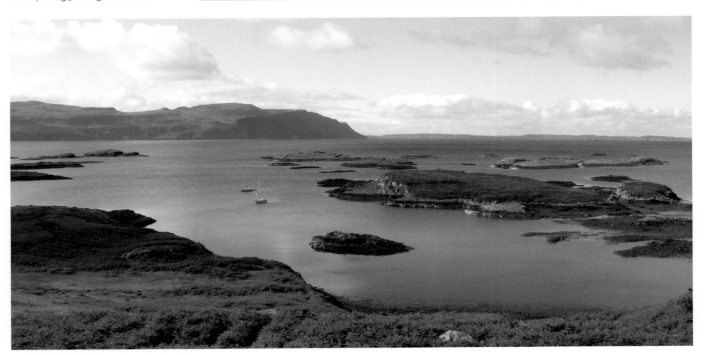

West Coast of Mull

'The navigation of the West of Mull requires considerable care. The whole coast is completely exposed to the SW, and though there are many clean bays which might be used as temporary anchorages, most of the sheltered harbours are rather difficult of access, owing to submerged rocks.'

This rather bleak assessment appeared in the Club's first entry for Mull, in the Sailing Directions of 1913, and has continued ever since; the only paragraph to remain totally unchanged. This is because it was, and still is, perfectly correct, the only difference being that with better equipment, including depth sounders, radar, GPS, chart plotters, reliable engines and of course Sailing Directions, it is a good deal easier and safer to enter 'the sheltered harbours' now than it was then. Even so, it is no place to be out sailing when a gale comes up from the south west.

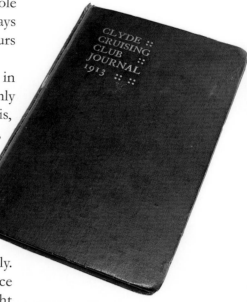

The Sailing Directions were in fact first printed in instalments, as part of the Club's Annual Journal, until 1922 when they were published as a separate book.

Between Iona and Rubh' a' Chaoil the Mull coast is indented by two lochs: **Loch Scridain** and **Loch na Keal**. Both offer magnificent scenery as they skirt the south and north sides of Ben More respectively. However they both suffer from the usual drawback of mountain lochs, fierce squalls and unpredictable winds, and are probably best explored in light weather under power when the several anchorages, within Loch Scridain at least, can be enjoyed.

However it is in the islands where the most interest is to be found: **Ulva** and its near neighbour **Gometra**, to which it is joined by a bridge, form the largest group and between them have the most anchorages. **Cragaig Bay** and **Ulva Ferry** on the south side both give good shelter and have access to good walking along a well-engineered track that links the two. Along the way you can explore the ruined village of Cragaig, less than half a mile from the anchorage, and look for the ruined watermill by the burn. At Ulva Ferry there is a small museum and a small restaurant. Lachlan Macquarie, governor of New South Wales from 1809 to 1822 and sometimes known as 'father of Australia', was born on Ulva where his family had owned the island for centuries. His mausoluem is to be found at Gruline at the head of Loch na Keal.

The Boathouse, Ulva Ferry provides a welcoming restaurant and has a small museum nearby.

Gometra has two good anchorages: **Gometra Harbour** on the south side and **Acairseid Mhor** at the extreme west end, which can claim to be the snuggest of them all. The Sailing Directions describe them all, including **Soriby Bay** on the north side of Ulva which can be reached by passing through the intricate and shallow **Ulva Sound**.

Due south of Ulva Ferry lies the much smaller island of **Inch Kenneth** where the wide open anchorage is ringed by beaches and drying reefs, all backed by the dramatic cliffs of Mull. Anchoring here in fine weather and visiting the ruined chapel and graveyard is highly recommended.

One of Lunga's much-photographed puffins

Further out to the west is **Staffa**, which is too well-known to need describing. As with Iona, try to land before the excursion boats arrive or after they have left but first make sure that no swell is running and either keep a very close eye on the boat or leave someone aboard as the anchorage can only be described as precarious.

Further out again lie the weirdly sculptured **Treshnish Isles**. The largest island, **Lunga**, has the best anchorage and well repays a visit ashore, especially during the breeding season when you will be able to get as close to a puffin (with as little effort!) as anywhere else in the Hebrides. Although often described as a temporary anchorage, staying overnight in settled weather is often quite possible and well worth it.

This scattering of islands has more attraction for the cruising sailor than almost any other part of the Inner Hebrides. Their historic and scenic interest is outstanding and the opportunity to observe wildlife is as good as you will find anywhere. Despite these assets, the area is generally uncrowded, with ample room in the many anchorages which can offer shelter from most weather, depending on their individual topography. Distances between these island havens are small so, even with the most relaxed of cruising plans, many could be visited in a couple of days. But why rush? Take a week over your circumnavigation of Mull and get to know all of them well.

Before returning to Tobermory you will have a few headlands to round and, to speed your passage, it is worth getting a fair tide and avoiding the race off Caliach Point. Once round this you will pass the final Mull anchorage, **Loch Cuan** (Loch a' Chumhainn) 3 miles east of the point. Entry looks fearsome on the chart but below half tide most dangers show and only in northerlies should it be avoided.

Gometra from the south with Loch Tuadh beyond, then Rub'a' Chaoil on the extreme left, Caliach Point and, in the far distance, Rum.

***Opposite**: Acairseid Mhor, Gometra is often acclaimed as one of the best small anchorages in the Inner Hebrides.*

Entering Loch Cuan the hard way

As you check your position on the GPS, furl up the genoa, drop the main and reach for the starter button spare a thought for Frank Cowper who sailed around Britain whilst researching his 'Sailing Tours' in a converted 48 foot Dover fishing lugger, sometimes with just a boy for a crew but often singlehanded.

'I reluctantly put up the helm, eased off the sheets, and steered by compass for Rhudha Cailleach again. It did not take long to pick this up, and then I thought of Sgeir Mor, and wondered if I could find my way into Loch Cuan, a complete stranger, in a fog, and with only chart No. 2515 to help me.

I decided I would try. So keeping well in shore and listening for the noise of the breakers, I groped my way until I saw a rock on my starboard bow, and heard a dull roar on the port. I must be inside something. Telling the boy to sound, I luffed up and shortened sail; we had six fathoms, and I did not know where we were.

When all was snug I once more turned E ½S until I heard the sea breaking right ahead. We had seven fathoms, and I steered more southerly. Then I saw an ugly reef close to me; but the sea was very quiet. I knew we must have got inside somewhere, and was preparing to let go when I heard voices, a cow lowing, a dog barking, and the thud of an oar.

"Hold on!" I said, as I let the yacht run on a little farther. Then I saw a mast. It was a fishing-boat at her moorings. We had three fathoms, and although I could see nothing else I determined to anchor. There seemed no tide, and the breeze was light and damp. The old ship lay easily to her anchor.'

Sailing Tours, The Clyde to the Thames, Frank Cowper, 1896

The old pier at Arinagour, with the anchoring area beyond and the visitor moorings out of sight to the right.

The visitors' moorings at Arinagour. Yes, it does rain sometimes!

Coll

The attractive island of Coll features on most cruising itineraries and **Arinagour**, despite its exposure to the south and east, is a popular stopping place. Part of the attraction is its visitors' moorings and a hospitable hotel serving good food. Beaches, bird life, fishing, interesting flora, golf in the machair and opportunities for walking add to the attractions but the drawback is the swell which can roll in with winds from south to east.

The landscape of Coll is of low rough hills interspersed with machair, the flat sandy pasture that develops on most west-facing Hebridean shores. It is partly the product of sand blown ashore over centuries, and partly of the changes in sea level since the last ice age. It has long been the most important asset of island communities, which go to great lengths to preserve it; a patch of damaged turf will soon become a wind-excavated hollow, a process that is hard to stop.

Bicycles can be hired from the shop which will provide information about routes to follow, one of which is down the east coast and back up the west, or vice versa. It is around 5 miles to the south end of the island and 4 to the north.

A small east facing anchorage between the north end of the island and **Eilean Mor** is an interesting fair weather stop beside the Cairns of Coll and, at the south end of the island, **Loch Breachacha** and **Crossapol Bay,** near the approach to Gunna Sound, are a good starting points for a passage to Barra.

Tiree

Often billed as the sunshine capital of the Hebrides because its low terrain does not generate cloud or rain as much as hillier islands, Tiree is more fertile than Coll, and has a much larger population. Unfortunately, like Coll, it lacks an all-weather anchorage, although **Gott Bay** is well sheltered from westerly winds. **Clach Chuirr** at the north end of the island in Gunna Sound is the only anchorage sheltered from the south and east at either Tiree or Coll but care must be taken as a submarine cable between the islands bisects the bay.

The island is now world-famous in windsurfing circles for its strong breezes and big seas, attracting hundreds of enthusiasts to its west coast where the annual Tiree Wave Classic is held each autumn. Cycling around such flat terrain is also popular and bicycles can be hired. There is a scheduled air service to Glasgow and a ferry service to Oban.

Hynish, at the south end of the island, was the base for the builders of Skerryvore lighthouse and Skerryvore Lighthouse Museum, run by the Hebridean Trust, is a worthwhile visit for anyone with an interest in the history of this engineering achievement. The outer jetty almost dries at LW but can be used at HW for a short stop, or you can anchor off.

Ornithologists also come to Tiree – to hear and possibly see the rare corncrake, as 200 birds spend the summer keeping the natives awake at night! Once you have heard the corncrake's incessant nocturnal cry, you will understand.

Hynish and the building of Skerryvore Lighthouse

The Signal Tower at Hynish was built to transmit and receive semaphore signals to and from the building works at Skerryvore.

It was also the transhipment point for the granite from the Ross of Mull that was used for the lighthouse's construction. The blocks were cut by a team of masons to their precise interlocking shapes before being delivered to the lighthouse site. The inner harbour (see adjacent photo), also built by Alan Stevenson, posed some problems as it kept silting up. Stevenson built a dam in the hill behind which enabled him to sluice the sand away from time to time. Ingenious, and still there to be seen.

Building what is now considered a perfectly proportioned light tower was a major engineering challenge, and took from 1839 to 1844. During the first winter all the preparation work was washed away! The finished lighthouse is almost 50 metres (156ft) high with a base diameter of 13 metres (42ft) tapering gracefully to just under 5 metres (16ft). The light was automated in 1994.

Those looking for solitude will find all they need amongst the skerries and islets off the north end of Tiree and in Gunna Sound.

3 Ardnamurchan to Cape Wrath

Rounding Ardnamurchan Point and making for more northerly waters opens a new and dramatic chapter in any west coast cruise.

Firstly, the rounding of **Ardnamurchan** (hill or point of the great sea) is not always the smoothest of passages, as the combination of Atlantic swells finding their way in from the west, and their subsequent reflection off the rocky shore, means it is best to keep a good offing in all but calm conditions.

Once that has been achieved a panoply of choices opens up, including visiting the Small Isles and then deciding whether to sail northward outside or inside Skye. The former course, perhaps via Canna to Loch Harport or Loch Dunvegan, is overlooked by the magnificent Cuillin, whilst the latter offers the diversions of the Knoydart lochs and the tidal challenges of Kyle Rhea before reaching the Sound of Raasay and the Inner Sound.

As one voyages northward beyond Skye, the mainland mountains of Torridon and Assynt become progressively more majestic, until the land finally stops at Cape Wrath where the Minch becomes the Atlantic. The name 'Wrath' is derived from the old Norse word for turning point, for this is where the Vikings altered course on their voyages between their Orkney stronghold and the west coast.

Even larger vessels can take quite a beating on occasion when rounding Ardnamurchan.

Passage Planning

The initial decision whether to go west or east of Skye, apart from any wishes to visit particular places, will probably depend on the weather pattern and forecast. The western route is more exposed once north west of Canna, and has relatively few havens to shelter from bad weather. On the other hand, the inner route via the Sound of Sleat and Kyle Rhea is sheltered by the island of Skye and has many stopping places en route.

Ardnamurchan Lighthouse. Built in 1849 by Alan Stevenson it is, reportedly, the only lighthouse in the world in the Egyptian style, though this is barely evident to the passing sailor!

Sunset seen from the anchorage in Sanna Bay. If heading south in conditions like these, why press on to Tobermory?

Looking over Sanna Bay to the Small Isles of Muck, Rum and Eigg (left to right) with Canna just visible on the horizon, far left.

Yachts heading for the Outer Isles will sail north westwards to Canna or beyond. Others aiming for the far north west will want to press on north, probably taking the shortest route through the Inner Sound, but those planning to go no further than Skye should, if the weather is looking good, take the opportunity to go outside Skye first and make a clockwise circumnavigation. However, if your plans are flexible and the weather is on the light side, why spend hours motoring north when there are so many islands and lochs to enjoy within a twenty mile radius of Ardnamurchan?

The Mainland Coast

The mainland coast south of Mallaig includes a number of small lochs which will reward exploration and, in some cases, provide a secure anchorage. The northern part of this area, between the Ardnamurchan and Ardnish peninsulas, is the Sound of Arisaig Marine Special Area of Conservation, formed to protect the unique seabed life in the area although this imposes no restrictions on cruising yachts anchoring.

The first anchorage is **Sanna Bay**, just a couple of miles north of Ardnamurchan Point, which is a handy lunch stop or overnight anchorage in settled weather. Sanna Bay is a good example of a white shell sand beach with, on a fine day, a turquoise sea reminiscent of a tropical island's. There are a few houses on the south shore but otherwise this is a sparsely populated area.

The circular form of solidified magma, know as a ring dyke, can be clearly seen here, stretching almost the full width of the Ardnamurchan peninsula. Sanna Bay is in the lower right corner of the picture.

The energetic can walk the 5km to Ardnamurchan Lighthouse where the Kingdom of Light visitor centre has a café, cottage accommodation and great views to the Small Isles, the Western Isles and the Skye Cuillin. Corrachadh Mòr, 1km south of Ardnamurchan is, at 6°13.4W, the most westerly point on the British mainland. This area is one of the finest unspoilt wildernesses on the Scottish coast, where you could see wildcats, pine martin, golden eagles and sea eagles. Those with an interest in geology might know that the Ardnamurchan peninsula is formed by a caldera, or collapsed volcano. This is not readily apparent from seaward but is illustrated dramatically by the aerial photograph above.

The engine room in the lighthouse section of the excellent museum in the former Head Keeper's house.

White Sand Bay and Loch Ceann Traigh, situated between Sanna and Loch Moidart, are also open bays with perfect beaches. **Loch Ceann Traigh** is easy to enter, unlike many anchorages on this predominently lee shore, and the pinewood backed, sweeping beach is generally deserted. Good holding and shelter make this anchorage a useful refuge if the wind is in the south or south west.

Loch Moidart

'The day was dying in a lurid, murky twilight born of portending storm. The Grey Wind of the west was massing its forces for the assault. It was a time for ships to be fleeing havenwards; to be hastening home, like the New Barge of Clanranald:

Back in gallop o'er to Moidart,
Past the hilly isles of caves,
Past the mountains dark and frowning,
Past the reefs so low and cold.

Where to steer for? That was the question. In all that rugged land of Moidart, where to find a haven of refuge? The name means "heights of the sea spray", and as we sped past Loch Moidart's narrow entrance, the aptness of the description was plain. For the rising seas were breaking heavily on Eilean Shona and the off-lying reefs, and though we knew that cradled in those dark wooded heights were still waters, where, beside old Castle Tioram of Clanranald, the winds might rave in vain, yet the roaring seas at the mouth, and the beaconless shoals within, daunted us. Still seeking, therefore, we held to the northward.'

Where did they end up? For the next instalment of this saga turn to p.121.

Loch Moidart is a favourite anchorage, overlooked by the ruins of the MacDonald Clan's Castle Tioram which stands on an island connected to the shore by a sandy isthmus. The castle is a scheduled monument, protected under the provisions of the Ancient Monuments and Archaeological Area Act, and is privately owned. The main loch entrance, south of Eilean Shona, is something of a pilotage challenge but, once inside, several well sheltered anchorages are available. The entrance north of Eilean Shona is even more complex and does not lead to the main anchorages near the castle, although there is a well sheltered pool called North Harbour for anchoring.

Loch Ailort, Loch nan Uamh and the Borrodale Islands are the remaining options between Ardnamurchan and Arisaig.

Opposite upper: Loch Moidart from above Castle Tioram. Two anchorages can be seen: that off the jetty on Shona, centre right, and the one to the north east of the castle, lower right.

Opposite lower: Going ashore from an anchorage in the Borrodale Islands.

Loch Ailort

'The upper reaches of Loch Ailort, like those of Moidart, are narrow and shoal with sunken rocks, and not to be recommended, while its lower reaches are wide, and open to the ocean's attack from the westward; but in the entrance is strung a group of four islands, the largest of which is Eilean Gobhar, and behind which is the most accessible and sheltered anchorage in the whole of the Ardnamurchan region.

Towards its proffered shelter we headed with all speed, for night was closing in, and the whine of the rising wind was charged with menace. The sunset had burned itself out to a low strip of dirty yellow, smoking with cloud, against which stood out darkly the outline of Muck. The sea, previously frolicsome and kindly, had grown suddenly dark and threatening, and was breaking with a sibilant roaring that filled the night with desolation. Running before the pursuing breakers we sped into the dark entrance of Ailort, swung round the bluff western end of Eilean Gobhar, and rounding to the wind, let go the anchor just as the storm, beginning in earnest, burst over the loch in a deluge of rain. All that night the wind came booming from the west, and whined and shrieked in the rigging. And as we rode to it on straining cable and heard the frightsome tumult of the breakers on the seaward side of Gobhar, we had good cause to feel grateful toward the sturdy little rock that shielded us from the Atlantic's rage.'

West Coast Cruising, John McLintock, 1938

Loch Ailort is a little longer than Loch Moidart, and reaches into the hills to the village of the same name at its head. Like many Scottish sea lochs, it is a typical product of the last ice age. The inner loch is very deep where the ice removed material and dumped it at the shallow and rocky entrance, where it has been no doubt added to by sea sediments. The Sailing Directions describe half a dozen anchorages at, or near, the entrance and there is another, some 4 miles within the loch, near the pier at the village.

Just a short distance to the north is **Loch nan Uamh**, within which the Borrodale Islands and the small loch at the head provide various pretty spots to drop the hook. These are frequently used by yachts based at nearby Arisaig. The impressive railway viaduct at the head of Loch nan Uamh is one of several built on the famous rail route from Fort William to Mallaig.

The Young Pretender, otherwise known as Bonnie Prince Charlie, landed here, possibly in the bay just to the east of the **Borrodale Islands**, in August 1745. The next year, after his defeat at Culloden, he returned as a fugitive with a price of £30,000 – £2.5m at today's values – on his head and fled to France on board one of two French ships which had been anchored in Loch nan Uamh for two weeks – the Royal Navy having left the west coast for Orkney.

A sandy beach on the Ardnish Peninsula on the north side of the entrance to Loch Ailort; a perfect fair weather anchorage.

The yacht moorings at Arisaig, Loch nan Ceall, with the Sgurr of Eigg in the gloom beyond.

The channel leading up to Loch nan Ceall is not only narrow in places, but also shallow.

Arisaig is the village at the head of Loch nan Ceall, another loch with a somewhat tricky entrance, but due to the popularity of the bay for yacht moorings and as a base for trips to the Small Isles, it is well marked with perches and leading lines and can be entered in all but the strongest onshore winds. There are sixty swinging moorings operated by **Arisaig Marine** (tel. 01687 450224) and, with good road and rail connections, it is an excellent place to leave a yacht at the end of a delivery passage. It is also a good place to use as a base for a family cruising holiday. With a bewildering choice of islands, lochs and sandy bays only a 2 to 3 hour sail away, all ages of crew should be happy and, for those days when there is no sailing, there is plenty to do ashore, especially if a car is also available.

Arisaig provides a choice of places to dine and a café/restaurant and hotel are both within the village. Other amenities include a shop and Post Office, the Fort William to Mallaig line railway station, a bus service and a 9 hole golf course.

The Land, Sea and Islands Visitor Centre is a community project which opened in July 1999 on the site of a derelict smiddy in the heart of Arisaig village. It has a viewing room overlooking the Small Isles, a souvenir shop, artefacts from crofting and fishing, a rebuilt forge, wildlife exhibitions and information about the secret activities in the area when Arisaig House and other buildings in this area were used by the SOE (Special Operations Executive) during the Second World War.

For about 4 miles north of Arisaig the coast is very foul and should be given an offing of at least 1½ miles until the **Morar estuary** is reached. More familiar to travellers on the old single track road to Mallaig than to yachtsmen, this extensive area of drying sand does offer attractions for shoal draft boats that can take the ground though, with any sea running at all, the bar could be a problem.

Until present plans come to fruition, berthing in Mallaig means rafting up with the fishing boats.

Mallaig was once the largest herring port in Europe and is still a busy fishing port and ferry terminal for the Isle of Skye, the Small Isles and Inverie in Loch Nevis. Local fishing boats now unload white fish as well as crabs, lobsters and prawns.

Because of all this activity, the advice given until recently was that it was best avoided by yachts unless bad weather, or the need for emergency repairs, necessitated a visit. This has now changed: yachts are welcomed and there are ambitious plans for pontoon berths in the inner harbour. If these come to fruition, it will become a valuable destination for repairs, stores, crew changes and a good place to leave a yacht unattended for a few weeks between cruises.

The Small Isles

The Small Isles, comprising the isles of Rum, Eigg, Muck and Canna, are probably the best-known of the smaller Hebridean islands. With each of them being large enough to support a population, yet small enough to sail round in a matter of hours, and each having its own distinct profile and character, they form an ideal group for the cruising yachtsman to enjoy over the course of a few days, despite none of them, apart from Canna, having a good all-weather secure anchorage. Add to this a few outlying shoals and banks, significant tidal streams and the odd magnetic anomaly, it is a wonder that they are so popular and yet, in the season, they will all have well-filled anchorages during any spell of good weather.

The view of the Small Isles from Arisaig is a classic for photographers, at all times of the day and in all weathers.

The mountains of Rum from the anchorage at Port Mor. As can be seen from this shot, and most of the others of the Small Isles, it is hard to take a photograph in this area without a dramatic silhouette!

Plotting the rocks

When using a GPS chart plotter, problems encountered in close-quarters pilotage, such as those mentioned below, may soon be a thing of the past. These are caused by the inaccuracies of old charts being transferred to otherwise highly accurate chart plotting software (see also p.184).

During the summer of 2009 CCC member Bob Bradfield and a team of helpers carried out detailed surveys in almost twenty west coast anchorages. Using data from a depth sounder linked to an accurate GPS, followed by checking with a side scan sonar, a profile of the seabed is built up which is then plotted by computer and finally superimposed on to a 'corrected' aerial photograph.

The results and progress of this project can be seen on *www.antarescharts.co.uk* and eventually will be available for downloading and use with compatible chart plotting software. For those who prefer to have it all down on paper, Bob has kindly offered to make his results available to the Club for use in the CCC Sailing Directions.

The approach to the Gallanach Bay anchorage on the north side of Muck. Whatever you do, do not rely on the chart plotter to pilot you through the reefs. Stick to the leading line, which is indicated by the mast of the yacht in the centre.

The **Isle of Muck** is the nearest to Ardnamurchan, although its modest profile does not attract attention as readily as that of its more assertive neighbours. It is about two miles long by one mile wide and has a population of approximately 38 people. There are two anchorages, **Port Mor** in the south and **Gallanach Bay** in the north and, between the two, shelter is offered from most wind directions. Both have rock-strewn approaches though Port Mor is now well marked and lit as a result of the new regular ferry service.

Muck is a pleasant island to walk around and is well worth a leisurely visit. Beinn Airein, its highest point, at 137m (450ft), is near the south west corner and overlooks Camas Mor (Big Bay) to the south, and Gallanach Bay and Eilean nan Each (Horse Island) to the north. Horse Island can be accessed at low tide to view puffins, other sea birds and seals. The Craft Shop and Café in Port Mor will sell you a map to guide you on your walk, as well as groceries and evening meals.

Port Mor House Hotel overlooks the pier and specialises in seafood using produce such as shellfish, lamb, game and vegetables from Muck itself. Visiting sailors are welcome for evening meals with prior booking. Anyone visiting the island is always more than welcome to attend ceilidhs, quiz nights or other social functions that might be taking place whilst they are on the island.

The Isle of Eigg, easily recognisable from almost every angle thanks to the dramatic silhouette of An Sgurr, is on the direct route between the Sound of Sleat and Ardnamurchan and it therefore attracts many passing yachts. Unfortunately the anchorage does not do the rest of this delightful island justice, it being shallow, not very well sheltered and subject to tidal streams. However, in moderate weather, this should not deter anyone from stopping there for a time. It is sometimes worth taking the extra trouble to gain access to **Poll nam Partan** at the north end of the bay in order to mitigate some of the foregoing drawbacks but, as the Sailing Directions say of all the anchorages: 'yachts should clear out in good time if heavy weather is forecast'.

The Sgurr of Eigg rising above Galmisdale Bay. Unless you are a rock climber, an ascent means a long walk, but it is worth the effort.

Possibly because of the limitations of the anchorage, Eigg is unusual in that the main centre of population does not cluster round the harbour, but is situated at Cleadale 2½ miles away on the other side of the island, looking over the magnificent Bay of Laig and across to Rum. This used to mean a long walk to the shop, but now there is a well stocked shop and Post Office by the jetty. As well as groceries and craft goods the shop sells walking maps of the island, and also books on its history, wildlife and geology. The 2 hour walk to the volcanic pitchstone summit of An Sgurr is along a waymarked path and reaches 393m (1,290ft) above sea level. The more level walk through to Bay of Laig is just over 2 miles.

The old harbour at Eigg, with the new ferry pier in the background.

In recent times the island has had a number of owners in quick succession but now the Isle of Eigg Heritage Trust is run by a partnership between the residents of Eigg, Highland Council and The Scottish Wildlife Trust. On 12th June 2007, the island celebrated 10 years of democratic ownership.

The sweeping silhouette of Rum seen from Eigg.

The interior and exterior of the romantic Kinloch Castle.

The **Isle of Rum** is the hub of the Small Isles, being no more than a 2–3 hour sail from any of the other three. It has been owned by Scottish Natural Heritage since 1957, when the nation bought it from the Bullough family. The island's mountains are mostly volcanic and the tallest is Askival at 812m (2,665ft), which is surrounded by lower but equally dramatic peaks.

Kinloch Castle, at the head of Loch Scresort, took three years to build, starting in 1897, and some 300 craftsmen were employed. The red sandstone was imported from Annan, Dumfriesshire and, in keeping with the inventiveness that had earned the Bullough fortune, this was the first private residence in Scotland to have electric power, generated by a dam constructed on the Coire Dhu burn. The castle cost the equivalent of £15m in today's money.

The only parts of the island not belonging to SNH are Kinloch village and the Bullough Mausoleum, on the west side of the island at Harris, a dramatic Doric styled Greek temple facing the Atlantic Ocean with the Rum Cuillin as a backdrop.

At the castle you can take a fascinating guided tour and buy art and craft products. The former servants' quarters are now a hostel and offer showers, a laundry and meals. The village shop is owned and run by the community and is open most evenings. It is well stocked with groceries, local crafts, and souvenirs. The Village Hall incorporates a café which is open daily during the summer.

Loch Scresort is the only secure anchorage on Rum but it is wide open to the east and well-endowed with weed. However, perserverance should enable reasonable holding to be found.

A rough passage to Rum

This account was written by Hugh Miller, the pioneering Scottish geologist, and recalls a three week cruise in the 'Betsey' with his old friend, the Reverend John Swanson, in the summer of 1844. Swanson was one of many ministers who left the Church of Scotland during the 'Great Disruption' of 1843 and who, prevented by the owner of Eigg from living amongst his parishioners in the Small Isles, took up residence on Skye at Isle Ornsay and carried on his ministry, winter and summer, by making use of the Free Church yacht, the 'Betsey'. This lasted for four years, with many near disasters, until, when presumably either he or the 'Betsey' could take no more, he moved to Nigg in Ross-shire in 1847.

'As the evening began to close gloomy and gray, a tumbling swell came heaving in right ahead from the west; and a bank of cloud, which had been gradually rising higher and darker over the horizon in the same direction, first changed its abrupt edge atop for a diffused and broken line, and then spread itself over the central heavens. The calm was evidently not to be a calm long; and the minister issued orders that the gaff-topsail should be taken down, and the storm-jib bent; and that we should lower our topmast, and have all tight and ready for a smart gale a-head. At half-past ten, however, the *Betsey* was still pitching to the swell, with not a breath of wind to act on the diminished canvass, and with but the solitary circumstance in her favour, that the tide ran no longer against her, as before. The cabin was full of all manner of creakings; the close lamp swung to and fro over the head of my friend; and a refractory Concordance, after having twice travelled from him along the entire length of the table, flung itself pettishly on the floor. I got into my snug bed about eleven; and at twelve, the minister, after poring sufficiently over his notes, and drawing the final score, turned into his. In a brief hour after, on came the gale, in a style worthy of its previous hours of preparation; and my friend, – his Saturday's work in his ministerial capacity well over when he had completed his two discourses, – had to begin the Sabbath morning early as the morning itself began, by taking his stand at the helm, in his capacity of skipper of the *Betsey*. With the prospect of the services of the Sabbath before him, and after working all Saturday to boot, it was rather hard to set him down to a midnight spell at the helm, but he could not be wanted at such a time, as we had no other such helmsman aboard. The gale, thickened with rain, came down, shrieking like a maniac, from off the peaked hills of Rum, striking away the tops of the long ridgy billows that had risen in the calm to indicate its approach, and then carrying them in sheets of spray aslant the furrowed surface, like snow drift hurried across a frozen field. But the *Betsey*, with her storm-jib set, and her mainsail reefed to the cross, kept her weather bow bravely to the blast, and gained on it with every tack.

She had been the pleasure yacht, in her day, of a man of fortune, who had used, in running south with her at times as far as Lisbon, to encounter, on not worse terms than the stateliest of her neighbours in the voyage, the swell of the Bay of Biscay; and she still kept true to her old character, with but this drawback, that she had now got somewhat crazy in her fastenings, and made rather more water in a heavy sea than her one little pump could conveniently keep under. As the fitful gust struck her headlong, as if it had been some invisible missile hurled at us from off the hill-tops, she stooped her head lower and lower, like old stately Hardyknute under the blow of the "King of Norse," till at length the lee chain plate rustled sharp through the foam; but, like a staunch Free Churchwoman, the lowlier she bent, the more steadfastly did she hold her head to the storm. The strength of the opposition served but to speed her on all the more surely to the desired haven. At five o'clock in the morning we cast anchor in Loch Scresort, – the only harbour of Rum in which a vessel can moor, – within two hundred yards of the shore, having, with the exception of the minister, gained no loss in the gale. He, luckless man, had parted from his excellent sou-wester; a sudden gust had seized it by the flap, and hurried it away far to the lee. He had yielded it to the winds, as he had done the temporalities *[his Church of Scotland living]*, but much more unwillingly, and less as a free agent. Should any conscientious mariner pick up anywhere in the Atlantic a serviceable ochre coloured sou-wester, not at all the worse for wear, I give him to wit that he holds Free Church property, and that he is heartily welcome to hold it, leaving it to himself to consider whether a benefaction to its full value, deducting salvage, is not owing, in honour, to the sustentation fund.'

The Cruise of the Betsey, Hugh Miller, 1858.

The setting sun wedged between the profiles of Eigg and Rum.

As **Canna** is the nearest of the Small Isles to both the Outer Hebrides and the north west of Skye, it is very well used by yachts on passage to a variety of destinations. It is fortunate, therefore, that it possesses the best anchorage of all of them, though this should be qualified by adding that this applies only once you get your anchor well set; it takes time and patience but, once achieved, you can sit back and be entertained for hours by watching the efforts of others.

The farm offers accommodation, toilets and showers. The tearoom was closed during 2009 but there are plans to re-open it. The western end of the island is wild and uninhabited – a challenge for determined walkers.

The island's dramatic coastline is a Special Protection Area, home to large colonies of seabirds including shags, puffins, razorbills, black guillemots and sea eagles which nest in the crags. For superb views of the Skye Cuillin, Rum and the Outer Isles it is an easy climb to the top of Compass Hill, 141m (462ft), so called because its iron-rich basaltic rock affects compasses.

Canna and Sanday were left in 1981 to the National Trust for Scotland (NTS) by their previous owner, the Gaelic folklorist and scholar John Lorne Campbell, and are run as a farm and conservation area. Canna House originally contained John Campbell's Gaelic archives, which were donated with the islands to the nation, but they are now housed in the converted Catholic Church – the St. Edward's Centre – which stands in isolation on the south side of the harbour.

South West Skye

The south west coast of Skye is nothing if not impressive. The Skye Cuillin overlook the whole sea area from Ardnamurchan Point to Neist Point, an inhospitable coastline with no all-weather anchorages and, apart from the limited shelter of The Small Isles, complete exposure to the Atlantic from the south west.

Point of Sleat to Neist Point is 35 miles, and the calling options are, according to weather, Lochs Eishort, Slapin and Scavaig, the island of Soay, and Lochs Brittle, Eynort, Harport and Bracadale. The last two lochs have a couple of decent anchorages each, but otherwise this coast needs the right weather for loitering. It either offers fabulous sailing in awesome scenery, or the opposite!

Opposite upper: Canna Harbour looking south east across the Sound of Canna to Rum.

An Coroghon, an isolated stack above the beach on the east shore of Canna, has a medieval prison turret clinging to its summit.

The Cuillin

The Skye Cuillin are not the highest mountains in Scotland (Sgurr Alasdair is 1006m, 3,300ft), but are certainly the most dramatic. Wherever you are around Skye, their peaks are always on the skyline, often capped by cloud, sometimes invisible in poor weather.

Their name is thought to be derived from the Old Norse word Kjöllen, meaning keels, and the spiky skyline certainly does look like a row of upturned keels. Many of the peaks in both the Skye and Rum Cuillin also have Norse derived names, such as Blaven, Askival and Hallival.

The range runs from Loch Brittle to Broadford, and is intersected by Glen Sligachan. North of this glen are the Red Hills (or Red Cuillin), lower rounded granite hills, whilst to the south lie the Black Cuillin, formed of basalt and hard gabbro rock which was eroded by glaciation and subsequently weathered to form their rocky peaks. The gabbro is the more durable, and forms most of the higher peaks.

Needless to say the Cuillin are a mecca for climbers as they offer demanding rock climbing, twelve Munros (see p.152) within the range and many places which require rock climbing skills. The Inaccessible Pinnacle, which at 986m (3,235ft) is the highest point of Sgurr Dearg, is the ultimate challenge, and must be scaled in order to complete a full set of Munros.

Opposite lower: The Skye Cuillin overshadow a pair of quite sizeable yachts anchored in Port Sgail.

Loch Eishort and **Loch Slapin** are not often visited by cruising yachts because, although they are much photographed thanks to the excellent views of the Cuillin, they have rather limited anchoring options other than in settled weather. The former has a rather tricky entrance and, above half tide, great care is needed, but the latter is straightforward and could be regarded as a useful alternative to Loch Scavaig if the anchorage there is too crowded. Like many Scottish lochs, both Eishort and Slapin have a number of fish farms but, thanks to the policy of the Crown Estate, which has recognised the need to preserve anchorage areas, the bays described in the Sailing Directions are clear.

There are small settlements on the shores of these lochs but, like most of the south west coast of Skye, there are really no amenities – just blissful peace and stupendous views.

Loch Scavaig is usually described by those who have visited it in expressive terms which depend on the weather when they were there: either dramatic and awe inspiring, or dramatic and terrifying.

The inner anchorage, called Loch na Cuilce, (cùil: corner, recess) is small enough to necessitate securing a warp to the shore in blustery conditions, prior to taking a run ashore to explore nearby Loch Coruisk, where pleasant walking into the heart of the mountains can be had, but without the need for mountaineering.

If bad weather is likely, forget it! You will be blown round and round your anchor by ferocious gusts that come vertically down from '... the rocky precipitous sides of the mountain [that] spring with a bold and rapid rise of black and naked cliffs in the wildest confusion, and altogether so steep that a stone loosened from its summit finds no resting place until it plunges into the sea...' So say the words of the 19th century Admiralty Sailing Directions, describing the scene rather more melodramatically than they would now allow themselves to do.

The anchorage in Loch Slapin has a grandstand panorama of the Cuillin, rather than the Worm's Eye view seen from the more popular Loch na Cuilce.

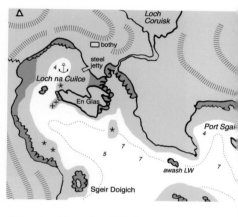

This extract from the CCC Sailing Directions shows that the entrance to Loch na Cuilce is by no means rock free but the accompanying text explains all.

Loch Scavaig

'Where we lay the hurricane was fortunately a steady one; the gales had to get through the anchorage at such a pace that they had no time to jostle each other, so that a boat that would lie quiet was comparatively safe as long as her cables did not part. But *Kelpie* was always a bad boat to anchor; she sheered about prodigiously, and broke her warps and dragged her anchors and only brought up a few yards from the rocks, with all her ropes and chains and every heavy thing spilled out into the bottom of the loch, and her masts stripped to a gantline, as the seaman puts it; that is, with all the gear unrove and only a single line left aloft to hoist it up again.

It seemed like almost certain destruction for my yacht, and I began to think about getting my valuables into a place of safety. Luckily it happened that *Molly* was straight up to windward of me, securely moored along-side to the island, and that all her lines joined together were just long enough to veer her boat, a good big one, down wind within my reach. I put my bag into the boat followed myself and abandoned ship. I don't know whether Botterill quite expected that; the weight of two of us even in his big boat made the passage back very wet and rather hazardous.

I spent that night in *Molly*; a very uncomfortable night, broken by the necessity of tending lines, and by being almost thrown out of one's bunk when the ship was heeled over by the force of the wind acting solely on the topmast, for the hull and lower mast were in the shelter of the island. And in the morning, wonderful to relate, *Kelpie* was still there. In the course of time the wind left Garbh-choirc and went off to worry some one else in some other loch; and as soon as it was safe *Molly's* crew retrieved my anchors, put my ship in order, and towed me clear; and I assure you neither of us wasted time in putting the miles between us and that infernal harbour of Scavaig.

The moral of all this is, of course, don't go up to Scotland single-handed unless you feel sure of meeting boats like *Molly* when you get into trouble.'

From Three Yachts, Conor O'Brien, 1921

Opposite: *A Bird's Eye view of Loch Scavaig with, in the centre of the picture, Loch na Cuilce and, below, left, the pair of yachts pictured on p.128 which are anchored in Port Sgail.*

Soay Harbour from the south. The channel through the bar can be clearly seen, and Maxwell's abandoned shark processing factory is on the east shore, just above the small bight.

In complete contrast to the Cuillin of both Skye and Rum, **Soay** is a low, sandstone island with little lochs scattered over it and generally few or no inhabitants. It was once owned by the author Gavin Maxwell who ran a shark fishing business there after the Second World War and which was continued by his wartime friend Tex Geddes, whose family stayed when the other inhabitants were evacuated in 1953. You can anchor in Soay Harbour after waiting for sufficient depth to enter, or in An Dubh Chamas (Black Bay) on the north side of the island. The bay on the south side of the island is exposed, and reported to have poor holding.

The ruined buildings by Soay harbour that were the base for Maxwell's shark fishing enterprise. The old railway engine boiler can just be seen to the left of the cottage.

Maxwell's first visit to Soay – July 1943

'I remember that it was a blue day, hot and still, and that it was lit for me with something of the vivid anticipation that belongs to childhood. My companions, whose home the yacht had been in peacetime, were wholly delightful, and the yacht itself had the orderly comfort of a neat cottage. We sailed from Mallaig in the morning. The islands swam in a pale blue sea, Eigg, Canna, and Rhum with white puffballs of cloud balanced above its peaks. There was not the faintest breath of wind, and the whole length of Sleat was mirrored in a still sea dotted with resting birds. In a little over an hour we rounded the point of Sleat and headed direct for Soay, on the same course as I was to follow times without number in all winds and weathers for four years. At that distance the island was barely separable from the bulk of the Cuillins – one would have taken it for an insignificant promontory of low-lying land at the foot of their long plunge to the sea. The eye was held by the great mountain massifs — to the north the regular scree-covered upthrust of the Red Hills of Skye, opened by Loch Slapin; a little to the west the solitary dark peak of Blaven, and straight ahead the great splintered ridge of the Cuillin itself. Not even North Norway's Troll Fjord can compare with the hills of Skye as they open, peak upon peak, across those eight miles of sea from Sleat to Soay.'

Harpoon at a Venture, Gavin Maxwell, 1952. Re-published by House of Lochar, 1998

Leaving Soay and rounding Rubh' an Dunain opens up first **Loch Brittle**, and then **Loch Eynort**. Both are pleasant to visit in settled weather and light offshore winds, but otherwise they cannot be considered tenable anchorages. Loch Brittle, however, is the closest point to the high peaks of the Cuillin so, if mountaineering is the objective of some of the crew, landing them here and then retreating to the security of Canna, ten miles to the south, might be an option. Sgurr Alasdair is just two miles away and two thirds of a mile high, so it is only a 20° slope to get there! It may not sound much, but don't try it unless you are a fit and experienced hill walker. There is a Youth Hostel just up the road from the settlement. The innermost mile of Loch Eynort is either shoal or shallow and there is no shelter in the outer part of the loch.

The sunflower raft in Loch Harport at the CCC Classic Malts Millennium cruise.

Six miles beyond Loch Eynort is the entrance to **Loch Harport**, which offers the only secure anchorage along this stretch of coast. It is generally clean and easy to enter, and not subject to the swell that plagues the other lochs. **Carbost** is a little off the beaten track, but it has a distillery, the only one on Skye, a visitors' mooring provided by the distillery, and a few amenities to tempt the visiting sailor. Talisker distillery has a visitor centre offering tours and sampling sessions. This is a good centre for exploring and climbing in the Cuillin, as it has transport links, life support of various sorts and a secure mooring on which to leave your boat unattended.

Showers and a drying room are available at The Old Inn, which caters mainly for climbers and walkers but is also happy to welcome sailors. A small village shop stocks essential provisions and it also has petrol and diesel pumps. A bus service operates infrequently, as does the Post Office which is part-time.

The 2009 Classic Malts fleet at anchor off the Talisker distillery.

On leaving Loch Bracadale, the three isolated rock stacks known as Macleod's Maidens are passed on the starboard hand, before carrying on up the coast to Neist Point.

Immediately north of Loch Harport, and sharing the same broad entrance from the Sea of the Hebrides, lies **Loch Bracadale.** Extending 4 miles inland, the loch is a series of fingers and islands and looks interesting on the chart, but nowhere is there a really good anchorage, as the more inland parts are shallow and contain several fish farms, and the rest are exposed to swell. The two best places are Loch Bharcasaig in the north west corner, and the bay on the north side of the drying causeway joining Ullinish Point to Oronsay.

Until 2007 the latter was qualified in the Sailing Directions as being suitable for 'small yachts'. Wondering 'How small is *small?*' the Editor recently entered it, cautiously, and was surprised to find that the bay was at least twice the size of Tinker's Hole (close by the Sound of Iona), clean, and with a level, sandy bottom. Research showed that this description originated in 1913, when 'small' might have meant anything under 60 feet. The entry has now been amended.

Looking south west to Oronsay from Ullinish Point, at the entrance to Loch Bracadale, showing the anchorage mentioned in the text above. The causeway to Oronsay is almost covered but dries across when the tide is about 3.7m above CD. The bay on the south side of the causeway is useful in northerlies.

North West Skye

Heading north from Loch Bracadale you pass Macleod's Maidens, a series of basalt stacks at the northern entrance to the loch, Macleod's Tables – distinctive flat topped hills inland – and finally Neist Point. The landscape of this area, like that of Mull, Staffa and the Antrim coast far to the south, is the remains of the huge Tertiary basalt flows that covered most of the north west fringes of what is now Europe. The result is a series of high cliffs and headlands with the one break being Loch Pooltiel, an anchorage which is only sheltered from winds east of south – a rare direction and one that can quickly veer.

Neist Point light, built in 1909 by David Stevenson.

After rounding Neist Point, one bold headland follows another: Dunvegan Head, Waternish Point and finally Rubha Hunish, with several intervening minor headlands just to deceive you. In between are the deep indentations of Loch Dunvegan, Loch Bay and Loch Snizort.

Looking over the anchorage in Loch More to Dunvegan Castle on the east side of Loch Dunvegan.

Being roughly halfway between Rona and Canna, **Loch Dunvegan** is well placed to act as a convenient anchorage if sailing round Skye, or alternatively as a jumping off point for the Outer Isles, as it is only about 15 miles from Dunvegan Head to Scalpay or Rodel. It is very well charted, to a scale of 1:25,000, and offers a variety of anchorages to suit all needs. Yachts wanting a temporary passage anchorage can use Gatrigill Bay, just a mile south of Dunvegan Head; those looking for a pleasant lunch stop off a beach on a lazy day could try the shallow bay north of the Lampay Islands; and those needing stores and a mooring should continue in to Dunvegan itself.

As a village, **Dunvegan** is unremarkable but being a busy tourist venue it has a range of shops, a bakery and several hotels. Further alternative anchorages are the bay to the west of the castle, which like all castles was designed to keep people out but is now one of Scotland's most popular visitor attractions, or **Loch More** on the west side of the loch, which offers secure anchorage and the opportunity for a meal at the well known 'Three Chimneys' restaurant at nearby Colbost.

The moorings at Stein in Loch Bay. The low island to the right is Isay with Dunvegan Head beyond.

The Isay Massacre

'In the early 16th century Roderick MacLeod of Lewis, whose daughter had married twice, decided to eliminate two entire families so that his own grandson should inherit the island of Raasay and the lands of Gairloch. He invited the families to a banquet on Isay promising that they would hear something to their advantage. They all turned up and during the meal Roderick said he wanted the private and personal views of everyone present on a matter of great importance. He left the room and each guest was summoned in turn to a room where Roderick had them stabbed to death.'

The Scottish Islands, Hamish Haswell-Smith, 1994–2008

Loch Bay is partially separated from Loch Dunvegan by three small islands, one of which, **Isay**, forms a sheltered anchorage off a ruined village. Here you might be interested in going ashore and ruminating on the bloodthirsty goings-on in the ruins of the large building at the south end of the village, described here by Hamish Haswell-Smith in his indispensable book, *'The Scottish Islands.'*

A little further into the loch is the village of **Stein**, which was developed by the British Fisheries Society in the late 1700s. The original layout was by Thomas Telford, who also designed the pier at the north end of the village. The one in use today, which is at the south end of Stein, was built in the late 1800s. The fishing station was not a success and much of the planned village was never built.

The village is a conservation area, having had few changes since it was built, so the traditional-style white painted buildings are very distinctive on the approach. There is a pub and a restaurant, a dive centre and an arts and craft shop. The Stein Inn is the oldest on Skye and it welcomes yachtsmen, who can use the visitors' moorings to make life easier, although they are exposed to a long fetch from the south and west.

Loch Snizort, a large, wide, and by the standards of other Skye lochs, rather featureless loch, offers anchorages at the Ascrib Islands, in the inner Lochs Greshornish and Snizort Beag, as well as Uig Bay, better known as the ferry terminal for the Tarbert, Harris and Lochmaddy services. The loch is reasonably clean and it allows good sailing in relatively sheltered waters. Nevertheless, all its secure anchorages are well south of any cruising route and it is little visited but, if time is not pressing, an excursion into it would make a change from other more popular destinations.

As with the rest of Skye, the vistas are impressive and the **Ascrib Islands** are as good a place as any from which to appreciate them. The islands are designated as a Special Area of Conservation on account of the breeding colonies of the common seal, but this does not impose any restriction on normal cruising activities, including anchoring. There are no other permanent inhabitants although there is a holiday house on South Ascrib.

Loch Greshornish's best anchorage is near to the village of Edinbane and the area offers several hotels and caravan sites, some village amenities and is on the bus route to Portree. Similarly **Loch Snizort Beag**, with several potential anchorages, is within walking distance of Carbost village. Landing may be difficult in both these lochs, for although they are sheltered and have adjacent settlements, there do not seem to be any slipways, piers or jetties.

Uig does not yet have any yachting facilities but there is a desire by local businesses to establish some. The bay is sheltered, and there are shops and eating establishments ashore, so a few visitors' moorings would be useful. However, despite the scattering of locals' moorings, which necessitate buoying your anchor if anywhere near them, space and shelter are available. A direct bus service to Glasgow make it a good place for crew changes.

Duntulm Bay is on the western side of the Trotternish peninsula, which is just one of the interesting landscapes on the island. The anchorage is behind the island and, though not sheltered from all wind directions, it is a convenient passage anchorage. Duntulm Castle overlooks the anchorage and the Duntulm Castle Hotel is nearby.

Trotternish

Trotternish is the large peninsula at the north end of Skye, separating the Sound of Raasay from Loch Snizort. Its coast has miles of cliffs, stacks, sea caves, natural arches and waterfalls, as well as much marine and bird life and can be better observed from the sea than from the land.

Its most famous feature is the Trotternish landslip, a massive landslide that runs almost the full length of the peninsula, some 30 km. The landslip contains two of Skye's most famous landmarks: the Old Man of Storr, an isolated rocky pinnacle, and the Quiraing, an area of dramatic and unusual rock formations. The summit of The Storr, on whose slopes the Old Man of Storr is located, is the highest point of the peninsula.

The Quirang is approximately two miles north west of Staffin, within reach of the anchorage in Staffin Bay. The Storr is a few miles north of Portree. It could be reached, in settled weather, by anchoring in or near Bearreraig Bay, but probably leaving your boat on a Portree mooring would be preferred.

Above: Uig Bay and the Calmac ferry pier.

Duntulm Castle (right) seen from the anchorage behind Duntulm Island. There is a landing beach below the two white buildings and the hotel is just out sight on the left.

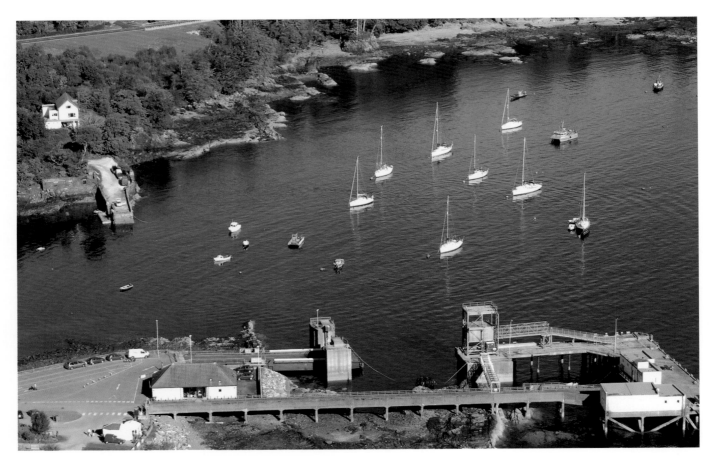

The moorings at Armadale from the south. The floating pontoon is alongide the stone jetty on the north side of the bay.

Sound of Sleat

The Sound of Sleat, running between Knoydart and Skye, is the direct route to the north and consequently is well used. Straight, well lit and comparatively hazard free, it presents few navigational problems and, unless the wind is strong from the south west, you are sure of a good sail in sheltered water although, like the Sound of Mull, the wind is invariably dead ahead or astern. The tidal streams are not commanding but, at its northern exit at Kyle Rhea, the opposite applies and the timing of your passage will be governed by that.

It is a little short of anchorages capable of providing good shelter in bad weather – Armadale and Isle Ornsay are probably the two best – but in fair weather, anchorages adajacent to, and within, the lochs to the east extend the options considerably. On the other hand, it is very well endowed with good places to eat and a gastronomic cruise within the Sound could last for almost a week without patronising the same establishment twice!

Armadale is near the southern end of the Sleat peninsula and is the charter base of Isle of Skye Yachts, who provide many useful yachting services that do not exist elsewhere in the area. Moorings are generally available, subject to charter yacht demands, as are fuel, water and the use of a half tide pontoon for loading. If you are unfortunate enough to need repairs, the yard are used to tackling the myriad problems suffered by charter yachts, and for crew changes the ferry to Mallaig runs from the pier and connects with train services to Glasgow.

Stores are available at **Ardvasar**, just ½ mile south of Armadale. This is a pretty village in a beautiful setting looking across the Sound of Sleat and its amenities include a hotel, both food and craft shops and a Post Office.

The nearby Clan Donald Centre, Armadale Castle Gardens and Museum of the Isles is an interesting place to visit and is set in the heart of a 20,000 acre Highland estate which was once part of the traditional lands of Clan Donald. The Clan Donald Trust bought the property in 1971, restored the gardens and part of the Castle, created the Museum of the Isles, founded a Study Centre, built holiday accommodation and established a visitor centre that appeals to all age groups. The old stables are now a licensed restaurant and shop.

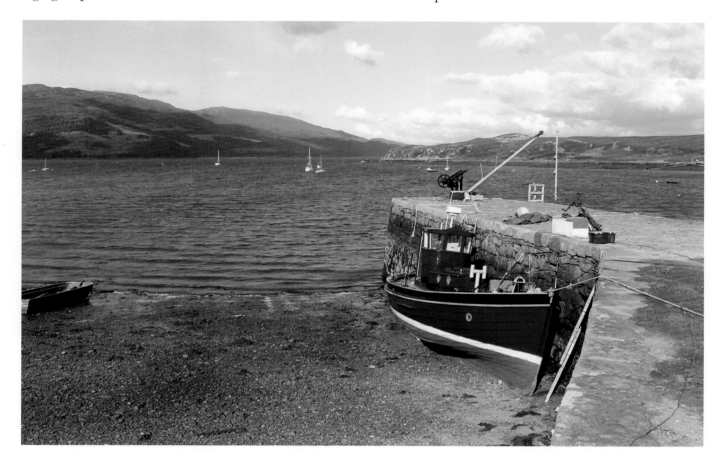

Isle Ornsay is one of the most attractive villages on Skye and is situated about halfway between Ardvasar and Kyle Rhea, where the tidal island of Ornsay creates a natural anchorage. The bay is shallow and it shoals a long way out from the head, but the holding is good and there is plenty of space. The Eilean Iarmain Hotel is small and intentionally old fashioned, has a restaurant and bar and is generally willing to let sailing folk use their amenities. Less than ½ mile further north brings you to Duisdale House, a luxury 4 star hotel standing in extensive grounds, which has moorings for patrons.

About a mile further north again is **Loch na Dal**, at the head of which is Kinloch Lodge, the hotel run by cookery writer Claire Macdonald, which has a renowned kitchen. Loch na Dal has never been rated very highly as an anchorage but recently the hotel has laid moorings for patrons so now you can relax and enjoy your meal without worrying whether your pride and joy is dragging slowly out into the sound.

A short sail across the sound brings you to two more well known eating places, both of which can be approached by boat only; and so the gourmet cruise continues...

Isle Ornsay pier at low water. The yachts are about as far in as most deep keel craft can expect to anchor. The entrance to Loch na Dal is just off the extreme left of the picture.

Isle Ornsay anchorage looking across the Sound of Sleat to Knoydart where, as ever, dark storm clouds are gathering.

Dun Ban Bay, a small bay at the end of the Knoydart promontory between the Lochs Nevis and Hourn, and almost opposite Armadale, offers an alternative passage anchorage when sailing through the sound, though not so well sheltered as Armadale. However it has other attractions which might well influence the choice between the two: the former clachan of Doune has been developed as a holiday centre and has an excellent restaurant. There are two yacht moorings provided for patrons near the south shore of the bay, and showers, telephone, weatherfax, water and diesel are available.

Sandaig Island lies at the point of the next peninsula, just north of the entrance to Loch Hourn. Although Gavin Maxwell did not reveal this location in his popular book *Ring of Bright Water*, it is where he lived whilst writing about Scotland's west coast and the otter he had acquired in Iraq and kept as a pet.

His house, Camusfeàrna, was burnt down in 1968 and the hills behind are now covered with dense conifers, but the beach, burn and waterfall where his otters once played remain. The bay is not well sheltered from the south west, but if you are early for the tide at Kyle Rhea and the weather is suitable, anchor at this magical place and go ashore.

Opposite upper: The moorings off Inverie in Loch Nevis. Compare this peaceful scene with that in the photograph at the foot of this page.

The memorial to Edal, the otter which died in the fire at Camusfeàrna.

Loch Nevis and Loch Hourn

Loch Nevis *(Heaven)* and Loch Hourn *(Hell)*, separated by the wildnerness of Knoydart, are aptly named. They are both surrounded by high mountains and are as remote from civilisation as anywhere in Scotland. There is no road into the village of Inverie in Loch Nevis, and getting to Arnisdale in Loch Hourn involves many miles of driving on single track roads.

However, if you are afloat, none of these difficulties arise. Both lochs are straightforward to navigate, with the aid of the Sailing Directions, and have a variety of anchorages. They are, however, very different in character, as their names imply.

W. H. Murray, whose detailed descriptions of the West Highlands and Islands should be on every cruising sailor's bookshelf, described them thus: 'Knoydart is still the wild west... whose peculiar quality is given less by its two great glens than by its two great sea-lochs and their mountain setting'.

Loch Nevis is probably more visited than Loch Hourn, being less overshadowed and with lower hills to the south giving it a sunnier aspect. Like most mountain lochs it is subject to squalls in windy weather and these are at their strongest in its inner loch. The best anchorage is generally thought to be off Glaschoille House, about two miles into the loch on the north side. However the attractions offered by the Old Forge Inn which, as well as providing good food and drink, has moorings for patrons in the **Bay of Inverie**, may well tempt many yachts to go the extra mile or so. Bear in mind though, that the bay is fully open to the south west and may not always be as placid as in the upper photograph on the opposite page.

Loch Hourn is surrounded by scree-covered mountains rising to around 1,000 metres (3,280ft), which shut out the sun and, in windy weather, can also produce violent squalls. In settled weather the fiord-like upper loch, **Loch Hourn Beag**, offers exploration opportunities; it penetrates many miles into the mountains through a series of four narrows, the last one in particular being tricky to navigate as it is tortuous and very shallow and relies on several shore marks which may not be easy to pick out. A passage at high water, preceded by an exploration in the dinghy, is recommended.

The old pier at Inverie during a November gale.

Opposite lower: Looking south west in Loch Hourn Beag, from an anchorage immediately before the third narrows.

The ferry at Kyle Rhea about to berth on the mainland. The Sound of Sleat lies beyond.

Opposite upper: The head of Loch Duich. The bay beyond the spit is Loch Beg.

Opposite lower: The view of Eilean Donan castle seen from the anchorage at Totaig, on the south side of Loch Duich.

The Kyle Rhea Ferry

The small ferry that crabs its way across Kyle Rhea every 20 minutes or so is the *Glenahulish*, the only remaining hand-operated turntable ferry in Britain. Since the tolls were removed from the Skye bridge it has been difficult for the ferry to be commercially viable but its value as a tourist attraction, offering a romantic and spectacular approach to Skye, has not been lost on the local community and it is now owned and run by the The Isle of Skye Ferry Community Interest Company.

Unfortunately there is not much a yachtsman can do to support this worthwhile enterprise, apart from keeping out of its way, but give it a cheery wave as you pass by!

Kyle Rhea to Kyle of Lochalsh

Having finally managed to escape from the culinary sirens of the Sound of Sleat, the way north appears at first to be totally blocked by mountains. However, approaching Glenelg, a narrow gap in the hills to port becomes apparent. This is Kyle Rhea.

Kyle Rhea is one of the tidal gates for which Scotland's west coast is famous. It is, along with the Dorus Mor, the Sounds of Luing, Cuan and Islay and the Gulf of Corryvreckan, a place where making progress against the tide is, by and large, neither practical nor, in some cases, possible. In other words, timing is everything. The Sailing Directions contain details of the time and direction of the tidal streams and as they run at up to 8 knots, this is vital information.

The narrows (Gaelic *Caol* anglicised to Kyle) is only about 500 metres wide and was once the main crossing for both people in boats and cattle, which had to swim. Notable persons who used this crossing in the past were Dr Johnson and James Boswell who, in their 1722 Journey to the Western Islands of Scotland, crossed to Skye from Glenelg before striking south to visit Coll and Mull. The tide in the Kyle of Lochalsh is much weaker, at one knot or less, and is subsequently less of a challenge.

As the tide spits you out of Kyle Rhea into **Loch Alsh** you have the option of making a short detour into **Loch Duich** which is another west Highland backwater striking deep into the mountains. This loch and its extension, Glen Shiel, is best known as the route of the trunk road from the Great Glen to Skye. This runs along its northern shore and over the road bridge which cuts off Loch Long to the north. It is also well known for the picture-postcard Eilean Donan Castle, standing on a small island off its north shore and which has adorned innumerable calendars and coffee table books. It was first constructed in the 13th century and rebuilt from a ruin in 1932.

Few yachts go all the way to the head of the loch but, if you do, you will not be disappointed by the surroundings and there are several anchorages to choose from. The anchorage off the castle is only a temporary one but immediately opposite on the other side of the loch there is a snug little bay known as **Totaig**, where you can see the castle but avoid the roar of traffic.

Maol Castle, Kyleakin, from the Skye bridge, with Loch Alsh beyond. The inlet where the yacht pontoons are located is hidden from view, behind the three white buildings next to the pier.

There are two suggested origins of the name **Kyleakin**. It is either the Strait of Haakon, the Norwegian king who was defeated at the Battle of Largs in 1263, or that of Acunn, a heroic Irish warrior of the second or third century. It is beyond the scope of this book to determine which it might be!

Kyleakin was for decades the southern terminus of the ferry to Skye from Kyle of Lochalsh, which has been superseded by the graceful and, for a while, controversial Skye bridge.

The harbour has a pontoon available for yachts and other small boats which is run and maintained by Highland Council, who charge for use of the facilities. These include fresh water at the pontoon but, at the time of writing, no electricity. In addition three visitors' moorings are available outside the harbour, between Kyleakin and the bridge.

The most prominent landmark is the ruined castle, once the seat of the Mackinnon clan. It controlled the sound between Skye and the mainland and its commanding position may have been used to enable a toll to be extracted

The replica Viking longboat, 'Havhingsten fra Glendalough' which sailed from Denmark to Dublin in 2007, pursues a 21st century super-yacht through Loch Alsh.

from ships using the route to avoid the exposed passage through the Minch. The present building dates back to the 15th century, but is traditionally reputed to be of much earlier origin.

The Skye bridge seen on the approach from the Inner Sound (above) and from the yacht pontoons at Kyle of Lochalsh (below).

Kyle of Lochalsh, on the mainland side, developed as the railway terminus of the line from Inverness, which still runs today, and which is considered to be one of Britain's finest rail journeys. The line was completed in 1897 and the ferries ran until 1995 when the new bridge took over as the link from the mainland to the Isle of Skye. It was a toll bridge until 2004.

Kyle Harbour's pontoon facilities are also provided by Highland Council and are managed by the same harbourmaster as at Kyleakin. They are well-situated for storing up at the town's shops before heading north to the Islands and other mainland harbours. Crew changes are easily carried out here thanks to the rail and bus links to Inverness and the south.

The Sound of Raasay

From the Skye bridge to the classic anchorage of Acairseid Mhor on South Rona is 17 miles across the Inner Sound and via Caol Rona, or 23 miles via the Sound of Raasay. The latter is a pleasant and sheltered cruising area, taking in Scalpay, Raasay and Portree on the way.

The first stage of a passage to the Sound of Raasay is either north or south of Scalpay. A glance at the chart will reveal that the former is a straightforward enough course past Pabbay and Longay and inside the buoyed Gulnare rock. On the other hand, going south of Scalpay involves an interesting piece of pilotage through **Caolas Scalpay** which can only be negotiated at or near high water.

Just west of the narrows, Skye Boat Centre has the only marine leisure facilities on this side of Skye before reaching Portree, with moorings in the sound, pontoon and slipway access for visitors, shower and washing machine ashore, and some boatyard services.

Broadford Bay and the Skye Lochs of Ainort and Sligachan are not high priority destinations as they lack comfortable anchorages, are rather encumbered with fish farms and their upper reaches are very shallow. **Broadford**, however, is the second biggest town on Skye and has shops, two hotels, some craft shops, a fuel station, a pier, and a nearby slip and yard used mainly by fishing vessels.

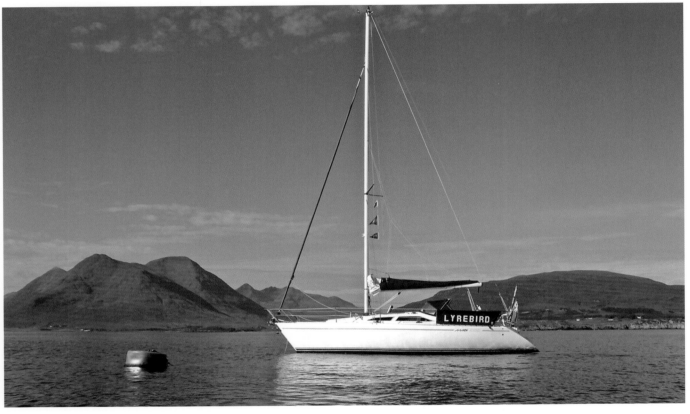

The visitors' moorings at Churchton Bay, Raasay have an excellent view of the Red Hills, sometimes known as the Red Cuillin. The entrance to Loch Sligachan lies roughly behind the yacht's mast.

Raasay is an important island, both historically and geologically. The rough, rocky but beautiful landscape of most of the island contrasts with the gentle area more suitable for habitation at the south west corner where the anchorage, visitors' moorings and a new ferry terminal are located.

The island is 14 miles long but only 3 miles wide and the highest point is the distinctive flat topped 443m (1,453ft) high volcanic summit of Dun Caan. The Isle of Raasay Hotel is situated near Churchton Bay and has a café and restaurant.

Apart from unlimited walking along the length of the island, things to do include seeing the Raasay Pictish Stone, Brochel Castle and Raasay House, which was badly damaged by fire in January 2009 during a restoration project. There are plans to resume the restoration of the house but this may take many years.

The unmistakeable outline of Dun Caan on Raasay.

Visiting the north end of Raasay to see Brochel Castle and Calum's Road is much easier if you use either of the two small anchorages at **Eilean Fladday** near the north west tip of the island.

However, before reaching the north of Raasay you will pass **Portree** on the Skye shore; the name comes from the Gaelic *Port-an-Righ* (Port of the King), after the visit of King James V in 1540. The entrance to the bay is between high headlands but inside the shelter is good in almost all wind directions, if

The pier and small boat moorings at Portree. The visitors' moorings are a lot further out into the bay, and can be quite exposed to southerlies.

somewhat gusty at times. The town is busy with tourists in summer and can provide most needs, although it requires some dinghy work and hill climbing to do the shopping. It is also an ideal base for seeing other parts of the island by car or bus. In a day's touring by hired car, you can cover the whole island and The Storr (see p.137) is only a short drive away.

Portree was developed as a fishing port by its laird, Sir James Macdonald, in the late 18th century and its pier was built by Thomas Telford 50 years later. Telford, who designed and built so much of Scotland's maritime infrastructure in this period, also built roads linking Portree with Uig and Kyleakin.

There are many visitors' moorings: eight in two trots of four well out in the loch, and a quite a few others closer in, though these are not of the familiar blue pattern. They are all administered by the Portree Moorings Association who maintain them and charge for their use. There is a pontoon for taking on water and stores at the main pier, but overnight mooring is not allowed.

The headland on the south side of the entrance to Portree. That on the north side is even higher.

Opposite: *Acairseid Mhor, Rona. The rocks in the approaches are just showing.*

The new pontoon at Acairseid Mhor.

South Rona, or more commonly just Rona when there is no likelihood of confusing it with its namesake way to the north, must surely feature in the top three anchorages of most west coast sailors. After all, Eric Hiscock rated **Acairseid Mhor** (Big Harbour), its principal anchorage, the second best anchorage in the world after Puilladobhrain (see p.91), and it was also described with great affection by Ralph Mowat, who edited the Club's Sailing Directions for many years.

One of the first yachtsmen to visit was Frank Cowper, who called during his cruise in the 1890s. His impression, described in his book *Sailing Tours*, was somewhat different. However, to be fair, it was probably raining at the time and anyone who can sail, shorthanded, an engineless 48 ft. converted fishing boat into Acairseid Mhor, guided only by the Admiralty Sailing Directions, is entitled to think that it is difficult.

The island, owned by the British Government since 1922, was inhabited until 1943 by when everyone had either migrated to Raasay or further afield. Rona, like the northern part of Raasay, is Lewisian Gneiss which does not produce a fertile soil: life must have been a struggle.

In the past the main centre of population was Acairseid Thioram (Dry Harbour), the ruins of which can still be seen a mile or so north of Acairseid Mhor. Several buildings have been restored by the island's current owner to accommodate holidaymakers. She has also restored Rona Lodge at Acairseid Mhor, where the island manager lives, and improved the landing jetty, all making a visit by yacht simpler. Walking on the island is easy because of the good tracks that lead both north and south from the anchorage.

Local stamps have been issued at Rona since 2003 so that visitors to the island can post their mail, which is then re-posted on the mainland. These unique covers are sought after by stamp collectors.

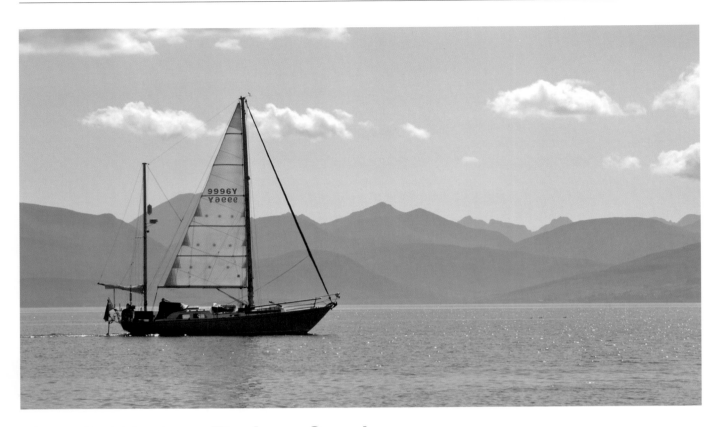

A Bowman 36 heads lazily north through the Inner Sound in the afternoon sun.

Looking eastwards from the drying creek at Plockton.

The Inner Sound

The most direct route northwards from Kyle is through the Inner Sound, which lies to the east of Raasay and is a large area of sheltered water offering welcome relief from the commanding tides and fluky winds that have ruled in Loch Alsh and Kyle Rhea. However, the Inner Sound does not really begin until you are past the Crowlin Islands and, before these, the wide mouth of Loch Carron opens up to starboard once you have left the buoys marking the fairway leading from the Skye bridge.

Loch Carron is seldom explored by cruising yachts although there is an anchorage at Slumbay, close to Lochcarron village, but access to it demands negotiating Strome Narrows where the tide can run at up to 3 kts. **Loch Kishorn**, which branches north eastwards from Loch Carron, is a simpler alternative but, again, you will rarely see a yacht in there as it very open to the south west. It was used for building oil rigs from 1975 to 1987, and was notable for producing the (then) largest man-made moveable structure: the 600,000 tonne Ninian Central Platform.

However, the main reason why Lochs Carron and Kishorn are unfrequented is probably because of the counter attractions of **Plockton**, arguably the most attractive village on the entire north west coast. Plockton is a National Trust conservation village and its natural harbour gives good shelter in most conditions. It is tucked in to the sheltered south west corner of Loch Carron and is popular as a base for cruising the north west, or as a port of call with good facilities. Yachts on passage from Kyle of Lochalsh to the far north, however, may find that the six or seven mile deviation takes more time than they wish to spare.

Plockton has an outer and inner pontoon, the former suitable for yachts but not for overnight berthing, the latter for small boats. The ten visitors' moorings are in two groups and there is space for anchoring in the middle of the bay.

The visitors' moorings at Plockton.

Payment for the moorings is made at the shops or hotels. The village has a restaurant and a take-away, and three hotels which offer showers to cruising sailors. Supplies are available from the village shops, or in the case of gas, fuel and chandlery, from Kyle of Lochalsh, a taxi ride away. Plockton station is on the famous and scenic Inverness to Kyle line, handy for crew changes.

Plockton was the location for the successful BBC drama series *Hamish Macbeth*. Three series were shot between 1995 and 1997 and it is still being shown throughout the world. This, like the Balamory children's series based on Tobermory, has boosted tourism and associated activities in a village that was little known before.

However, for yachts not wanting to make the diversion into Plockton there are several good anchorages on the direct route north. The nearest to Kyle is the anchorage in the **Crowlin Islands**, a group of three uninhabited islands lying near the northern entrance to Loch Carron between which a narrow and quite shallow creek provides total shelter in a landlocked pool. A walk over the hill to the north east of the anchorage leads to the ruined village which was once home to crofters who opted for island hardship rather than emigration following the Clearances.

A few miles north on the mainland shore lie the anchorages of **Poll Creadha** and Poll Domhain. The former is entered through a maze of rocks and needs care, especially if some of the half dozen or so perches are missing, but **Poll Domhain** is easier to approach and gives good shelter. Ashore, the short walk over the Ardban peninsula will bring you to a pair of remote cottages by a beach with outstanding views over to Skye and Raasay.

The Butec Range

Heading north from Poll Domhain, the notes on the chart and in the Sailing Directions concerning weapons testing in the Inner Sound should be taken seriously, as this range, the British Underwater Testing and Evaluation Centre, is in frequent use. Information about the day's testing is given on Ch. 8 at 0800 and 1800 each day and Range Control can be contacted on Ch. 16 or 13. When testing is in progress yachts will be asked to stay out of the restricted zones shown on the chart, which in effect means keeping within about half a mile of the Raasay or mainland shores. Transgressors will be approached by the range patrol boat and asked to leave the zone.

A good path leads you from the Poll Domhain (Poll Doin) anchorage to this quiet bay on the west side of the Ardban peninsula.

Opposite: Two contrasting views of the anchorage between Shieldaig village and Shieldaig Island, which can just be seen on the left of the lower picture.

The Munros

Strangers to Scotland may be puzzled by the frequent mention of 'Munros'. This explanation, taken from the excellent walkhighlands.co.uk website, should enlighten them.

The Munros were first listed by Sir Hugh Munro (1856–1919) in his 'Munros Tables', published in the Journal of the Scottish Mountaineering Club (SMC) in 1891. Sir Hugh divided the summits into 283 separate mountains (now known as the Munros), whilst 255 further summits over 3,000 feet (915m) were considered to be only subsidiary 'Tops'. His list caused quite a stir at the time, as it had previously been thought that there were only around 30 mountains of that height.

Sir Hugh never managed to complete the ascent of all the summits on his list, and it was left to the Revd A. E. Robertson to complete the first round of the Munros in 1901. Since then, attempting to ascend all the peaks ('Munro-bagging') has become a popular pursuit among British walkers and mountaineers.

Sir Hugh had been planning to revise his list of Munros, and after his death the SMC took over the job of keeping the list up to date. The first revised edition was published in 1921, and several further changes were made – the most recent revision being in 2009. There are currently 283 Munros and 227 Tops.

A well-made track on the south side of Upper Loch Torridon affords excellent views of Beinn Alligin and Liathaich, both Munros, on the north side of the loch.

Northwards from Skye

Beyond the northern tip of Rona, the Inner Sound begins to open out and once Skye is left behind you are into the Minch. Although the whole coast is in the lee of the Outer Hebrides, the wind and wave fetch progressively increases as you sail north and, as Cape Wrath is approached, you are effectively sailing in the Atlantic. The mainland coast north of Skye is characterised by a series of prominent headlands with deep bays and loch systems between. These headlands, from south to north, are Rubha Reidh, Point of Stoer and Cape Wrath.

As well as a multitude of sheltered and very beautiful lochs, the coast offers a succession of useful staging ports: Gairloch, Ullapool, Lochinver and Kinlochbervie. These have varying levels of facilities, ranging from the bustling town and ferry port at Ullapool, to the quieter harbour at Kinlochbervie, where fish is landed for transport to the south. They can all provide at least the essentials of a berth, village facilities and a friendly welcome.

Wind, rather than tide, is the main consideration on this coast. With a fair wind the passage from Kyle to Cape Wrath will take less than 24 hours or, if broken with stops en route, two or three days. In less than favourable conditions the headlands of this coast can be a challenge. Each, as headlands do, usually produces increased wind and seas, so a fair wind direction is worth waiting for. If wind over tide conditions cannot be avoided these headlands should be given a wide berth.

Loch Torridon

Loch Torridon and its two inner lochs, **Upper Loch Torridon** and **Loch Shieldaig**, will take you right into the heart of some of the most magnificent mountain scenery in Scotland. In all, it contains over a dozen anchorages, those in the Upper Loch being more suitable for settled weather when the mountain scenery can be appreciated, and there is an absence of squalls. The anchorages on the south side of the outer loch give good holding and protection from most wind directions. Unfortunately many anchorages will have to be shared with fish farming equipment, but space can usually be found.

Shieldaig, the principal settlement in the Torridon area, is mainly concerned with tourism, given its location amidst some of Scotland's most spectacular mountain scenery. The hotel and store are on the village's main, and only, street which fronts the anchorage behind Shieldaig Island.

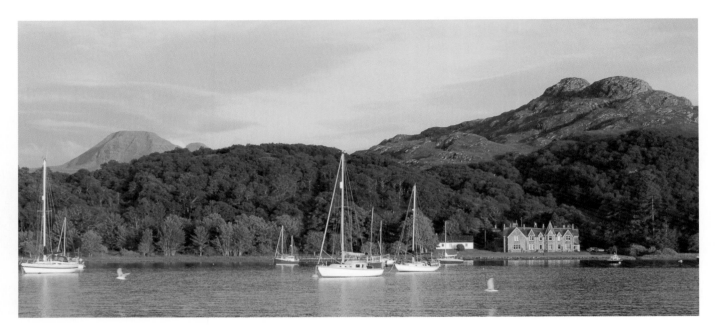

The anchorage and moorings in Loch Shieldaig, with Shieldaig Lodge by the water's edge.

Loch Gairloch (Gearr or Short Loch)

After the dramatic surroundings of Loch Torridon, Loch Gairloch is altogether different, a throwback to the more gentle landscapes of the lochs south of Ardnamurchan. Moorings, hotels, caravans, cars and all the trappings of tourism are also in evidence, although they do not spoil the natural beauty of the loch. Make the most of the facilities on offer here, as further north things soon revert to the rugged character of Loch Torridon.

Unlike many Highland lochs, Gairloch only bites a few miles into the land, making its harbours and anchorages easily accessible without a long sail in and out again. Even at its head, in **Loch Shieldaig** – not to be confused with its namesake in Loch Torridon – you are less than five miles from the entrance. Here there is a secure anchorage, a number of visitors' moorings and easy access to the Shieldaig Lodge Hotel.

The slip and drying moorings at Badachro, taken from almost in front of the inn. The far side of the slip has adequate depth for coming alongside at HW, but beware of the fast flowing burn. Eilean Horrisdale is in the middle distance beyond the yachts.

Further west on the south shore of Loch Gairloch, **Badachro** is a very sheltered, picturesque and therefore popular anchorage. It lies on the southern shore of Gairloch, and its northern entrance is straightforward although the eastern one requires very careful pilotage, as detailed in the Sailing Directions. However, large yachts use this spot so the average cruising boat will have no difficulty. The Badachro Inn offers two free moorings for patrons plus a range of other facilities for those visiting by sea. The inn has long been known as a convivial waterside pub, a favourite with cruising sailors for many generations. It offers a bit of local history, a cosy bar and, of course, food, drink and other facilities for seafarers.

Looking north west to the Aird across the anchorage at Badachro.

Badachro, like many west coast places, owes its original existence to fishing and Island Horrisdale, which encloses the natural harbour, was originally a fishing settlement. Then, it was deep water white fish but now the catch is predominantly shellfish: lobsters, crabs and prawns. Also, the local fleet and activity is now centred at nearby Flowerdale, leaving Badachro to leisure craft and holiday sailors.

The view south eastwards from the Flowerdale pontoon, with the Torridon hills beyond.

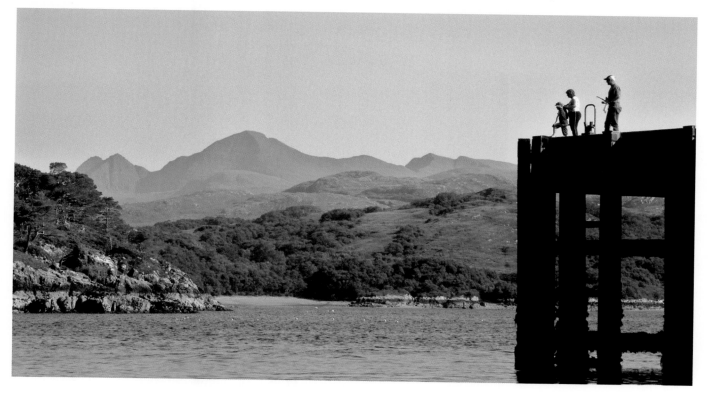

Gairloch Harbour, otherwise known as **Flowerdale**, is situated at the south end of the village in the north east corner of Flowerdale Bay about a mile due north of Loch Shieldaig. It is a busy working port for inshore fishing and local and east coast fishing boats land their catch most evenings. Highland Council, who operate the harbour, have installed approximately 60 metres of pontoons making this a good port of call for storing, watering ship and obtaining fuel.

The pontoon at Flowerdale.

A pleasant diversion from sailing is the waymarked walk up sheltered Flowerdale Glen, the English name given by the Mackenzies of Gairloch (the owners of the estate) to Kerrysdale due to its impressive displays of wild flowers. The route starts right in the village centre, and the distance is around 4–5km. It is mostly easy walking on waymarked paths to a pretty waterfall.

The small island of **Longa** guards the northern exit from Loch Gairloch. It is uninhabited now but supported half a dozen families in the mid-19th century. The anchorage on the north coast – Camas nam Rainich – is a pleasant bay and although not sheltered from northerly winds it makes an ideal passage anchorage. The approach channel from Gairloch, Caolas Beag, is less than quarter of a mile wide due to extensive shoals both from the island and the mainland shores.

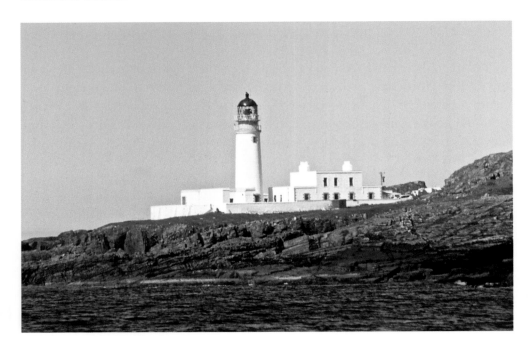

The lighthouse at Rubh Reidh.

Rubh Reidh to Cape Wrath

Rubh Reidh

The headland is not particularly dramatic although, against wind and/or tide, the stretch between Longa and Rubh Reidh seems to go on for ever! Its main feature is the elegant lighthouse and buildings. The light was first proposed in 1853, but its construction was deferred for financial reasons until 1908, when the Board of Trade sanctioned the expenditure of £14,900 on the establishment of a light and fog signal on Rubh Re point and the light was first lit in January 1912.

The foghorn and clockwork mechanism are now in the Gairloch Heritage Museum along with the lens and lighting equipment which was removed in 1985 prior to automation of the Station in 1986. The keeper's house has now been converted to holiday accommodation.

As you leave Gairloch and head towards Rubh Reidh you will be aware that not only are you sailing along a much more exposed coast, but also that the number of other yachts has decreased markedly. Gairloch is about the northern limit for an ambitious two week cruise for boats based on the Clyde or a comfortable two weeks from the Lorn marinas. From here northwards, most of the other boats you will meet will either be locals, longer term cruisers or those on passage to the Orkneys and beyond. Crowded anchorages should no longer be a problem.

Rubh Reidh, also known as Rubh Re, is the dominant headland between the Inner Sound and more northerly cruising grounds. Not only does it project into the Minch, meaning accelerated tides, it also has no havens for the 20 or so miles from Gairloch to Loch Ewe, although the latter is a good loch to duck into if conditions become unpleasant as it contains anchorages affording shelter from most wind directions.

Once Rubh Reidh and Greenstone Point, which is north east of Rubh Reidh, have been rounded, sixty miles of interesting cruising lie ahead. Bounded in the north by the headland-like island of Eilean an Roin Beag just north of Loch Inchard, it includes Loch Broom, the Summer Isles and their satellite islands, with Ullapool as a cruising base. North of Rubha Coigeach lies Enard Bay and the port of Lochinver. The next landmark is Stoer Head, another commanding headland, leading on to Eddrachillis Bay, Loch a Chairn Bhain, Handa Island and Loch Laxford. Finally, Kinlochbervie is the west coast's most northerly port and is the last staging post before Cape Wrath.

Loch Ewe

This is a large and rather featureless loch, but it is quite hazard free and easy to enter. Of the six or seven anchorages it offers, one of the best is **Camus Angus** (Acairseid Mhor on the chart) on the east side of the north point of Isle of Ewe, which gives good shelter from westerlies and is not too far up the loch. A little bay in the south west corner of **Loch Thurnaig** gives shelter from all wind directions, but soft mud and rock make the holding problematical and there is quite an array of fish farming equipment to avoid.

Loch Ewe was an important wartime anchorage for the Royal Navy and it still has a small naval base just south of **Altbea**, the principal village on its east shore. Altbea is a pleasant village with a shop and a hotel, and the fertile Isle of Ewe supports a couple of families.

The famous Inverewe Gardens are located at the south end of the loch and if the weather is settled you can try the temporary anchorage in **Camas Glas**, where there is a jetty and steps, although landing is reported to be tricky. This is conveniently within the Gardens which are under the management of the National Trust for Scotland.

Loch Ewe looking north west. The Isle of Ewe is in the centre with Camus Angus on the right.

The drying stone pier at Aultbea.

Loch Ewe

Loch Ewe was of strategic naval importance in the Second World War following the sinking in Scapa Flow of HMS Royal Oak in December 1939. The loch served as a fleet base and then as a convoy assembly point. Between February 1942 and December 1944 nineteen Arctic Convoys sailed from Loch Ewe for Archangel. Altogether 481 merchant ships and over 100 naval escort vessels left for Russia to face the onslaught of enemy U-boats and surface ships. Allied losses were significant with over 100 merchant ships sunk with their crews numbering over 800. However much needed supplies reached the hard pressed Soviet Union and in the battle of the North Cape in December 1943 the battlecruiser *Scharnhorst*, the pride of the German navy, was sunk.

Gruinard Bay and Little Loch Broom

Loch Camus Gaineach, in the south east corner of Gruinard Bay, is a pleasant sandy bay that would appear to have some merits as an anchorage in offshore or settled weather.

Gruinard Island was infamous as a no-go area following a wartime experiment with the deadly anthrax bacillus. Landing was prohibited for fifty years, until the land was de-contaminated and declared safe in 1990. It is, of course, uninhabited, save for some (healthy) sheep and rabbits, but as it has no sheltered anchorage there is no incentive to visit.

The Sailing Directions mention one or two temporary anchorages around the shores of **Gruinard Bay** itself. They are little used and might be subject to swell, but in fair weather could be worth exploring as an alternative to the better known anchorages in the area.

Little Loch Broom has precipitous hills on either side, so although it has dramatic scenery it is also subject to strong downdraughts and squalls in windy weather. You can anchor off **Scoraig**, just inside the north point at the entrance, but few people do, given the proximity of Ullapool for landward comforts, and the Summer Isles for classic cruising anchorages.

Fishing boats jostle for position on the pier at Ullapool, with the yacht moorings beyond.

Loch Broom

White painted houses along the shore at Ullapool, with Ben Mor Coigeach in the background.

Opposite: Moored yachts in Loch Broom, Ullapool.

Like Tobermory, **Ullapool** was founded as a fishing station at the end of the 18th century by the British Fisheries Society to take advantage of the vast shoals of herring that regularly visited Loch Broom. More recently it was the anchorage for many Eastern European factory ships which took fish straight from the local trawlers, but now it is mainly a base for inshore fishing boats.

Ullapool is very much the regional focus of this part of the coast and is significant as the ferry terminal for Stornoway, an important if perhaps declining fishing port, and increasingly as a stopping port for cruising yachts. To encourage this, the Harbour Trust has recently installed 16 moorings suitable for visiting yachts of up to 15m. Soundings are very deep for anchoring and, as the pier is usually very busy, the new moorings – and the pontoons which are planned at the time of writing – will be most welcome.

The concrete slip at the local sailing club is a good place to land by dinghy. Showers etc. are available at the swimming pool and leisure centre and the town, being a major tourist centre, has a wide variety of shops, eating places and other useful services.

The anchorage on Tanera More, known as 'The Cabbage Patch'. It is fairly full of moorings, but the large yacht nearest the camera seems to have found a place.

Plan of the Tanera Beg anchorages taken from the CCC Sailing Directions.

The Summer Isles

The Summer Isles, named for their use as summer pasturage, lie just south of the village of Achiltibuie, about ten miles north west of Ullapool. The principal islands, which are part of a National Scenic Area, are **Tanera Beg** and **Tanera More** and between them this miniature archipelago contains more than half a dozen attractive and sheltered anchorages offering protection from most winds and, for yachts on passsage to the north, accessible without having to make a downwind diversion.

The naturalist Frank Fraser Darling, an important figure in the development of Scottish conservation, lived on Tanera Mor for two years in the 1930s. His book *Island Years* (1940) records his time there. He found much of interest here, as will the visiting cruising sailor.

Since 1970 the Summer Isles Philatelic Bureau has been issuing stamps of the islands for the many tourists who visit each year. They place them on mail which is then posted on the mainland. The stamps of the Summer Isles are keenly sought after by collectors and can be bought from the tearooms on the north side of the large bay on Tanera More.

The anchorage between Tanera Beg and Eilean Fada Mor from the south west (see plan above).

Although not one of the Summer Isles, **Isle Martin**, which lies just north of the entrance to Loch Broom, has a well sheltered anchorage off some cottages on the east side. The anchorage also has the benefit of a pontoon which has been installed by the local Isle Martin Trust, who own the island, and can be used by visiting yachts for a small charge.

Approaching this anchorage from the south, a shallow spit has to be crossed with only a narrow channel through it. Chart 2500 describes the leading line as: 'Dark streak on face of cliff in line with E extremity of Isle Martin 000°', to which the Sailing Directions helpfully add: 'The dark streak is reported difficult to identify'. This must be the understatement of the century, as the navigator is confronted by a multitude of streaks in every shade of darkness.

However help is at hand. In 2009 a chance combination of calm weather and bright sunshine from the ideal angle allowed the Editor to capture what he hopes is the definitive photograph of the leading line. As it may be a while before a new edition of *Ardnamurchan to Cape Wrath* allows this photograph to be published, it is included below.

Isle Martin from the anchorage showing the pontoon on the right.

The leading line into the Isle Martin anchorage from the south. The white arrow indicates the dark streak on the cliff, and the black arrow the eastern extremity of Isle Martin.

Isle Ristol lies between the Summer Isles and Rubha Coigeach and provides sheltered anchorage between the island and the mainland, and also off its north east corner, in a wide bay off Loch an Alltain Dubh. Leaving Isle Ristol, going north, Rubha Coigeach is soon rounded bringing you into Enard Bay.

The small boat anchorage inside Isle Ristol, much of which dries. The deep water anchorage is some distance further out.

Garvie Bay. One of four sandy bays on the south west side of Enard Bay, which give good shelter in offshore or light weather, with the added bonus of the imposing Assynt skyline.

Enard Bay

Enard Bay is dominated by the distinctive silhouettes of Stac Pollaidh in the south and Suilven to the north. The majority of yachts entering the bay make for the busy fishing port of Lochinver, but for those looking for quieter anchorages there are several in the south west corner which give good shelter, and whose only drawback might be swell in westerly or northerly weather. The best of these are **Garvie Bay**, **Lag na Saille** and **Loch Sailainn**.

As well as expanding its commercial facilities, **Lochinver** can now provide deep water pontoon berthing for visiting yachts in the small marina that has been created in the shelter of the breakwater. In the village there are two self-service stores, a butcher, chandler, gift shops, garage, bank, medical centre, pottery, newsagent, restaurants and a leisure centre where showers can be taken. Diesel can be obtained at the quay near the ice plant. Easily approached by day or night, it is an ideal departure point for Lewis or the north coast, and could be considered as a place where a yacht might be left after a delivery cruise.

An alternative nearby anchorage, without the benefit of any civilisation, is **Loch Roe**, the narrow entrance to which is two miles north west of Loch Inver. Here it is possible to lie in perfect peace in a small pool sheltered by a steep knoll to the south west.

Opposite upper: *Suilven rears above the fish quays at Lochinver.*

Opposite lower: *The Lochinver yacht pontoons have recently been extended. The white buildings on the left are the start of the main part of the village, on the other side of the bay, which is about a fifteen minute walk from the pontoons.*

Assynt

Assynt, the area around and north of Lochinver, is justly famous for its spectacular mountain scenery and also as the first crofting area to be bought by the local crofters – the Assynt Crofters' Trust. This 1993 event led to a change in land ownership in Scotland and laid the framework for many other community buy-outs, including those at Knoydart, Eigg and Gigha. The whole of the Assynt and the Coigach region is a National Scenic Area.

The Assynt Foundation's aims are to 'create local employment and safeguard the natural and cultural heritage for the benefit of the community and future generations, and for the enjoyment of the wider public'. The 18,000 hectare estates of Glencanisp and Drumrunie are managed by the Assynt Foundation on behalf of the Assynt community.

The backdrop from seaward is of Assynt's evocative and distinctive mountains: notably Suilven; Stac Pollaidh; Canisp; Quinag; and Ben More Assynt. These isolated peaks of reddish-brown Torridonian sandstone, often topped, like a cake, with a layer of pale quartzite, spring from an low landscape of Lewisian Gneiss. Only Ben More Assynt is in the Munro category, at 998m (3,274ft), but as all these individual peaks rise from low land, they are all the more dramatic.

The geological interest is more than just the hills: this area is designated the North West Highlands Geopark, as it contains rock formations of outstanding interest which span over 3,000 million years and therefore include some of the oldest rocks in Europe. The Geopark is the tourist theme for the area, and if you have a day to spare hire a car and set off on The Rock Route, which takes in twelve locations of great significance. Explanation boards make sense of it all for the non-geologist. If you only have a an hour or so to spare, the excellent Assynt Visitor Centre in Lochinver has interesting and informative displays on the history, culture and natural environment of the area, in addition to a mass of information on local businesses, services and accommodation.

The Old Man of Stoer seen from the south, when approaching Eddrachillis Bay.

Eddrachillis Bay

Point of Stoer is the next challenge on the route north and like the other major headlands on this coast is best rounded in benign weather, or at least with favourable wind and tide. In good weather, passing close to the shore provides the opportunity to admire and photograph the Old Man of Stoer, a 70m sandstone stack standing just north of the lighthouse, which was built in 1870. Round this corner lies Eddrachillis Bay which, together with Badcall Bay, contains an archipelago of a dozen skerries and small islands giving both island and loch anchorages. The whole area is an ideal cruising destination where, if time allows, several days can be spent exploring the variety of anchorages before beginning the long haul back home.

Loch Nedd

'Loch Nedd had been recommended to us by a man in Tarbert harbour. "I went in, and it was such good shelter I left my boat there all winter" he said. "Oh, if you get wind, please don't forget Loch Nedd. Really, don't." So, since another six hours beating to Loch Laxford would have been legitimate cause for reporting us to the NSPCC, we had threaded our way through the rocks of Eddrachillis Bay to his favourite haven. And he was right: that nameless, passing acquaintance, how we blessed him. Loch Nedd is one of those miracles of Western Scotland, a long, crooked sea-loch which takes the wave-tossed sailor straight off the open Atlantic and the polar swell, and brings him within ten minutes into a still inland lake. The wind still blew Force Five or Six but Nedd's upper loch was smooth as a mirror, ringed with trees, crossed by paths of spongy boggy heather, beautiful as a dream. Inland birds sang, mellower than the wild seabirds who had swooped around us out by the headland; salmon jumped in the stream at the loch's head, and we were in paradise. The children poked around a wrecked ship's lifeboat on the foreshore, and shot their new potato-guns at imaginary foes; Paul and I lay on the sweet-smelling grass, forgetting the sea. There are Mediterranean harbours like this, with stunted olive trees not unlike the small Highland birches around us; but they are nowhere near so beautiful as a Scottish loch in the sunshine. Loch Nedd brought an end to Paul's nervous anger, to my gloomy musings, and to the children's worst behaviour of the trip. Here we cooked toad-in-the-hole and were tolerant and sweet to our children. Rose made an appalling mess with a bucket and toy boat long after her bedtime; Nicholas battered the ship's bell in a complicated private game. We drank quantities of whisky and smiled on their misdeeds, and refused flatly to listen to the weather forecast. Nothing could hurt us in Loch Nedd, and nothing could make us sail tomorrow for the north.'

One Summer's Grace, Libby Purves, 1989

Loch Nedd is very attractive, but this is marred by several hulks and wrecks littering its shores, and an increasing number of houses.

Eddrachillis Bay is given six pages in the Sailing Directions so only a selection of the anchorages can be mentioned here. As might be expected, the best shelter is offered by those on the south shore, **Culkein Drumbeg**, **Loch Dhrombaig** and **Loch Nedd** being the best. The latter, because of its ease of entry, good holding and all round shelter, is the place to go if caught out by bad weather in this area.

As a contrast, inland lies **Loch a Chairn Bhain**, which leads to Kylescu Bridge (24m clearance) close to which are two anchorages and the Kylescu Inn. The inner lochs of **Loch Glencoul** and **Loch Glendhu** can be explored from here though preferably not in strong wind conditions when heavy squalls will make life difficult among the mountains. However, in better weather, you can be assured of a quiet night in **Loch Beag** at the head of Loch Glencoul with not a house or road in sight and the highest waterfall in Britain, approximately 200m (656ft), just a short walk away.

Loch Dhrombaig with the anchorage in the lower part of the picture. The entry channel is off to the left.

Almost three miles north of Loch a Chairn Bhain, the attractive anchorage of **Badcall Bay** is sheltered by a rash of small islets which looks impenetrable at first sight, but which is easily navigated through to gain access to a sheltered bay which is taken up by only a few local moorings.

The award-winning Kylescu Bridge, which replaced the ferry in 1984, spans the entrance to the inner lochs of Loch Glencoul and Loch Glendhu.

The anchorage at Badcall Bay, with Quinag in the far distance.

The northern point of this pattern of islands and lochs is **Handa**, which lies just south of the entrance to Loch Laxford (fiord of the salmon). The island is an important bird sanctuary and it can be visited quite easily as there are anchorages on either side of its south east tip. Bird life is spectacular in early summer.

Handa is owned by the Scottish Wildlife Trust and was inhabited by a St. Kilda-like community until the 1848 potato blight made subsistence impossible. The village ruins lie on the south facing slope overlooking the Traigh Shourie beach. Beyond the ruins a footpath leads to the north west point of the island, where there are spectacular views of the cliffs, and in particular the Great Stack, 115m (377ft) high, and pierced through its base by three caverns. The Stack, like the rest of the island, is Torridonian sandstone.

The northern cliffs are the breeding place for thousands of seabirds, including the largest guillemot colony in Britain, and are best viewed from the sea. However, the sound between the island and the mainland is rock strewn and should be used with the utmost caution, as not all the obstructions are accurately charted.

Beware of Bonxies! When walking across Handa take care not to upset the Great Skuas; they guard their nests energetically.

Loch Laxford

Loch Laxford, as its name suggests, is a major salmon farming centre and there are many cages and mussel ropes to be avoided within the loch. **Loch a' Chadh-fi** is an offshoot to the north and is the base of Cape Adventure, founded by John Ridgway who, along with Chay Blyth, was the first to row the North Atlantic. It is now run by his daughter Rebecca and her husband, who was one of the original instructors at Ardmore. Visiting sailors are welcome to use the centre's facilities. The anchorage in Loch a' Chadh-fi is, thankfully, free of fish farms.

The approach is overlooked by another clutch of the north west's mountains: Beinn Stack, Ben Arkle and Foinaven. Once in the loch, Laxford has perhaps half a dozen anchorages to choose from, but none have ready access to stores or facilities. This is, after all, wilderness cruising.

Entering Loch Laxford. The rocks on Rubha Ruadh on the right are noted on Chart 2503 as 'remarkably red'! Ben Stack, on the right, is the conical mountain which dominates the loch.

Opposite: *An ornithologist perches precariously above the cliffs on the north of Handa.*

Loch a' Chadh-fi looking east. Cape Adventure is based on the south side of the inner part of the loch which is mostly too shallow for anchoring.

The narrow entrance, between perches, into Kinlochbervie. The new pontoons are hidden behind the point in the foreground.

Loch Inchard

Using **Kinlochbervie** as a staging post will reduce the exposed and perhaps daunting passage around Cape Wrath to Loch Eriboll to just 30 miles. Kinlochbervie has a safe approach in any weather, offers complete shelter and has some recently installed pontoons to make life easier for visiting cruising yachts.

The harbour, once home to a busy fishing fleet, has diversified in recent times and there is now an import trade from the Faroe Islands. Faroese trawlers bring fish to the market and also land Faroes produced fish food for the salmon farming industry.

Fuel and water are available and nearby are a general store and an hotel and restaurant. The Deep Sea Fisherman's Mission is on the quay. There is a pleasant walk around nearby Loch Innis and a longer one to Sandwood Bay, a renowned beach on the coast to the north west.

A night time shot of the old Kinlochbervie yacht pontoon, at the head of the harbour.

The new Kinlochbervie yacht pontoon which is on the west side of the harbour next to the ice plant.

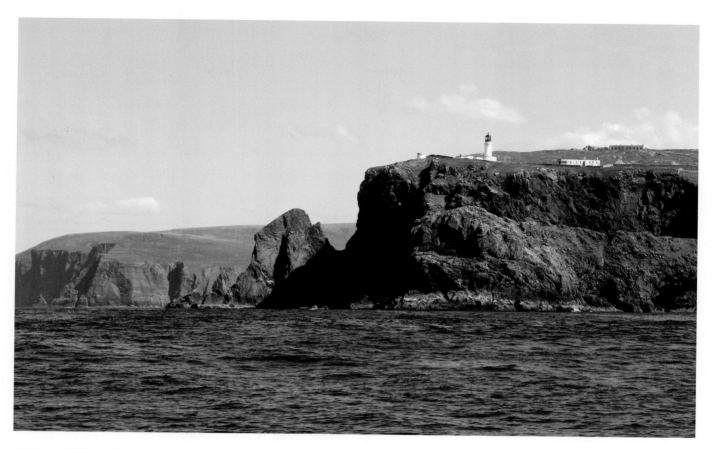

Cape Wrath

A good day to round Cape Wrath!

The yachtsman on passage around the Scottish mainland's north west point is greatly privileged as Cape Wrath is no easy place to reach by other means. To do so you must cross the Kyle of Durness by ferry, and then walk, cycle or take a minibus for the journey of around 11 miles to the lighthouse.

The lighthouse was established in 1828 and stands over 121m (396ft) above sea level. Unsurprisingly, it was one of the earlier lighthouses to be built, not so long after the first in Scotland at Kinnaird Head in 1786, and the Bell Rock in 1811.

The Cape Wrath MOD range, which is used by all three UK forces for bombing and gunnery practice, can provide spectacular entertainment as one sails east from Cape Wrath. However, the range is closed during July and August. The Clo Mor cliffs, just east of the Cape, are the highest on the British mainland at 195m (640ft), and further to the east the hill of Cnoc Carn is a near cliff of almost 300m (984ft).

Kyle of Durness is the nearest inlet to Cape Wrath but is effectively un-navigable by deep draught vessels. Fortunately it is just 15 miles from the Cape to **Loch Eriboll**, where good anchorages can be found. For an on-passage stop in settled weather you can choose one near the entrance, the alternative being a five mile sail into the loch to **Ard Neakie**, where the sandy isthmus connecting the island to the mainland provides a choice of shelter from north or south winds. Overlooking the southern bay are large and long disused lime kilns and a pier from which their product was shipped.

Tir na n'Og, or Valhalla

This mythical land, fabled in Irish, Scottish and Viking culture, may lie beyond Cape Wrath, a place beyond the edges of the map, located on an island far to the west, which can be reached by either an arduous voyage or an invitation from one of its fairy residents.

Here sickness and death do not exist as it is a place of eternal youth and beauty, happiness lasts forever and there is unlimited food and drink.

So sail on to the ultimate cruising destination!

4 Outer Hebrides

The Long Isle, to give it its romantic name, stretches like a breakwater for one hundred miles from Barra Head to the Butt of Lewis, sheltering the mainland west coast and islands from Ardnamurchan almost to Cape Wrath. This shelter has made the Sea of the Hebrides and the Minches the fine cruising ground that it is.

The islands themselves offer contrasting attractions. From the south, the islands of Berneray (Barra Head) to South Uist vary from now uninhabited and wilderness places like Mingulay, to the busy islands of Vatersay and Barra, and the navigational complexities of the Sound of Barra.

The Uists have two very different faces. To the west is an uncompromising thirty mile strand with no anchorages or refuges, whilst the east coast is indented with many lochs and havens, a fine setting for the cruising sailor.

Next is the Sound of Harris, the main route to the Atlantic. The Sound is in places rock-strewn, but the newly buoyed Stanton Channel along the Harris shore is an easy route to the west, whether heading for the west coast of Harris and Lewis, or to visit St Kilda, the ultimate destination for many yachtsmen.

The mountains of Harris seen from the north of Skye on an evening which promises fine weather for the crossing of the Little Minch.

The east coast of Harris and Lewis, like that of the Uists further south, has lochs, some quite long, to explore and anchor within. Stornoway, unless one is bound northabout past the Butt of Lewis or for the Faroes, generally marks the limit of cruising endeavour, for the coast north of the Eye peninsula has little to offer the recreational sailor.

What the proposed super-quarry at Ròineabhal in South Harris might have looked like had the project gone ahead, showing also the dock which was to be created out of the small anchorage north of Lingarabay Island. The planning application for the project was refused after a public inquiry.

Wild flowers blooming in the machair on the Atlantic coast of South Uist.

Geology and Topography

The Outer Hebrides are mainly composed of Lewisian Gneiss, one of the oldest rocks on the planet, which have been not only to the south pole and back as the continents drifted around during the 4,500 million years since the planet was formed, but also down towards the centre of the earth for some serious cooking before returning to the surface as a hard and resistant basement rock to form Scotland's western islands and much of the north west mainland coast.

In one place, Ròineabhal, in South Harris, the hill is composed of anorthosite, which also forms the uplands of the moon! This stone is much prized by roadbuilders and the outcrop narrowly escaped destruction when a public inquiry upheld the arguments of the objectors, who included Scottish Natural Heritage.

The hills of the Outer Isles, which are generally of between 200 and 600 metres, are generally of gneiss or sometimes granite, able to resist the forces of glaciation that have otherwise planed the island surface to a bumpy flatness, ideal for the formation of peat bogs, lochans (small lochs), and wild areas that are a haven for wetland wildlife.

On the west coast, where this flat land slopes into the sea, the formation of sand beaches backed by sandy pasture, known as machair, is the focus of most agricultural activity and, as a result, much of the population is on the windy west coasts, not on the sheltered east coast lochs.

A night passage to Barra

'Sanday slipped astern, its beacon already flashing to the eastward, and then the shore of Canna fell back at the wide bight of Tarbert Bay. There the waves were still falling in rhythmic crashes of sound, for although the seas had ceased to break outside, they were still running fairly high. Away behind Canna rose the faint dark shapes of the majestic Cuillins, while the goblin Rum brooded aloof and forbidding astern. Two miles ahead a white light flashed every six seconds. It marked Humla Rock, and for it we steered so as to escape the Belle and Jemima sirens that lurk unmarked between it and Canna. A little to the south of Humla, three quick flashes every half-minute came from the high beacon that guards the lonely Hysgeir.

The darkness deepened. The Cuillins vanished, then Canna. Orval on Rum remained for a time, a darker bulk against the black arras of the east; then he, too, vanished, and we were alone on a restless sea where a thousand sibilant voices spoke. Humla and Hysgeir became the only realities in our world. The black pit that had swallowed the Cuillin giants could not annihilate them. That was a comforting thought. Those yellow winking beacons of night are among the most companionable things on the sea.

All night the wind blew steadily, and, just able to lay her course for Barra, the yacht went swinging out to the west. Humla and Hysgeir dwindled astern, and a new star rose in our navigational firmament – Barra Head Light, high on its cliff on Bemeray, the southernmost of the Outer Isles. Towards it we held our way, till a grey light stole into the east whence we had come, and revealed the sea, a tumbling waste of steely waters, empty and desolate. The sky had two cloud strata; the lower, thin and wind-blown, the upper, cirrus wisps of a pale pink hue, apparently motionless. Low in the north-east, cold and green as an iceberg, glittered a strip of clear sky, notched by the crests of far-off seas.

The light increased and discovered over the bow a number of slaty shadows – the Barra Isles. Dowsing the now superfluous side-lights, we bore steadily on while the islands, imperfectly seen in the dawn light, seemed to change shape, to waver, and vanish, and reappear, like the Green Isle in the legend. The sun rose and shone on the swelling hills of Muldoanich as we passed; and soon we were picking our way among the rocks and into Castle Bay, where, off Kishmul's Castle, famous in story, we anchored, and slept.'

West Coast Cruising, John McLintock, 1938

Shamrock, CCC

Passage to the Outer Hebrides

Westward passages to the Outer Isles vary from the fifteen mile hop from Skye to North Uist, to the near forty miles from Coll to Barra, or from Loch Broom to Stornoway. These latter courses begin to have the feel of real voyages, for the low island hills will not begin to grow out of the sea until you are halfway across the Sea of the Hebrides or the North Minch.

As usual, the key factor is the weather. The Long Isle may shelter the Minches and the Sea of the Hebrides, but the depressions that track north east past Britain must still be taken into account. On the other hand, being at the northern end of Britain has its advantages too, for when a series of depressions track further south, the north of Scotland enjoys easterly winds and often long spells of clear, dry and sunny weather.

Tides are only a serious factor at the Shiant Islands and in the Little Minch, where the tidal stream can reach 2½ knots on the Skye side of the channel. In the more open waters to the north and south the rate is seldom above 1 knot.

A glance at the chart will confirm that the best departure point for Barra and Lochboisdale is Canna, just 25 miles from the destination. Coll is an alternative, but this can require a diversion through Gunna Sound before the crossing can begin. North of Skye the passages from the mainland to Harris or Lewis are also longer – a day's sail in a small cruising yacht – and with no real option for shortening the passage. A diversion en route, however, is a visit to the Shiant Isles: not a haven in bad weather, but a fascinating group of islands at which to break the journey.

The western anchorage off the gravel spit joining Garbh Eilean and Eilean an Tigh in the Shiant Islands, pictured on one of the rare days when it is tenable.

Islands to the South of Barra

We start at **Berneray**, the southern extremity of the archipelago, and best known for its lighthouse, Barra Head, perched at the top of the western cliffs. It is so high at 200m (656ft) that on misty nights the light can be obscured by cloud.

The lighthouse pier provides a landing place at the eastern end of the Sound of Berneray, a narrow fiord-like passage between Berneray and Mingulay. There is a temporary anchorage off the pier, from where a track leads up to the lighthouse.

For a few years, in the late 1960s and early '70s, there was an offshore race from the Clyde to Tobermory via, of all places, Barra Head. This involved rounding the Mull of Kintyre at night, a simple task compared with negotiating the Sound of Berneray, sometimes also in the dark – the very dark! If a rite of passage was to be devised, this might have been it. Fortunately, no one came to grief on this demanding event, but very few did the race a second time!

Barra Head lighthouse on Berneray with Mingulay in the middle distance and Pabbay, Sandray and Barra beyond. Built by Robert Stevenson in 1833, it was automated in 1980.

Opposite: *The old lighthouse pier on Berneray, where it is possible to anchor off and go ashore in moderate weather. Note that many of these redundant facilities are no longer maintained by the NLB and great care should be taken if using them.*

The ruined schoolhouse on Mingulay overlooks the landing beach and anchorage.

Another island that can be visited relatively easily is **Mingulay**, next in the chain. It has an east facing bay, although it can be difficult to land without getting wet, as it is subject to swell. The island is hilly and was inhabited until a century ago. The remains of many houses can still be seen. The island's main feature is its precipitous western coast, which can best be seen from the sea, of course, although the energetic can walk overland from the bay to view them from above.

Perhaps the best way to view these islands is to circumnavigate them. Pick a settled day, and either cut through to the Atlantic south of Vatersay, or return that way. You will be rewarded by seeing some spectacular sea cliffs, stacks, geos and other coastal features.

You might see climbers on these cliffs, which are now recognised as offering some of the best climbing experiences in Scotland, partly on account of the hard and stable Lewisian Gneiss from which they are formed and also for the challenge in getting there. Early in the summer the bird life, particularly on the cliffs of Mingulay, is spectacular, whilst on the hill slopes wild flowers bloom in profusion.

Cliffs on the west side of Mingulay on a day with virtually no swell running.

Meanish Bay on Sandray gives reasonable shelter from the west but is open to south and east.

A final bonus would be to come across the sealife that once sustained island communities. The waters around these islands are sometimes full of fish, and when this happens it attracts pods of cetations and flocks of seabirds. The birds are the clue – if you see a lot of aerial activity, the chances are that dolphins, minke whales, porpoises or even orca (killer whales) might be spotted too.

Pabbay and **Sandray** lie between Mingulay and Vatersay. They are, and generally have been, uninhabited and neither have particularly secure anchorages. Meanish Bay on Sandray is the better, having less swell and fewer sunken rocks to contend with. The name Pabbay usually designates a priest's isle, so this was probably a retreat, like the Garvellachs in Argyll, and the few archeological remains would confirm this. There were crofts on Sandray until around 300 years ago, and traces of earlier habitation too.

Vatersay is no longer a separate island, having been linked to Barra by a causeway in 1990, following the much publicised drowning of a prize bull when the cattle had to swim across the Sound of Vatersay to reach Barra. This causeway now gives welcome shelter from south westerlys, to which Castle Bay on Barra is totally exposed. However, much better shelter in more congenial surroundings is offered by the magnificent **Vatersay Bay** to the south. It is protected from the west by a sweeping beach and a narrow spit of sand dunes, on the other side of which another extensive beach, Traigh Siar, faces the Atlantic swell. The bay has long been a favourite with yachtsmen, and it was well filled in 1985, when the 75th Anniversary muster of the CCC was held there. Many more boats will anchor in the bay when the CCC Centenary Cruise fleet arrives in 2010.

Looking down on a single yacht anchored in Vatersay Bay. It takes quite a stretch of the imagination to picture 200 yachts anchored here!

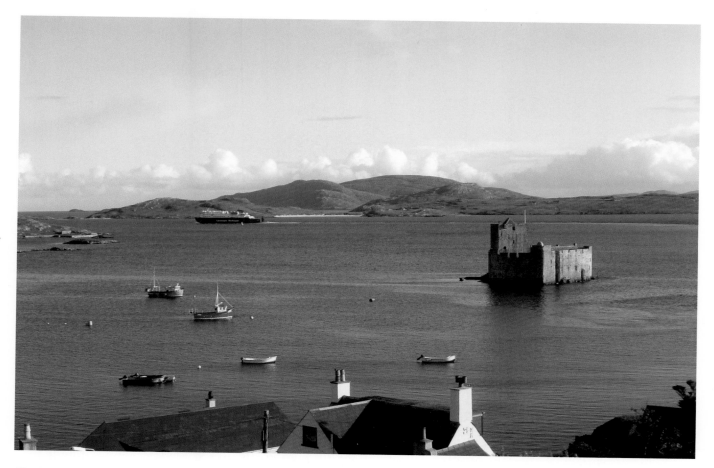

Barra

To many people Barra is an ideal island destination. Small enough to comprehend easily and get to know well, and yet large enough to support a lively community and meet most of the victualling requirements of a cruising yacht, with a supermarket, butcher, grocer, bank, hotels and a Post Office all in **Castlebay**, the main settlement. Communications with the mainland and other islands are as good as anywhere, with ferry services to Oban and the islands to the north, and air services to Glasgow and Benbecula from the unique beach airfield at the north end of the island.

Unfortunately it is not well provided with anchorages, Castle Bay and North Bay being the only two. However, Castle Bay has many visitors' moorings, a total of 12 in all, but as mentioned previously they are very exposed to the south and south west, though for most of the time they are well used. Between Castle Bay and North Bay the coastline is foul with offlying rocks and this does not encourage close inspection from seawards without local knowledge. By far the best way to explore both the east and west coasts is to hire a bicycle and take a few hours on a circular tour of the island. On returning to Castlebay, visit Kisimul Castle which is in the care of Historic Scotland, who describe it as 'The only significant surviving medieval castle in the Western Isles'.

North Bay provides good shelter in Bagh Hirivagh (see p.179) but, as this is the working anchorage of the island, much of the space is taken up by moorings and the fish processing factory at Ardveenish dominates the shoreline. However it is well marked and lit and can be a secure refuge in bad weather. A more secluded alternative in the same vicinity is **Sgeirislum**, just north of the island of Fuiay at the entrance to North Bay.

The classic view of Kisimul Castle in Castle Bay, with Vatersay and Sandray beyond.

The domestic character of the Kisimul Castle courtyard contrasts unexpectedly with the stern exterior.

The Sound of Barra looking north across to South Uist from near the Boat Harbour at Eoligarry.

Sound of Barra

This is a wide but shallow stretch of water, bordered by extensive beaches and well filled with small islets and rocks. Even though it is buoyed and well charted it is infrequently used by yachts as the nearest good anchorage beyond it is in the Monach Islands, about 30 miles north, and St Kilda is almost double that distance. Pilotage through makes use of distant transits and shore marks and care and good visibility are needed to ensure that they are correctly identified. The Sailing Directions say it all in their advice: 'Due to the shallow patches and shifting sands, passage through is best made on a rising tide'.

At the eastern entrance to the Sound lie a pair of small islands, **Hellisay** and **Gighay**, between which there is a sheltered anchorage providing total protection and seclusion. It is also strewn with rocks, especially in its two entrances, and avoiding them all is a considerable challenge. Nonetheless it appears to have a magnetic attraction for yacht skippers, and it is rare to meet one who has sailed in the Hebrides for any length of time without having been in there. Whether they avoided all the rocks is another matter!

A sailing dinghy or sea kayak is the ideal craft for exploring the anchorage between Hellisay and Gighay.

Opposite upper: *Fishing boats mirrored in the calm waters of Bagh Hirivagh, North Bay, Barra.*

Opposite lower: *Acairseid Mhor, the anchorage on Eriskay with the pier and new pontoon on the left.*

The anchorage between Hellisay and Gighay. Taken from Gighay looking over Eilean a Ceud towards the narrow western entrance.

The recently installed and well used pontoon in Acairseid Mhor, Eriskay. The visitors' moorings are opposite and towards the far side of the pool.

The unusual altar in the Catholic church at Haun is made from the bow of a lifeboat lost overboard from HMS 'Hermes' and washed up on South Uist.

An extract from the CCC Sailing Directions showing the Sound of Eriskay, now blocked off by the causeway, and the wreck symbol NW of Calvey marking the position of the remains of the SS 'Politician'.

North of Gighay lies the island of **Eriskay** which protects the larger part of the Sound of Barra from the east. This small island, now connected to South Uist by a causeway and Barra by a vehicle ferry, is best known as the place where Bonnie Prince Charlie first set foot on Scottish soil on his way to raise the clans for the 1745 rebellion. The island is also famous for inspiring the book *Whisky Galore!,* written by Compton Mackenzie.

Eriskay is known to yachtsmen as possessing one of the best natural anchorages in the Outer Isles, **Acairseid Mhor** on the east coast. Entry to it is not straightforward as there are several sunken rocks in the approach but the leading line, once recognised, is invaluable. Inside the anchorage there are two visitors' moorings and the new pontoon makes life much easier when taking on water or diesel, both of which are available by hose. A walk of 1½ miles will bring you to the church on the hill and the village of Haun, by the old jetty on the Sound of Eriskay. On the way you will pass the well stocked shop and the pub, *Am Politician,* and will be able to look down on the west coast beach where the Prince landed.

The Prince and the Whisky

Two very different historical events have taken place on Eriskay. In 1745 Bonnie Prince Charlie first landed in Scotland prior to leading his ill-fated cause of reclaiming the throne of the United Kingdom for the Stuart lineage. In 1941 during the Second World War the doomed cargoship SS *Politician* foundered in the Sound of Eriskay due to an unexplained error of navigation while attempting to avoid the attention of enemy U-Boats west of the Outer Hebrides. As part of her cargo there were no fewer than 264,000 bottles of whisky.

Evidence of both events can be found: firstly the attractive sea-pink convolvulus wild flower grows just inland from the strand of white sand on the west side of the island. It is said that these wild flowers grow from seeds which the Prince dropped when landing from the French frigate which had carried him from France. Secondly, within the pub aptly named *Am Politician* there are artefacts, including original bottles, which vouch for the removal of the whisky by the islanders from the *Politician,* immortalised in the film *Whisky Galore!* From the official records of the cargo of the *Politician* held in the Public Records Office, it appears that a sum of hard cash in the form of nearly 290,000 ten shilling notes, equivalent to £5,000,000 today, was also on board. Had any part of this item of cargo been discovered by the islanders their good fortune might well have extended beyond having a sufficiency of whisky!

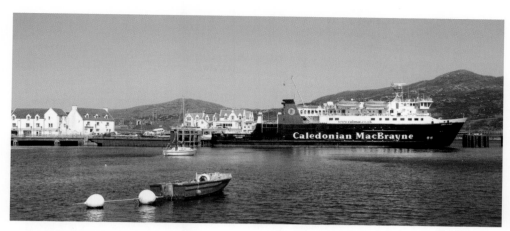

The Oban ferry berthed at the Lochboisdale pier.

South Uist

Whilst the classic tourist image of South Uist is of seemingly endless sandy beaches backed by the machair, the cruising yachtsman usually sees the more rugged side of the island. The east coast is fringed by cliffs and rocks overlooked by a chain of mountains and punctuated by three long lochs which penetrate through towards the west. These lochs all offer sheltered anchorages but differ in character.

Approaching from the south, the first is **Loch Boisdale**. Although the loch has several anchorages, many of these are occupied by either fish farming gear or moorings. In practice, most yachts use one of the six visitors' moorings in the bay to the north east of the pier. The loch is straightforward to enter and well lit so, combined with the moorings, it makes a good refuge in bad weather.

The village of Lochboisdale is centred principally around the Calmac ferry terminal and consists of a hotel, a bank, the tourist information office and a few houses. Those needing provisions will have to make the trek three miles inland to the shop at Daliburgh.

The next loch, **Loch Eynort**, five miles north, is a much more challenging proposition. It is divided into an upper and outer loch by a tortuous narrows, where the tidal stream can reach 7 knots and the channel at its narrowest is little more than 30 metres wide. Entry at slack water is definitely recommended. Once inside the upper loch there are numerous unmarked rocks but the shelter and scenery may make the excursion worth while. However it is not for the faint-hearted, who may prefer to settle for the Cearcdal Bay anchorage in the outer loch.

The Birlinn of Clanranald

Loch Eynort was the starting point for the epic voyage to Carrickfergus of the Birlinn of Clanranald. This poem, the longest in the Gaelic language, was composed by Alasdair Macdonald in the mid-18th century for the Chief himself, Clanranald who, in the extract here translated by Hugh MacDiarmid, is listing the duties of the various members of his crew. His sentiments will be appreciated by the skippers of many family cruising yachts!

I'll have at my ear a teller
  Of the waters;
Let him keep close watch windward
  On these matters;
A man somewhat timid, cautious,
  Not altogether
A coward however!—Keeping
  Stock of the weather. . .

Clamorous at the least threat of danger
  This man must be,
And not fear to give the steersman
  Any hint of hazard.
– But let him be the one teller
  Of the waters heard,
And not the whole of you bawling
  Advices mixed,
A distraught steersman not knowing
  Who to heed next!

A Birlinn or Galley as shown on the 16th century tomb in St. Clement's Church at Rodel, South Harris. Vessels similar to this design were based on Viking models and continued little changed for centuries.

Continuing up the coast and around Usinish Point brings you to **Loch Skipport** which is regarded as one of the classic anchorages of the Hebrides. It has a number of branches and pools in which to anchor, the two best known being Caolas Mor (Kettle Pool) and Wizard Pool. Both have their devotees though there is not much to choose between them and opinions are probably influenced as much by the weather on the holder's last visit as by technicalities. Behind them, on the south side, stands Hecla, 606 metres (1,988ft) high, which provides both a good hill to climb and a source of ferocious gusts in southerly gales.

By contrast with the difficult entrance to Loch Eynort to the south and the intricacies of Benbecula to the north, entry to Loch Skipport is simplicity itself and can be made in all weathers. Being only 28 miles from Canna, and with the daymark of Hecla or the prominent light on Usinish Point to aim for, Loch Skipport is a excellent landfall to choose when crossing the Sea of the Hebrides.

A lovely evening at anchor in the Wizard Pool, Loch Skipport, but cloud is beginning to cling to Hecla. The next day proved to be wet and windy!

Opposite upper: *The entrance to Loch Eynort showing, in the centre of the picture, Strue Beag, the narrows. Bo Dearg, the long rock in the approach channel to the narrows is off the photograph to the lower right and none of it is showing. Entry to the loch is easier when it can be seen.*

Opposite lower: *Looking over the entrance to Loch Skipport from the south with the Kettle Pool on the left and the Wizard Pool on the right.*

Another good anchorage in Loch Skipport is Poll na Cairidh, but the gusts from Hecla are just as strong.

183

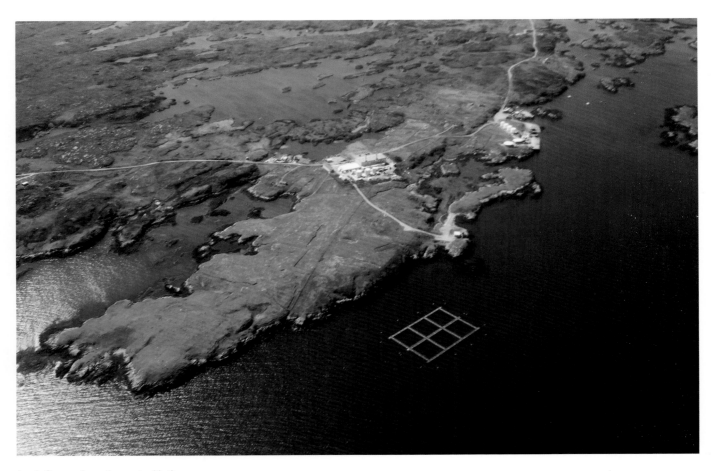

Loch Carnan from the east with the power station in the centre and the yacht mooring upper right.

Looking across the South Ford in the direction of Wiay and Peter's Port.

Benbecula

North of Loch Skipport, South Uist falls away rapidly to a lochan-studded landscape which merges imperceptibly into the sea. Benbecula to the north is similar, its highest point reaching an insignificant 124 metres (407ft) and its east coast fringed by a profusion of small islands interspersed by an intricate pattern of waterways. It is separated from both the Uists by wandering, drying channels which penetrate through to the Atlantic, although now all three islands are joined by causeways.

Both on the chart and from the sea it is all a bit baffling to the sailor used to the clearly identifiable summits, headlands and other marks generally found on the west coast; even in moderate visibility it is possible to sail past Benbecula and see nothing at all! However, it is charted to a good scale and with the benefit of GPS it is now possible to be certain at least of your position before making an approach although, like many rocky anchorages in this part of the world, it would be unwise to rely on GPS or a chart plotter for close quarters navigation (See 'Chart Accuracy' on the previous page and also p.124).

Before leaving South Uist you pass **Loch Carnan** which is the location of a power station, now only used as a backup for mainland supplied electricity. Apart from having a buoyed entrance channel and a visitors' mooring, it is hard to see why a yacht would want to call here, it having neither the true wilderness character of the Benbecula anchorages further north, nor any services or supplies other than water.

The anchorage at Peter's Port.

Across the South Ford from Loch Carnan is the island of **Wiay** which, although not circumnavigable by deep-keeled vessels, shelters a number of remote anchorages between it and Benbecula. **Peter's Port** on the south side is a good anchorage which can be approached reasonably easily, using the Loch Carnan landfall buoy and the two buoys laid in the channel for the benefit of the few local boats.

North of Wiay lie **Loch a' Laip**, **Loch Keiravagh** and, 1½ miles further on, **Loch Uskevagh.** They all have innumerable unmarked rocks, both in their approaches and within, and should be entered only in settled conditions and good visibility. However all three offer intriguing opportunities for exploration in the right weather and, preferably, by a shoal draft boat.

Further north again is the island of **Ronay**, to the west of which is the busy fishing harbour of **Kallin**. This, having been built in 1985 and recently extended in 2008, is well used and water and diesel are available and some repairs might also be possible. Although there is no village where supplies can be bought, shellfish are available in abundance from the factory at the pier.

The harbour and new pier at Kallin where berthing alongside a fishing boat may well be necessary.

Evening light in the Bagh a Bhiorain anchorage in Loch Eport.

Taigh Chearsabhagh -
The Lochmaddy Arts Centre

Situated within 100metres from the pier terminal this award winning centre provides attractive insights into the culture, arts and heritage of the Outer Hebrides. There are art and craft workshops and an extensive photographic collection. During the year exhibitions and concerts provide an interesting blend of the art and history of the islands.

Additionally, a sculpture trail has been developed which leads visitors to remote locations on North Uist.

Some of the visitors' moorings are astonishingly near the ferry pier!

North Uist

Before arriving at North Uist, which is easily recognised by the wedge-shaped profile of Eaval rising gradually from Benbecula and Ronay, two more small but interesting anchorages can be investigated: **Acarseid Fhalach** a small pool off **Flodday Sound** is well described in the Sailing Directions and the north anchorage in **Poll nan Gall** allows for easy access to Eaval, 345 metres (1,132ft), from the summit of which is a bird's eye view of the complex pattern of water and land that is Benbecula and Loch Eport to the north.

At the extreme south east point of North Uist another challenging anchorage is **Bagh Moraig**, a small landlocked pool approached via a narrow 'hairpin' bend before crossing a drying rocky bar. Those who found Loch Eynort too easy might try this one, but wait until slack HW.

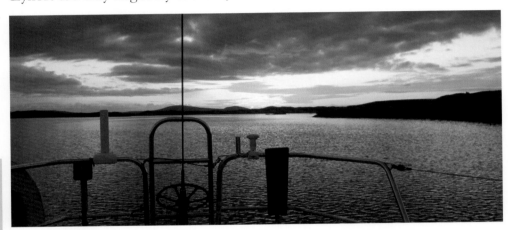

After these two, **Loch Eport**, 2 miles up the coast, is relatively simple, although from outside the 6 cables long, ½ cable wide gap in the rocks can look a little daunting. It is however deep and steep-to and presents no problems. These begin once inside but, providing the leading lines shown in the Sailing Directions are recognised and followed carefully, all will be well. The most popular anchorage here is in **Bagh a Bhiorain** on the south side of the loch, just inside the entrance, although there are many others further up the loch for the intrepid to discover.

After all the rock dodging since leaving Loch Skipport it is with some relief that the comparatively clean and well-marked haven of **Loch Maddy** is reached. This is the ferry port linking the island with Uig on Skye and, unlike Lochboisdale, the village of **Lochmaddy** has grown with the development of roll-on roll-off ferries and the increased trade, including tourism, that has come with it. There is a tourist information centre, two hotels offering bar meals and restaurants, various shops, a café, and a bus service to other parts of the island. Since 1995 there has also been an excellent museum and arts centre which also has a craft shop and restaurant.

For visiting yachts there is a total of nine moorings, split among three locations. The majority are near either the pier or the village but for those wanting security together with seclusion, there is a pair on the south shore in **Ardmaddy Bay**. Away from the village and the moorings the loch develops into a rash of low lying islands which enclose between them several anchorages, though it must be said that the holding in many of them is rather poor in soft mud. **Loch Portain,** an arm of Loch Maddy extending to the north east, is reported to have better holding than most.

Sound of Harris

The Sound of Harris is both a miniature cruising ground in itself and the main route through to the west. As Cowper says, it is 'beset with sunken rocks' and its navigation is far from straightforward, as can be seen by over a dozen pages being allocated to it and its anchorages in the Sailing Directions. However these, and the many buoys and beacons now in place, do mean that a pilot is not needed!

The **Stanton Channel**, along the south shore of Harris, has been upgraded by the Northern Lighthouse Board by the addition of four new buoys. It is now the preferred channel from the Minch to the west, replacing the **Cope Passage** which has a potentially dangerous bar at its western end, although the latest reprint (2009) of the Sailing Directions gives precise instructions as to how the best channel through the bar can be found. However the southern part of the Cope Passage, as far as the ferry route, forms part of the approach to the island of Berneray and therefore is well used, though there is a possibility that the Cope buoys to the north of the ferry route may eventually be removed.

Berneray, although a little tricky of access and needing a good rise of tide, is well worth the effort to visit. It has three visitors' moorings in **Bays Loch**, and a small harbour on its south side, near to the village. The island is just three miles by two and can easily be explored on foot. On the east side, tracks and lanes meander amongst the croft houses, reaching the low, 93m (305ft), hill of Beinn Shleibhe at the north end and affording fine views of the Harris hills and the islands to the west, amongst which is, of course, St Kilda. The west side of the island is an unspoiled continuous beach backed by dunes, inland of which is Loch Bhrusda, a freshwater loch. The island found fame when the Duke of Rothesay (Prince Charles) stayed there for a while to learn about island and crofting life.

An alternative approach to Berneray is through the Reef Channel, seen here marked by two poles where it passes through a narrow gap in the reef extending south east from Berneray.

Other good anchorages in the south eastern approaches to the Sound of Harris are in **Vaccasay Basin**, **Bagh Chaise** and **Cheese Bay**, where excellent holding can be found. In the centre of the sound, the anchorage east of **Groay** is good and probably the easiest to approach in the whole sound. Those looking for a pilotage challenge might care to try the **Grey Horse Channel**, which starts from **Opsay Basin** just to the north of Vaccasay. This is fully described in the Sailing Directions and used to be one of the main approaches to Berneray before the establishment of the buoyed route for the ferry.

The origins of Leverburgh

The yachtsman who has crept cautiously into Leverburgh must wonder why anyone would ever dream of establishing a major port in such a rock-bound place. He might know of Lord Leverhulme (the Lancashire soap tycoon and founder of what is now Unilever) and his abortive ventures to make first Lewis, and then Harris, into thriving centres of industry and commerce, with fishing as their basis; but just how the small village of Obbe came to be the focus of his ambitions for an Atlantic port is a little known tale.

However, for all Leverhulme's misguided obsessions, it is ironic that over eighty years after his death, the Northern Lighthouse Board is about to light at least one of his beacons, and Caledonian MacBrayne are now using Leverburgh as the Harris terminal of their ferry across the Sound.

The beacon on the Red Rocks, erected as part of Leverhulme's development. The NLB plan to establish a light on this mark.

'Leverhulme did not search long for the site of his harbour. He found it at Obbe. It was a pity that he and his advisers did not give the matter further thought before embarking on the engineering works, for Obbe was not the best possible site. Tarbert would have been preferable, for it had deep sheltered water, and it would not have been beyond Leverhulme's scope to dig a canal through the narrow isthmus linking the East and West Lochs Tarbert, and so provide his boats with access to the seas on both sides of the Hebrides. This proposal was urged on him at an early stage by Duncan Maciver; and his personal representative in Lewis, Colonel Walter Lindsay (who had apparently not heard of Maciver's idea), raised it again in October 1920. "It struck me yesterday," he wrote to Leverhulme, "that it would be a great advantage if a canal could be cut at Tarbert, as there is extremely good anchorage in both lochs." But it was in that very month that work at Leverburgh began in earnest. Why Leverhulme discarded the obvious claims of a Tarbert canal is not clear. Perhaps he feared its proximity to Stornoway, or did not wish to harm the interests of the thriving community of fishermen on the isle of Scalpay at the entrance to the east loch. Or perhaps it was for the more personal reason that once the decision had been taken to rechristen Obbe "Leverburgh", it became unthinkable to abandon it.

The great disadvantage of Obbe lay in the dangers of the Sound of Harris. One who knew it well wrote in 1923:

Leverburgh as it is today. Leverhulme had plans to expand it to a town with a population of 10,000, but in the end only a handful of houses were built.

> "The Sound of Harris is considered very dangerous for the navigation of vessels. It is full of rocks, numbers of which are sunken at a short distance from the surface of the water; and again, the current is always so strong during a calm that there is great difficulty in keeping a vessel off those dreaded skerries."

The engineers of the Scottish Fishery Board told Leverhulme that Obbe was quite unsuitable. So did the skippers of MacBrayne's steamers. So did the Northern Lighthouse Commissioners. Halliday Sutherland, who saw Leverhulme on the site in 1923, found him quite unrepentant, even after he had himself run aground at the entrance to the harbour on one of his journeys from Skye:

> "In vain the local sailors—and they are amongst the most fearless I ever knew—told him that the Sound of Harris with its thousand rocks could not be navigated at night in winter. The persistent old man replied, 'If the Harris men cannot sail my ships, I will get English sailors, and if necessary, I will put a light on every rock in the Sound of Harris."

Determined not to be thwarted by a mere accident of geography, Leverhulme blasted away some of the rocks and put gas-beacons on others. He saw only the gap in the long ridge of the Outer Hebrides that opened up between South Harris and North Uist, presenting him with his much-needed avenue from east to west, and attributed the experts' apprehensions to a want of vision. He was always complaining that they were incapable of thinking big. The rocks and small islands were a protection, not an obstacle:

The small harbour at Berneray where diesel and water are available.

> "I do not know why the pessimists should wail over the prospects of Leverburgh. I stood on the scaffolding at the end of the pier on Saturday, and you could not get a view of the open sea in any direction. Whichever way you looked there were intervening islands blocking the way. These islands produce a bay for Leverburgh, and I am confident that any vessel can ride out the storm there as well as in Stornoway harbour."

Leverburgh was never tested as a fishing-harbour under winter conditions, but the distrust of its approaches among local and mainland skippers was one of the reasons for its abandonment on Leverhulme's death.'

Lord of the Isles, Nigel Nicolson, 1960

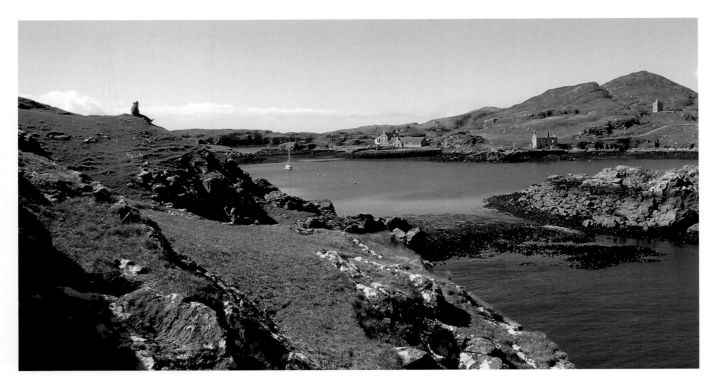

Poll an Tighmhail at LWS. The Rodel hotel is in the centre, and the tower of St. Clement's church on the extreme right. The Sea channel in the foreground is almost dry and the Bay channel in the background has dried totally.

Opposite: *Loch Scadabay is one of the smallest of the South Harris lochs and is entered through a narrow cleft in the rocks, which opens out into a perfectly sheltered pool. This is shallow, but soft mud allows fin keels to sink in at low water.*

St Clement's Church

St Clement's Church, which by medieval Hebridean standards was a grand building, was built by Alexander MacLeod in 1520. He was, in due course, buried in it in 1548 having had his tomb built twenty years earlier. It has magnificent carvings of knights, castles and, of particular interest to sailors, a medieval galley (see p.181). It appears to have 17 oar ports which implies at least 34 oarsmen, is fully rigged and has the high prow and stern of its predecessor, the Viking longboat.

South Harris

The east coasts of Harris and Lewis are similar to the coasts further south – hills overlooking rocky shores, but punctuated by many lochs and inlets. South of Scalpay the coast of South Harris is intricate, with small inlets and islets providing a fascinating cruising ground bounded in the north by East Loch Tarbert, and in the south by the Sound of Harris. There is one harbour on South Harris that faces the Sound of Harris: Leverburgh, whose origins were recounted on the previous page. **Leverburgh** is no place of beauty but is a useful jumping off point for St Kilda or other destinations on the west, and diesel, water and provisions can be obtained there. Two breakwaters have recently been built and give shelter to local boat moorings, but access to the area within the breakwaters is not easy without local knowledge and not recommended for visiting yachts.

Once out of the sound and after rounding Renish Point heading north, you arrive immediately at **Loch Rodel** and its adjacent natural harbour, **Poll an Tighmhail**. This is an interesting place that offers good shelter, three visitors' moorings and a hotel right by the edge of the landlocked pool, which is only accessible after a good rise of tide. The ancient church of St Clement (see side panel) is a short walk up the road and well worth a visit. The whole of the inner pool and the drying channels were recently surveyed in detail by the same team and in the same manner as Loch Tarbert, Jura (see p.75), and now, for the first time, the information on depths over the entrance cills can be relied upon.

The lochs and inlets of the South Harris coast are on a much smaller scale than those found on the Uists, or further north on Lewis. Unfortunately they are only shown at a scale of 1:100,000 on chart 1757, but the plans in the Sailing Directions give much more detail as they are based on unpublished Admiralty surveys and are quite suitable to use for exploration. The anchorages they depict are not of the 'wilderness' variety, as many of the lochs are surrounded by crofts which are served by the quiet road – known as the *Golden Road,* another legacy from Lord Leverhulme – which wanders up the coast.

The first shelter north of Rodel is the small inlet of **Lingara Bay**, which was to have been part of a super-quarry project (see p.172) but, fortunately for the yachtsman, was reprieved by the Planning inquiry and is still available as an anchorage. A mile and a half further north is **Loch Finsbay**, which is probably one of the better anchorages on this coast, being reasonably easy to enter and offering good shelter and holding. Two miles north again are **Lochs Flodabay, Beacravik** and **Gheocrab**, all of which offer anchorages of the 'occasional' variety, best enjoyed when the weather is kind and suitable for picking your way through the rocks that are scattered around their approaches.

The small fishing harbour of Poll Scrot with Caolas Beag and Stockinish Island in the background.

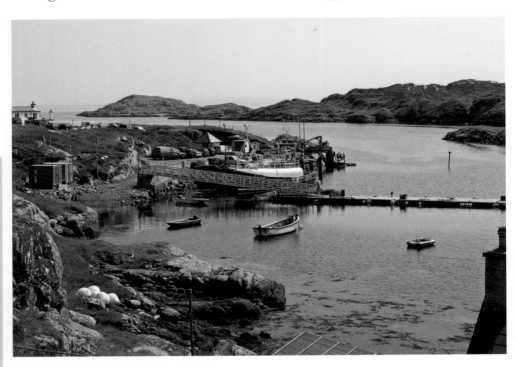

Harris Tweed

Traditionally tweed was made by the islanders, for warm woollen clothing, from local sheep's wool. Vegetable dyes, especially lichens, gave it its characteristic soft colours and odour, with subtle variation of tone. The wool was then combed, carded and spun and woven on hand looms in a close, twill-like pattern.

The distinctive, somewhat hairy, water repellent texture became popular with sportsmen and production increased from the middle of the 19th century until the peak was reached in 1966. In the 20th century spinning and dyeing became mechanised and only the weaving was done in the home.

Harris Tweed is now defined as being hand woven by the islanders at their homes in the Outer Hebrides and made from pure virgin wool dyed and spun in the Outer Hebrides.

Harris Tweed has recently enjoyed a revival of acclaim as a fashion fabric, and an attempt by a Yorkshire firm to control the industry by reducing the range of patterns to four appears to have been unsuccessful. A new enterprise, Harris Tweed Hebrides, currently accounts for about 95% of the tweed produced.

Loch Stockinish, which is immediately adjacent to the above and shares some of their offlying rocks, is easy to enter if the passage north of Stockinish Island, Caolas Beag, is used. This will take you past the inelegantly named, but very welcoming and very small fishing harbour, **Poll Scrot**. Here you will find a pontoon and supplies of diesel and water, which may, or may not, be available by hose. When the boats are in, space is very tight but during the day there is good chance you will find a berth at the pontoon for a short stop. The anchorage at the head of the loch is good for an overnight stay.

The last two lochs with anchorages on this friendly coast are **Lochs Grosebay** and **Scadabay**, which is pictured on the previous page. Loch Grosebay does not offer the best shelter but has a nearby garage and engineers who could prove to be very useful in a crisis. Scadabay has no such facilities and used to be a centre for the weaving of Harris tweed, with several crofts able to be visited where weaving could be seen and tweed bought. Sadly, this is no longer the case.

Rounding Rubha Bhocaig brings you into **Braigh Mor**, a large area of islet studded water between the island of Scalpay and Harris which leads eventually to **East Loch Tarbert** and the Uig ferry terminal at Tarbert itself. Including Scalpay, this contains at least a dozen anchorages and two or three days could be spent quite happily exploring what it has to offer. Although it is lit and buoyed for the ferry, the anchorages are not and care needs to be taken in several of them, such as **Plocrapool**, where rocks abound.

Tarbert, a common name in Scotland, means place of portage where sailors can drag their boats from one sea to another. In this era, the village is primarily the ferry port for the service from Uig on Skye, and has several hotels, shops and other useful services. There is not a lot of room to anchor, as the ferry needs space to turn and there are quite a few moorings. The pier, like most other ferry piers in the area, does not provide any facilities for other types of vessel but carrying the ferry timetable will indicate whether a brief shopping trip is on the cards.

An alternative is to slip across to **Scalpay** where the anchorage in North Harbour is both more spacious and better sheltered. Water and diesel can be obtained here but the shop has recently closed, a casualty of the bridge which opened in 1997, linking the island to mainland Harris. However, a bus service into Tarbert runs every two hours or so if the need for shopping is overwhelming. Scalpay also has another well sheltered anchorage at South Harbour which is only a short walk from the village.

Looking down on Scalpay North Harbour with Caol Scalpay and the new bridge beyond.

Tarbert ferry terminal, moorings and, on the extreme right, the anchorage.

South Harbour, Scalpay.

Opposite upper: The Shiants, looking along the cliffs and screes on the eastern side of Garbh Eilean from Eilean an Tigh towards the arch at the northern end, off which a yacht is anchored.

Opposite lower: At anchor in the pool known as Tob Bhrollum, on the east side of Loch Bhrollum, framed by scenery which is typical of the lochs on this coast.

South East Lewis

Emerging from Braigh Mor or the Sound of Scalpay, one of the most obvious landmarks in anything like decent visibility, are the Shiant Islands 10 miles to the east. Their dramatic outline marks the northern limit of an area of isolated shoals and rocky outcrops that stretches across the Little Minch from the northern point of Skye to south east Lewis. This makes the otherwise short crossing to the Outer Hebrides – 18 miles from Duntulm Bay to Scalpay – a little less simple, as the uneven seabed and increased tidal streams can lead to confused seas in conditions of wind over tide. This is especially the case in the **Sound of Shiant**, the passage between the islands and the Lewis shore, where a massive undersea shelf can cause dangerous seas in some weathers and an uncomfortable motion at almost any time. It is true to say that the triangle between Loch Bhrollum, the Shiants and Loch Shell is probably the only area on a passage from Barra to Stornoway where tidal strategy is of overriding importance.

The **Shiant Islands** themselves are a fascinating destination and are worth a considerable detour in the right weather. The owner permits landing and whether your interest is natural history, archeology, geology, or just wandering and marvelling at the view, you will not be disappointed. One isolated fact out of many is that they are home to 240,000 puffins, or one in eight of the British total. Presumably the puffins flourish on what is brought to the surface by the turbulent waters which cause the yachtsman such trouble!

Although they have separate names, Lewis and Harris are one island, which is the largest in the British Isles. The northern part of the island is Lewis, the southern, Harris, and the boundary between them is difficult to determine, as different sources suggest a different line. None of this matters to the cruising yachtsman but for the purposes of our journey northwards it is assumed that the boundary is at **Loch Seaforth**. This loch is the longest of the half dozen or so major lochs between Scalpay and Stornoway, several of which penetrate many miles inland. Probably because it is slightly off the direct coasting route, and maybe because the entrance is not as straightforward as the others, it is less visited by cruising yachts. It is also in the immediate lee of the highest hills with the inevitable ferocious squalls.

The next three lochs, **Loch Claidh**, **Loch Valamus** and **Loch Bhrollum** all offer secure anchorages in true wilderness surroundings with not a road, track or occupied dwelling in sight. Frank Cowper must have had them in mind when, in dismissing the Outer Hebrides, he wrote:

'As regards a cruise among the Outer Hebrides, personally... I do not think that, unless one has unlimited time, the scenery is worth the trouble. Rocks, endless rocks; land, barren, bleak... '

For those who agree with him, these three lochs are best given a miss, thereby making complete solitude all the more likely for those for whom it is the essence of cruising.

A few miles further north, **Loch Shell** and **Loch Odhairn** are busy in comparison, both having small settlements within them. In particular, Lemreway in Loch Shell has quite a number of houses and several moorings for working boats at the head of **Tob Lemreway**, which is also a good anchorage. Both these lochs are good landfalls if crossing the North Minch. They have no offlying rocks and can be entered in all winds without having to cross the potentially bad seas in the Sound of Shiant.

Loch Mariveg, looking down on to the anchorage of Camus Thormaid, from the north. It must be assumed that the anchored yacht is of shoal draft as the Sailing Directions say: 'the pool W of the islet shoals rapidly and is full of weed'. The cover photograph is also of Loch Mariveg.

East Lewis

A little over two miles north of Loch Odhairn, Loch Erisort branches off westwards for six miles or so inland. Just before you enter it, you will pass a hidden loch of which you would have been unaware unless you had read the chart or the Sailing Directions. This is **Loch Mariveg** which consists of a series of interlinked lagoons offering at least six anchorages in a variety of delightful bays. The two entrances to the loch are not easy to see but neither are they difficult to navigate, though the southern one is best taken above half tide as it has only 1.6m and a rock in the channel. Once inside, caution is still needed as there are several shoals, but the whole place is so sheltered and free of tidal currents that you can take your time and choose your spot according to wind and mood.

Loch Erisort, including its branches **Loch Thorasdaidh** and **Loch Leurbost**, offers a wide choice of anchorages, both secluded or otherwise. Three of the best, **Camus Orasaidh**, **Tob Cromore** and **Peacam** can be entered from the outer loch with no trouble, but entry to the inner loch needs care in negotiating the shoals at its mouth.

The anchorage at Tob Cromore seen from the west. The access from Loch Erisort is off to the left.

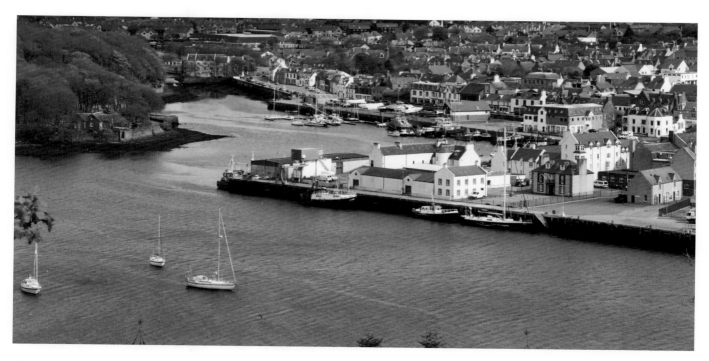

Stornoway

There are no harbours with facilities in the 25 miles between Tarbert and Stornoway, but plenty of good anchorages, so most yachts heading north of Erisort are either planning on replenishing their stores or changing crew. As Stornoway is approached there is more settlement on the coast – crofts whose inhabitants usually combine a part time job for the bread-winner with some fishing, a few sheep and a little basic agriculture if the ground permits.

Stornoway is a fine natural harbour and the capital of the Outer Isles. Like most Hebridean and west coast harbours, it grew around the herring industry which began in the 17th century and reached its zenith in the 19th when the exploitation of this now scarce resource arguably destroyed it.

Today, the town has around 8,000 inhabitants, is linked by sea and air to mainland Scotland and is the administrative centre of the islands. There is a good selection of shops, services and tourist facilities, all made more accessible by the visitors' pontoon in the inner harbour, although this is invariably taken up with local boats. A regulation call to the Harbourmaster will, as often as not, result in a berth being allocated at the base of pier No. 1, conveniently close to the Harbour Office. There are currently plans to extend the pontoons though it may be some time before they come to fruition.

If time does not permit a cruising visit to the west coast of Lewis and Harris, an alternative is to hire a car, leave your yacht in the security of Stornoway harbour and explore the islands. The Butt of Lewis, Loch Roag, Dun Carloway Broch and the Standing Stones at Callanish are all just a short drive away.

North of Stornoway the coast is quite different in character. There are no havens worthy of the name between the Lewis capital and the Butt of Lewis and none on the west coast between there and Loch Roag, meaning a near fifty mile stretch of inhospitable coast. The Butt of Lewis is a formidable headland with strong tides and rough seas, with the result that yachts and small craft rarely venture north of Stornoway unless on passage to places further afield. However, one fictional yacht did venture up the coast north of Stornoway; read on overleaf...

Stornoway Harbour in autumn. In high season the No. 1 pier, where the large yacht is berthed, can have several yachts berthed abeam. The marina pontoons can be seen towards the top left in the inner harbour.

Lews Castle, Stornoway, seen from a berth at the No. 1 pier.

Ransome's drawing of the coves (Mac's Chart of the Cove) with a leading line shown at the top.

Although the current Admiralty chart shows only a single bay full of drying rocks, the 1849 chart shows something similar to Ransome's coves, but smaller.

The Admiralty chart of Loch Valamus and the adjacent inlet.

Arthur Ransome's *Great Northern?*

Inspired by a bird-watching friend, AR's 'Scottish Book', as members of The Arthur Ransome Society call it, was the last he completed in the Swallows and Amazons series. He deliberately jumbled the geography 'to prevent the inquisitive reader from learning the exact place where the *Sea Bear* was scrubbed and the Ship's Naturalist made his discovery', but if ever there was a carrot...

The harbour in *Great Northern?* (first published in 1947) has now been identified as Stornoway, and what he calls 'the Head' as Tiumpan Head on the Eye Peninsula. At the beginning of the book, the cutter *Sea Bear*, borrowed from 'Uncle Mac', sails round this, laying a course for 'Scrubber's Cove', where her approach in dense fog is real hold-your-breath stuff which can teach the modern, computerised yachtsmen several tricks worth knowing.

Sea Bear herself really existed, and maybe still does. Designed by G.L. Watson along the lines of a typical Colin Archer, she is listed in the 1960s issues of Lloyd's Register of Yachts, owned by a then member of the CCC (not 'Mac'-anything by name). Her photograph in the 1965 CCC Journal shows her painted black and ketch-rigged, but with the same number of portholes in her coach-roof as drawn by Ransome.

'Scrubber's Cove' itself is almost certainly one of the twin rocky indentations at the foot of Gleann Tholastaidh (Tolsta), a few miles up the Lewis coast from Stornoway. The entrance lies 4.3 nm. from the latter's lighthouse, well fitting the story's timings. Sadly, it was back in 'the year of the Foot & Mouth' when Judy and I drove our motor-caravan down the un-fenced lane down the eastern side of the glen shown in 'Mac's Chart of the Cove'. Where it finally curves left towards the clachan, a notice forbade strangers from walking down to the twin coves themselves. So how accurately Ransome depicts the two inlets I cannot say, nor if there is a cliff, never mind a 'Pict house', on the northern side of the entrance. (I'd love to know!)

Tolsta Glen (steeper and deeper than Ransome suggests) has no lochs near its foot – the nearest are far inland, beyond the modern main road. In fact, what he calls 'the lower loch', with its islet where in the book young Dick Callum discovers a pair of great northern divers to be 'nesting for the very first time in Britain,' is now known to be one that Ransome loved to fish, whilst holidaying at Uig Lodge – on the Atlantic side of Lewis. Perched above Loch Roag, with its battlemented tower at one end, the lodge is unmistakably 'Dorothea's Castle' – lair of the fierce 'McGinty' and his kilted son, the un-Scottishly spelled 'Ian', but supposedly close to 'Scrubber's Cove'.

The road heading southwards from Uig Lodge bridges the outflow from the real 'lower loch' (and others). You can see the split waterfall Ransome sketched, depicting the children portaging *Sea Bear's* folding dinghy up its right-hand bank, from the bridge.

And finally, the folding boat was no invention either; it was one of the Berthon Boat Company's folding canvas dinghies of Ransome's day – a brochure for which Judy and I found tucked among the pages of his original typescript in the Ransome Archives in Abbot Hall Museum, Kendal. He obviously sketched how it was unfolded directly from the brochure's photographs. (Berthon, incidentally, built the 'collapsible lifeboats' for RMS *Titanic*.)

All twelve of Arthur Ransome's Swallows and Amazons books are still in print, widely and repeatedly read by adults as well as children. But then, there's a lot of undeniably good sailing in them.

Jim Andrews 2008

Editor's footnote:

Not wanting to let matters rest here we decided to investigate further. It was a hot day at the end of June 2009, the sea was like a millpond and it had taken us four hours to motor round from Stornoway. Entering the northern cove first, it was immediately clear that nobody could ever land here, let alone dry out, as it was steep-to on all sides. Nor could you anchor easily; it was so small that we had to go astern to extricate ourselves. The southern cove was slightly bigger, with a beach at the head but somehow it didn't add up. Even though the location fitted perfectly with the story, the hills were too low, the coves were too small and nothing felt 'right'.

In the knowledge that Ransome usually based his descriptions and drawings on places he knew, it still seems fair to assume that somewhere in the Hebrides there is a pair of small lochs or coves which will come closer to those he described in 'Great Northern?' Is he recalling the 'wilderness' lochs of south east Lewis? None fit his description precisely but there is on the chart an inlet close east of Loch Valamus (Bhalamuis) where it might be possible to dry out and maybe even see into the Valamus anchorage from the crosstrees! If anyone knows it, or If readers have any other suggestions, please get in touch.

The West Coast and St Kilda

Unless the west coast has been approached from the southern end of the isles, or around the Butt of Lewis, the usual westward route is via the Sound of Harris. Historically this stretch of water has been considered a navigational challenge for a number of reasons: the disrepair of the navaids in the Stanton and Leverburgh channels; the shallow bar at the west end of the Cope Passage, which was buoyed for shallow draft landing craft en route to St Kilda; and not least the peculiar orientation of the Admiralty chart, which was printed to suit the paper size rather than to have north at the top!

Today, most of these difficulties have been addressed, spurred perhaps by the establishment of a ferry route from North Uist to Harris, which required a safe channel amongst the shoals and rocks of the Sound.

The Sound of Harris may be a launch pad for the west, but the tidal limitations of Berneray and Rodel make **Leverburgh** (see pp.189–190), or the anchorages on the east shores of **Ensay** and **Killegray**, the best bet for waiting to get off to the west without tidal constraints. The Ensay and Killegray anchorages are the nearest to the west end of the channel.

Ensay House and the small Chapel are both close to the landing beach.

Croic Harbour between Ceann Iar and Ceann Ear is the best anchorage in the Monach Islands.

The nearest point of all to St Kilda is the **Monach Islands**, which aside from this attribute, are an interesting group of islands to visit. The most westerly, Shillay, is the location of the newly re-commissioned lighthouse, whilst the other two islands, Ceann Iar and Ceann Ear (east and west island) are a bird sanctuary. The **Sound of Shillay** anchorage tends to be very crowded with moorings, but **Croic Harbour** on the north side of the islands is both sheltered from the prevailing winds and beautifully remote.

Strategies West of the Hebrides

It goes without saying that the weather is the commanding factor when planning to sail west of the Hebrides. For most cruising sailors a period of settled weather is important, if only because there are few hurricane holes on this coast, although there are lots of good anchorages for normal conditions. Seeking shelter by entering the Sound of Harris, or the other Harris lochs, from the west in a rising gale could be fraught with difficulty and East Loch Roag, which is lit, is the best option.

The Monach Islands

Despite the commanding lighthouse on Shillay Island at the west of the group, and some fishing boats moored nearby, this is a classic Hebridean wilderness. Looking west may reveal St Kilda, and further west lie Rockall and America!

The small group of five islands is tucked into the north west corner of North Uist, separated from it by three miles of shallow water. Folk memory says that they were connected until the land was washed away more than 500 years ago. The Monachs had a population of around one hundred people at one time, but they dwindled and all had left by 1948.

The Monachs National Nature reserve was created in 1966 on account of its diverse range of species. A large grey seal population of 10,000 breeds here each autumn, as do a large number of seabirds in the spring and early summer, particularly black guillemots and fulmar. The fulmar unusually nest in the dunes, and are surprisingly tame – but don't get too close! The Monach Isles support some of the finest summer flower meadows in the Western Isles, with over two hundred types of plant recorded.

Strategies tend to fall into two categories: a passage to the St Kilda archipelago, and cruising the west coasts of Harris and Lewis, with the added possibility of visiting the remote Flannan Isles. Given adequate time and good weather, these can all be achieved, for the distances are not very large. The triangle from Sound of Harris to St Kilda, Loch Roag and back to the start is somewhat less than 150 miles, with approximately 60 of these being the passage from St Kilda to West Loch Roag.

The St Kilda Archipelago

This famous and remote group of islands is probably on every cruising yachtsman's list of places he or she aspires to sail to, drop anchor and explore. It comprises the main island of **Hirta**, which together with Dun and Soay forms the main landmass. The offlying and dramatic island of Boreray together with nearby Stac Lee and Stac an Armin, and Levenish stack just east of Hirta, complete a unforgettable seascape.

The islands are the remains of a volcano, active 65 million years ago, and now eroded until only the most resistant rocks, granite and gabbro, remain as jagged peaks, sea stacks and spectacular cliffs. One of these, Conachair, at 430m (1,400ft), is the highest in Britain. This activity was contemporaneous with the eruptions that formed Skye, Rum and Ardnamurchan, and the lava flows that formed Mull and Staffa.

The whole, however, is more than the sum of the parts. As well as its scenic impact, the islands have a fascinating history, a huge concentration of seabirds and some unique flora and fauna. This unique place is recognised as such by its designation as a double World Heritage site for both its land and its surrounding seas, and as a National Nature Reserve. The islands are owned and managed by the National Trust for Scotland.

Opposite upper: Looking down on Village Bay, Hirta, St Kilda, with Oiseval behind.

Opposite lower: The deserted buildings lining the street on Hirta, with the circular burial ground on the lower left.

Seabird colonies include one of the largest gannetries in the world on Boreray, and prodigious numbers of most other seabird species. Ashore, the St Kilda mouse and the St Kilda wren are unique variants of their species, and the Soay sheep that wander freely are an ancient and isolated species brought from the adjacent island of that name.

Those who lived on St Kilda could perhaps also have been regarded as unique variants. How stone age people made their way here and survived is beyond our knowledge, but evidence exists, in the shape of a bronze age structure, that man lived and left his mark around 3,000 years ago on Hirta.

Stac an Armin, the most northerly of the St. Kilda group, is 194m (635ft) high and Boreray in the background is 382m (1,253ft)

Life was not any easier down the succeeding millennia but the St Kildans survived, even if they did not prosper. The population fell steadily from almost two hundred in the 17th century to 36 at the time of evacuation, when the impact of modern life forced them to capitulate and opt to settle on the mainland in 1930. Ironically, although most St Kildans had never seen a tree, most of the evacuated people were taken to Morvern and given jobs by the Forestry Commission!

Since 1957 Hirta has been a tracking station for the Benbecula firing range. The resources provided by the base make the National Trust's task of maintaining the village and the islands a good deal easier.

The St Kilda group has roused the curiosity of travellers and writers down the years. The first visitors of relatively modern times were, of course, the Vikings. In 1549 Dean Donald Monro visited and wrote about St Kilda, as part of his descriptions of no less than 209 Hebridean Islands. He observed 'In this fair ile is fair sheipe, falcon nests, and wylde fouls biggand, but the streams of the sea are starke, and are verey eivil entring in aney of the saids iles'. Very much as it is today!

In 1697 Martin Martin paid the archipelago a visit in the course of his Hebridean journeys. He left from Ensay in an open boat and took several days to reach the island, where he and his party stayed for three or four weeks and explored every aspect of the topography, the wildlife and the people. His account, *A Voyage to St Kilda*, is fascinating. These writings of Martin and Munro are available as a paperback from Birlinn publishers under the title *A Description of the Western Isles of Scotland* (see bibliography).

The Clyde Cruising Club's Sailing Directions contain all the detailed information needed when cruising the archipelago.

The lighthouse on the Flannan Isles.

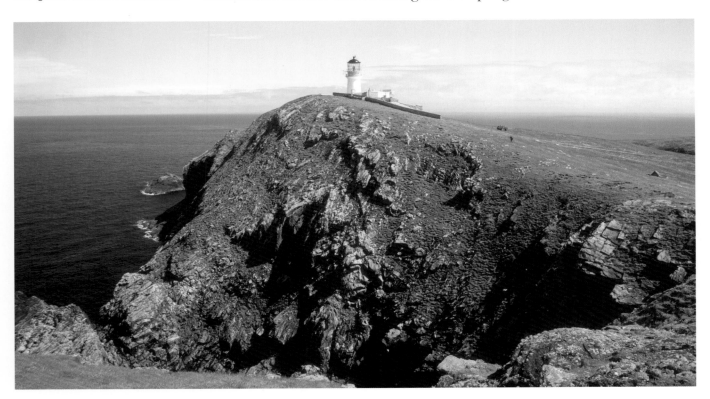

Damaged landing steps on Eilean Mor (see text).

The Flannan Isles

This group of seven rocky islands lies around 20 miles from Lewis to the west of Loch Roag, and has the alternative name The Seven Hunters. Like the St Kilda group, they are volcanic in origin.

The lighthouse, established in 1899 and automated in 1971, is the principal feature although the islands are also used for summer grazing.

The islands, however, are remembered for the Flannan Islands Mystery. On 15th December 1900, just a year after the light was commissioned, all three keepers disappeared in mysterious circumstances. A routine visit by the lighthouse tender *Hesperus* ten days later found no sign of life, and no clues as to what might have happened, except that some recent exceptionally bad weather may have washed all three into the sea.

Landing at the islands is not easy, but use might be made of the old lighthouse landing place on Eilean Mor, located on the east side of the island. However it must be realised that the NLB no longer maintains this landing and cannot accept any responsibility for injury. Landing is entirely at your own risk.

The West Coasts of Harris and Lewis

On leaving the Sound of Harris and heading north there are two main cruising areas: the bays and islands between West Loch Tarbert and Loch Resort and, further north, the Loch Roag complex. Between these is a 15 mile stretch of rugged coast between Scarp and Gallan Head without much shelter.

The beach at Taransay looking towards Toe Head, centre right, at the entrance to the Sound of Harris.

You will arrive at the first of these once Toe Head, at the north western corner of the Sound of Harris, is rounded and Taransay comes into view. This is a wonderful small cruising area of anchorages in sheltered inlets and sandy bays backed by the North Harris mountains. Often bypassed in a rush to reach the ultimate destination of Loch Roag, it is little known but will repay exploration. Off the mouth of West Loch Tarbert and around Scarp, navigation requires care as there are several groups of rocks to avoid. Some show, many dry and others break in any swell, but none are marked and constant vigilance is needed in poor visibility.

It will be a long time until **Taransay** is liberated from its connection with the 1999 BBC series *Castaway,* which observed 36 volunteers trying to make their home there and was billed as a social experiment, but which was perhaps an early form of reality TV. It was also the setting for scenes for the film *The Rocket Post*, although the event the film is based on actually took place on Scarp. Now, as then, there is no permanent population but there are some holiday cottages.

A deserted village on Taransay above the landing beach.

The island is egg timer shaped, with the narrow isthmus formed by sand dunes, and the southern bay of this feature provides a good anchorage. Apart from opposite the mainland, where a sand spit extends almost halfway across the narrows, the shores are rocky. Thanks to ample shell-sand blown ashore to cover the underlying gneiss and granite this island is fertile, and supported around 75 people a century ago. In 1695 Martin Martin reported '...Taransay, very fruitful in corn and grass, and yields much yellow talk'. What this yellow talk was is not known.

The stone pier, West Loch Tarbert.

The Whaling Station

'The crew was very keen to see the whaling station in West Loch Tarbert. The Skipper told us that it was about a mile from the village and warned us of the very bad smell there. On our way there we found that the Skipper had underestimated the distance, it was a good three miles, and when we got there we found that he had not given full value to the smell either. We were very disappointed to find that there were no whales in, so that our chief recollection of the place must necessarily be the indescribable stench, which seemed to increase in power in each fresh shed we entered. It is the type of odour which has to be smelt to be believed, and we were thankful to be once more out of range and breathing fresh air unpolluted by whale blubber, whale oil, whale meat and whale-bone manure.'

The Log of the Blue Dragon III
C. C. Lynam 1924. Edited by
Jim Pitts, 1999

The 'stack-like rock' marking Loch Leosavay, that 'Suilven' had such trouble in identifying, is here highlighted by the setting sun.

North of Taransay and on the Harris shore, **West Loch Tarbert** cuts deep into the Harris mainland to within about ½ mile of Tarbert village on the east side. Good anchorage can be found west of the stone pier at the head, and this is probably as good an opportunity as any to visit shops, and civilisation generally, whilst you are on the west coast of Lewis and Harris. Branching north off West Loch Tarbert are three lochs which all offer alternative anchorages.

The most easterly of these, **Loch Bun Abhainn-eader** is used for mooring by local fishing boats and provides good shelter off the site of the old whaling station. **Loch Meavig** is shallow at its head but is surrounded by the Harris mountains and is a spectacular stopping place. Perhaps the best haven is **Loch Leosavay**, a little further west, where there is a small settlement, a pier, and several anchoring options, one of which is in the bay overlooked by the imposing Amhuinnsuidhe Castle which was built in the 1860s by the Earl of Dunmore when he bought Harris. Nearby **Soay Mor** has a sheltered bay at its north point, although the entrance may be encumbered by fish cages.

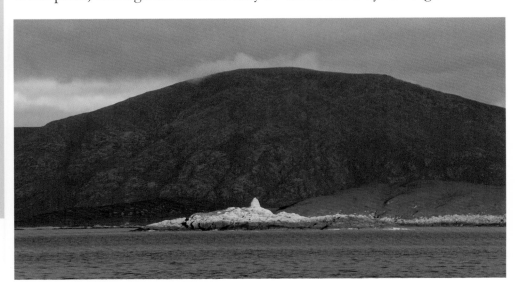

A bad night in Loch Leosavay

'We had decided to run in to the tiny natural harbour formed by Loch Leosavay, but in the gathering darkness we could not see the entrance. The Admiralty Pilot rather led us astray by its mention of a stack-like rock marking the entrance to the loch. This eventually turned out to be a flattish island and was not at all the miniature Ailsa Craig which we had expected.

The Farmer came up to help find the entrance but his airy suggestions were not taken seriously. We were running at about 6.5 knots with the trisail gybing about until it finally wrapped itself up against the mast.

I had almost decided that we would be forced to seek shelter for the night in the lee of Taransay and was about to announce this decision when we discovered our elusive harbour. The Mate was the first to see the lights of Castle Amansuidhe, which stands at the entrance to Loch Leosavay, and with the certainty of a snug anchorage so near our spirits soared. The West Coast Pilot advises anchoring off the castle, but a heavy swell was setting into the loch, and we preferred to sound our way into the inner loch.

We anchored in three fathoms L.W. past the point on the east shore. The wind had been gradually backing round to the SSW and the glass was dropping like a stone. The wireless forecast spoke of a deep depression which was approaching the Hebrides and told us to expect westerly winds of gale force.

It was one of those nights when it is better to be at anchor, for by midnight the wind screeched and raged in the rigging and the glass reached dead bottom at 28.82 (975.9mb). I don't know what strength the wind reached that night, but I do know that my double forestays, which are held apart by wooden blocks, were twanging together like banjo strings. I had about fifteen fathoms of cable out, helped by a forty-pound lead weight, and if there had been more room I would have given her another fifteen fathoms. Fortunately the holding ground was excellent, and our marks against the castle showed that we had not dragged. As we were undressing for bed John said, "I pity anyone at sea to-night" ... '

At the Tiller, Iain W. Rutherford, 1933 (A shakedown cruise in the Herreshoff 6 metre *Suilven*)

The narrow entrance to Loch Tamanavay which is generally steep-to apart from the small bay at the head where there is a narrow shelf.

North of Scarp one is still amongst the mountains of North Harris, with splendid scenery and very little habitation. **Loch Resort** has a wilderness anchorage on the south shore, beneath the ruined settlement at the head of a small bay. **Loch Tamanavay** offers shelter east of the promontory, but as reported in the Sailing Directions, the bay may be foul and the anchor should be well buoyed. This loch is not quite so isolated as there is a road around the head of the loch. Nearby Loch Tealasavay is not recommended; it has neither shelter from westerlies, nor any natural havens in which to anchor.

Looking across from the south side of West Loch Tarbert to Loch Bun Abhainn-eader. The brick chimney of the old whaling station is slightly left of centre.

Like Taransay, **Scarp** has a modern story to tell. It was the site of an experimental mail rocket firing in 1934 by Gerhard Zucher, an amateur German rocket builder. He chose Scarp to try to interest the British government in the idea. After a misfire, the second, and last, experiment was successful and history was made, although the idea was never developed either in Britain or Germany. A film, *The Rocket Post,* was made in 2004, but most of the filming took place on Taransay.

The island is uninhabited and unremarkable but it has three good anchorages: two in Caolas an Scarp, north and south of the sand bar, and a superb one at the north end, protected by the small island of **Kearstay**. This bay is not only sheltered from south east to north west, but has one of the finest beaches in the area. Seclusion is almost guaranteed as there is no easy overland access. Ashore there is a cave and a waterfall to explore and it is also the nearest point to the island's 308m (1,010ft) summit.

About 10 miles north of Scarp, the rocky shoreline opens up at **Camus Uig** to reveal the Uig sands some distance away. Temporary anchorage can be made, in the right weather, south of the small islet of Holm allowing the possibility of exploring the inland settings of *Great Northern?*, described on p.198

At anchor in the Sound of Scarp (Caolas Scarp).

Opposite upper: Scarp separated from Harris by the Sound of Scarp with Loch Resort leading up into the mountains beyond (top right).

Opposite lower: The anchorage between Kearstay and the north end of Scarp is not to be missed.

The anchorage in Camus Uig

Rounding Gallan Head two miles beyond Camus Uig brings you to **Loch Roag**, consisting of two north west facing inlets, West and East Loch Roag, separated by the island of Great Bernera which is linked by a bridge to Lewis. This is classic Hebridean land and seascape and an intricate cruising ground with many nooks and crannies to explore, as well as containing much of archeological interest.

It is hard to say which is the more attractive of the two; West Loch Roag probably has more and better anchorages but **East Loch Roag** has the the attraction of two archeological sites of international importance. You come first to **Dun Carloway Broch** which can easily be visited by anchoring in Loch Carloway. It is one of the best preserved of these unique defensible dwellings which were in use during most of the first millennium AD. There is a visitor centre quite close to the anchorage.

The **Standing Stones at Callanish**, near the village of Callanish, are much more ancient, dating from around 2,500BC, and used for religious and astronomical purposes until after 2,000BC. This is just part of a complex of such structures in the area but the others are not as well preserved. Here too is a visitor centre with a jetty close by. The best anchorage is east of the Bratanish Islands which lie about 2 cables east of the south end of Eilean Kearstay, and the jetty is just around the mainland point. The Callanish Standing Stones are of particular importance as they pre-date both the Pyramids of Egypt and Stonehenge, indicating a civilisation of considerable significance but about which little is known.

The Dun Carloway broch.

The Callanish stone circle.

Above this small beach on Little Bernera there is a ruined chapel with a burial ground by the sea.

Bernera Harbour

'I've been here only once
  before, cold and tired.

You turn coastwards where Old
  Hill floats

like a bread loaf out at sea. Wind
  and waves

fall as you sail into the shelter of
  the loch:

you no longer have to shout
  above the noise.

You drop anchor close inshore:

clatter echoes round the rocky bay

then silence falls. It's still:

what *haven* means.

There were otter cubs.

All evening on deck and no dark.

I could take exactly the same
  photo I took then

but now there's a museum in the
  school and a notice:

*Algal Toxins at this Location above
Permitted Level.'*

Places Like This, Jane Routh,
2004

Opposite: *The southernmost of the two bays on the east side of Pabay Mor in West Loch Roag, where there is also a ruined chapel on the shore.*

An attractive anchorage can be found in **Bernera Harbour** between Great Bernera and Little Bernera, although some of it is taken up by a fish farm. Diesel and water can be obtained at **Carloway** or **Kirkibost**, where the anchorage of Dubh Thob gives good all round shelter.

Local boats pass through to **West Loch Roag** from Bernera Harbour via an extremely narrow and shallow channel, Caolas Cumhang, but without careful examination from the dinghy and sufficient rise of tide this is not recommended for strangers, which means retracing your steps outside the islands to get there. Here you could happily spend days exploring the loch and its many anchorages. The island of **Pabay Mor** has two delightful bays off its east coast – see the photograph opposite and p.10 – and for the intrepid, a lagoon at its north end which is not yet in the Sailing Directions!

Diesel and water can be obtained at the pontoon at **Miavaig**, a sheltered inlet in the heart of the loch, and for those wishing to penetrate even further there is always the narrow channel of **Little Loch Roag** to explore. In fine weather either of the two anchorages off the island of **Shiaram Mor**, near Valtos, will give access to the magnificent beach of Traigh na Berie. Good shelter can be gained by tucking in behind **Eilean Teinish** just over the hill and many more anchorages can be discovered by looking at the excellent large scale chart.

Retrospect

In many ways the attraction of cruising to the west of the Outer Hebrides is that it is the most challenging area on Scotland's west coast. The lure of the Monach Islands and particularly St Kilda, the feel of the Atlantic swell below the keel bringing the boat alive and the vistas of the the west coast of Harris all combine to be the pinnacle of Scottish cruising. Yet these waters are empty. That extra touch of remoteness, combined with the vagaries of Hebridean weather are undoubtedly a disincentive but one that is worth striving to overcome. If this little stretch of coast was just 500 miles further south, it would be alive with recreational craft. It isn't, so take advantage!

Gaelic glossary

Introduction

In order to find the word you want it is helpful to know a little bit about Gaelic grammar. Gaelic words change in a number of ways to form the plural, feminine, possessive, the dative and vocative case of nouns, the past tense of verbs etc. Changes will be found at the beginning, at the end and also in the middle of a word, for example:

cinn see *ceann*

eich genitive and plural of *each* horse

mara genitive of *muir* sea

The change most likely to cause difficulty in looking up a word is the insertion of *h* after a consonant at the beginning. This alters the sound of the preceding letter (*bh* and *mh* and pronounced like English *v*, *ph* is pronounced *f*). Thus if you are looking for a word beginning with *bh, ch, dh, fh, gh, mh, ph, sh, th,* look it up in the list without the *h*, for example:

bhàn see *bàn*

ghlas see *glas*

mhòr see *mòr*

Meanings of common Gaelic words

In the entries which follow: Gaelic words are in bold; English equivalents follow in bold within square brackets; information about case, plurals etc. are italicised and the meanings in English are in regular text.

àird, àrd height, (high) promontory
abhainn [avon] river
acarsaid anchorage
achadh [ach] field
àilean [aline] green field
aiseag ferry
allt [ault] burn, stream
aonach hill, moor
aoineadh steep rocky brae
aonach (steep) hill, moor
àrd see **àird**
àros house
àth ford
ault see **allt**
avon see **abhainn**
bà see **bò**
bac (sand)bank
bàgh bay
baile town, village, farm
bàn white, pale, fair
bàrr top, summit, height
beag [beg] little

bealach (mountain) pass, gorge
beàrn gap, crevice
beinn [ben] mountain, hill
beithe birch-tree
binnean pointed hill, peak
bò, *possessive and plural* **bà** cow
bogha, bodha [bo(w)] submerged rock, rock on which waves break
bodach old man
breac [breck] *adjective* speckled, spotted; *noun* trout
bruach bank, hillside
buachaille herdsman, shepherd
buidhe yellow
caileag girl
cailleach old woman
caisteal castle
caladh harbour
calltainn hazel
camas, camus bay, creek
caol, caolas, [kyle] narrow(s), strait
carraig rock
ceann, *possessive and plural* **cinn [ken]** head, point

cill [kil] church, monk's cell
clach stone
clachan village (with a church)
cladach shore, beach
cnap [knap] (small) hill, lump
cnoc [cnok, knock] hillock
còig five
coille wood, forest
coire [corry] kettle, cauldron, whirlpool, steep round hollow in hillside
coll hazel
craobh tree
creag rock, crag, cliff
crois cross
cruach stack, rick-shaped hill
dà two
darach [darroch] oak
dearg red
deas south
dòbhran otter
doirlinn isthmus, (connection to) an island which is accessible at low tide
domhain deep
donn brown
drochaid bridge
druim back, ridge
dubh black, dark
dùn fort, mound
each, *possessive and plural* eich horse
ear east
eas waterfall
eilach mill-race; mound
eilean island
fada long
faich meadow
faing sheep-pen, fank
fasgadh shelter
feàrna alder-tree
fèith bog
fiacal tooth
fear, *possessive and plural* fir man
fireach moor, hill
fliuch wet
fraoch heather
garbh rough, harsh
geal white, bright
geòdha, geò deep cleft in cliffs, chasm
gil glen, water course
glas, grey, green
gleann glen, narrow valley
gobhar goat
gorm blue, green
gualainn shoulder; slope of hill
iar west
iasg fish
inbhir [inver] river mouth, confluence
innis [inch] island, river meadow
iolaire eagle

ken see ceann
kil see cill
kyle see caol
lag hollow, pit
leac slab, flat stone
learg hillside, plain
leathan broad, wide
leth half
liath grey
linne pool, channel
loch lake, arm of the sea
lochan small loch, lake
long, *possessive* luinge ship
machair sandy grassed area behind a beach, low-lying plain
maol [mull] headland, bare rounded hill
mòinteach moorland, mossy place
mol, mal shingle (beach)
mòr [more] big, tall, great
muir, *possessive* mara sea
mullach summit
òb (sheltered) bay, harbour
odhar dun-coloured
oitir sandbank
òrd, ùird hammer
òs river mouth
plod, pool, pond
poll, puill pool
port port
rath fortress
rathad road
rhu see rudha
rìgh king
rinn promontory
ròn seal
ruadh red, reddish-brown
rudha, rubha [rhu] point of land
seachd seven
seann old, ancient
sga(i)t skate
sgarbh cormorant
sgeir skerry, rock
sgùrr rocky peak
sròn nose, (nose shaped) promontory; jutting ridge
srath strath, low-lying valley
sruth current
taigh, tigh house
tarbh bull
tioram dry
tobar well
tràigh beach, strand
trì three
tuath north
tulach hillock
uamh cave
uaine green
ùird see òrd

Bibliography

Admiralty, Hydrographer, *West Coast of Scotland Pilot, NP66 16th Edition*, 2009.

Atkinson, Robert, *Island Going*, 1949.

      Shillay and the Seals, 1980.

Barrett, Richard, *Walking on Harris and Lewis*, 2010.

Blake, George, *The Firth of Clyde*, 1952.

Blake, John, *Sea Charts of the British Isles*, 2003.

Bathurst, Bella, *The Lighthouse Stevensons*, 1999.

Bray, Elizabeth, *The Discovery of the Hebrides. Voyagers to the Western Isles 1745–1883*, 1986.

Brooke, Dennis & Hinchliffe, Phil, *Scotland's Far West, – Walks on Mull & Ardnamurchan*, 2005.

Boswell, James, *The Journal of a Tour to the Hebrides*, 1785.

Campbell, John Lorne, *Canna: the Story of a Hebridean Island*, 1984.

Carslaw, Dr. R.B. *Leaves from Rowan's Logs*, 1944.

Clyde Cruising Club, *Firth of Clyde*, 2004 (with updated reprints to 2009).

      Kintyre to Ardnamurchan, 2007 (with updated reprints to 2009).

      Ardnamurchan to Cape Wrath, 2006 (with updated reprints to 2009).

      Outer Hebrides, 2005 (with updated reprints to 2009)

Cooper, Derek, *Road to the Isles. Travellers in the Hebrides, 1770–1914.* 1979.

      The Road to Mingulay, 1985.

Cowper, Frank, *Sailing Tours, The Clyde to the Thames Round North*, 1895.

Darling, F. Fraser, *Island Years*, 1942.

Darling, F. Fraser & Boyd, J. Morton, *The Highlands and Islands*, 1964.

Dillon, Paddy, *Walking on the Isle of Arran*, 2008.

Drummond, Maldwin, *West Highland Shores*, 1990.

Edwards, Peter, *Walking on Jura, Islay and Colonsay*, 2010.

Faux, Ronald, *The West. A Sailing Companion to the West Coast of Scotland*, 1982.

Gibson, John S. *Ships of the '45*, 1967.

Gifford, John, *The Buildings of Scotland, Highlands and Islands*, 1992.

Grimble, Ian, *Scottish Islands*, 1985.

Haswell-Smith, Hamish, *The Scottish Islands*, 1996.

      An Island Odyssey, 1999.

Hedderwick, Mairi, *An Eye on the Hebrides*, 1989.

      Sea Change, 1999

Hiscock, Eric C. *Wandering Under Sail*, 1939.

Historic Scotland, *Iona Abbey & Nunnery, Official Souvenir Guide*, 2001.

Jamieson, Isobel, *Skeletta and the White Knight*, 1925.

Johnson, Alison, *Islands in the Sound. Wildlife in the Hebrides*, 1989.

Johnson, Samuel, *Journey to the Western Isles of Scotland*, 1775.

Knox, John, *Tour of the Highlands of Scotland and the Hebride Isles*, 1787.

Bibliography

Lawrence, Martin, *Clyde to Colonsay*, 2007.
   The Yachtsman's Pilot to Skye and Northwest Scotland, 2002.
   The Yachtsman's Pilot to the Isle of Mull and adjacent coasts, 2008.
   The Yachtsman's Pilot to the Western Isles, 2003.
Lynam, C.C., *The Log of the Blue Dragon*, 1909.
Lynam, C.C. & Pitts, Jim, *The Log of the Blue Dragon III*, 2000.
MacCulloch, Dr. J, *The Highlands and Western Isles of Scotland*, 1824.
Macdonald, Angus & Patricia, *The Hebrides, An Aerial View of a Cultural Landscape*, 2010.
McLintock, John, *West Coast Cruising*, 1938.
McKirdy, Alan, Gordon, John & Crofts, Roger, *Land of Mountain and Flood*, 2007.
Marsh, Terry & Sparks, Jon, *The Magic of the Scottish Islands*, 2002.
Marsh, Terry, *The Isle of Skye – Over 50 Walks and Scrambles*, 2009.
Martin, Martin, *A Description of the Western Islands of Scotland*, 1703.
Maxwell, Gavin, *Harpoon at a Venture*, 1952.
   Ring of Bright Water, 1960.
Mitchell, Ian, *Isles of the West*, 1999.
Moir, Peter & Crawford, Ian, *Argyll Shipwrecks*, 1994.
Munro, Dean Sir Donald, *Description of the Western Isles of Scotland*, 1549.
Murray, W.H., *The Islands of Western Scotland*, 1973.
   The West Highlands of Scotland, 1988.
Nicholson, Christopher, *Rock Lighthouses of Britain*, 1995.
Nicolson, Adam, *Sea Room, An Island Life*, 2001.
Nicolson, Nigel, *Lord of the Isles*, 1960.
Pennant, T., *A Tour in Scotland and Voyage to the Hebrides*, 1776.
Purves, Libby, *One Summer's Grace*, 1989.
Ransome, Arthur, *Great Northern?*, 1947.
Ratcliffe, Dorothy Una, *Swallow of the Sea*, 1937.
Rea, F.G., *A School in South Uist*, 1964.
Redfern, Roger, *Walking in the Hebrides*, 2003.
Reynolds, Henry, *Coastwise–Cross-Seas*. 1921.
Ritchie, Graham & Harman, Mary, RCHM, *Exploring Scotland's Heritage, Argyll and the Western Isles*, 1983.
Scottish Mountaineering Club, *North West Highlands*, 2004.
   The Islands of Scotland (including Skye).
   The Central Highlands, 1994.
Shaw, Margaret Fay, *From the Alleghenies to the Hebrides*, 1993.
Shea, Michael, *Britain's Offshore Islands*, 1981.
Steel, Tom, *The Life and Death of St. Kilda*, 1975.
Thompson, Francis, *Crofting Years*, 1984.
   Harris and Lewis, Outer Hebrides, 1968.
   The Uists and Barra, 1976.
Walker, Frank Arneil, *The Buildings of Scotland, Argyll and Bute*, 2000.
Walmsley, Andy, *Walking in Scotland's Far North*, 2009.

Acknowledgments

Photographic Credits

Clyde Cruising Club Publications is grateful to all those photographers, amateur and professional, who responded to the Editor's frequent requests for specific shots and who took the time to seek them out and present them in the appropriate format. In particular we would mention the participants in the photographic web site www.geograph.org.uk who were, without exception, unfailingly helpful and co-operative in allowing us to use photographs from their unique archive under the Creative Commons Licence and, in addition, provided us with the high resolution files needed for printing.

We are also very grateful to Rhu Marina, Kip Marina, Largs Yacht Haven, Clyde Marina, Troon Marina, Oban Marina and Diageo/Classic Malts for either providing or sponsoring photographs.

Allan, John, 134 lower, 148, 192

Allison, David, 102 lower

Anderson, John, 18–19, 69 lower, 73, 79 upper, 80 upper, 90 upper, 92 upper, 93 upper, 94 both, 100 lower, 102 upper, 105 upper, 106 upper, 108 upper right, 109 both, 110 upper, 111 centre & lower, 112, 113, 117 upper, 128 upper, 143 upper, 151 upper, 172 lower, 177 lower, 179 both, 185 lower, 191

Balmforth, Mike, 20, 26 both, 29, 30, 31 centre & lower, 36 upper, 39, 41 both, 45, 46, 49 lower, 50 both, 53 lower, 54 centre, 55 lower, 58 lower, 59 both, 67 upper, 77 lower, 85 upper, 89 lower, 106 lower left, 136, 137 upper, 139 upper, 147 upper, 155 upper, 156, 158 centre, 160 upper

Bark, Billy, 40 upper

Barlow, Rosy, 81 lower, 90 lower

Brookes, Mike, 140 upper

Brown, Gordon, 72 upper, 82 upper & centre

Buchanan, Ian, 10, 14 upper, 61, 149, 209

Burgess, Anne, 189 centre

Cape Adventure, 167 lower

Carr, Barbara, 180 centre, 184 upper

Carter, Steve, 153 both

Clyde Maritime Trust, 40 lower

Coe, Randal, 91 lower, 131 upper, 190

Coleman, Christopher J Stacey, 207 lower

Cottier, Finlo, 186 upper

Croker, Dave, 154 lower

Dera, John, 206 lower

Douglas, John, 14 lower, 17 both, 120 lower, 176 upper, 185 upper, 186 lower

Envision 3D Ltd/Patricia & Angus Macdonald, Aerographica/SNH, 172 upper

Forrester, Tim, 49 upper, 51, 52 upper

Gillibrand, David, 66 centre

Goldthorp, Steve, 8, 12 both, 13 upper, 15 upper and centre, 16 lower, 18 upper, 19 centre, 67 lower, 123 both, 125 upper, 132 lower, 139 lower, 146 lower, 167 upper & centre, 168 upper and lower right, 199 lower, 200 lower, 201 both

Hall, Katie, 174

Hardley, Dennis, 89 upper

Hartland, Mike, 71 lower

Hatton, Gordon, 65 lower, 157 lower, 161 lower, 162, 184 lower

Herald & Times, The, 142

Heron, Paddy, 158 upper

Highland Council, 168 lower left

Houston, Arthur, 87 lower, 88 lower, 115 lower, 152

Houston, David, 110 lower

Hughes, John, 178 centre

Jones, Bob, 66 lower, 175 upper, 193 lower

Kingairloch Estate, 98 upper

Kip Marina, 37 lower

Lalor, Séamus, 31 upper

Largs Yacht Haven, 35 upper

Lawrence, Martin, 74 upper, 75 both, 79 lower, 84 lower, 99 lower, 107, 132 upper

Leask, Fiona, 207 centre lower

Lepêtre, Bernard, 76

Macdonald, Patricia & Angus, Aerographica/SNH, 119 upper

Macdonald, Donald, 96 lower, 98 lower, 106 lower right, 154 upper, 183 lower

Mackenzie, Douglas R., 165 lower

MacLachlan, Roger, 157 upper

MacLennan, David, 205 lower

MacLennan, John J., 205 upper

MacLennan, Michael, 121 lower

MacLeod, Iain, 35 lower

Marinas.com, 25 upper, 32, 138 upper

Acknowledgments

Mason, Edward, Cover, 2–3, 7, 16 centre, 24 upper, 47 both, 63, 64 upper, 65 upper, 68 upper, 69 upper, 70 both, 74 lower, 77 upper, 82 lower, 83, 84 upper, 85 lower, 86 upper, 87 upper, 88 upper, 91 upper, 95 lower, 96 upper, 97, 101, 103 lower, 104 upper, 108 upper left & lower, 111 upper, 114 both, 124 both, 129, 135 upper, 137 lower, 140 lower, 141 upper, 143 lower, 144 lower, 145 upper, 147 lower, 150 upper, 151 lower, 155 centre & lower, 158 lower, 160 lower, 161 upper & centre, 163 lower, 164 upper, 165 centre, 166, 169, 171, 173 lower, 175 centre & lower, 178 lower, 180 upper, 183 upper, 195 both, 196 both, 197 lower, 203 upper, 204 both

McManmon, Tommy, 141 lower

Medcalf, David, 25 upper

Morrison, Hugh, 71 upper

Oban Marina, 93 lower

Oystercatcher, The, Otter Ferry, 56 upper

Philip, David (www.hebridean-wild.co.uk), 78, 80 lower

Ransome, Arthur (Trustees of)/Jonathan Cape, 198 upper

Reeves, Clive, 36 lower, 58 upper, 118 upper, 146 upper, 188, 189 lower, 199 upper, 202 lower, 203 lower, 207 upper, 207 centre upper, 208

Rhu Marina/John Guthrie, 38

Rigby, Gavin, 130

Roach, Patrick, 27 both, 28 upper, 33 upper, 34, 54 lower, 182 both, 193 upper, 206 upper

Robertson, David, 118 lower, 120 upper, 122 upper, 127 lower, 159

Royal Marine Hotel, 44 lower

Royal Northern & Clyde Yacht Club, 44 upper

Sclare, Duncan, 176 lower

Scott-Wakeling, Susan, 93 centre

Scottish Viewpoint, 24 lower, 25 lower, 28 lower, 42, 43, 53 upper right, 54 upper, 56 lower, 57 all, 60 all, 92 lower, 100 upper, 126 centre (both), 135 lower, 145 lower, 150 lower, 181 upper

Sheard, Karen, 86 lower

Spreiter, Christine, 19 upper, 21 both, 64 lower, 68 lower, 105 lower, 128 lower, 133 both, 134 upper

Swannie, John, 122 lower

Tait, Charles, 202 upper

Tillyard, Ruth, 15 lower, 16 upper, 125 lower, 126 upper & lower, 214 lower, 216 upper,

Tobermory Harbour Association, 104 lower

U. K. Hydrographic Office, 198 lower

Watts, Frances, 178 upper

Waugh, Barrie, 23 lower, 48, 52 lower, 53 upper left, 67 middle, 99 upper, 103 upper, 115 upper, 117 lower, 177 upper, 200 upper

Webb, Richard, 187 upper

Webster, Hugh, 144 upper, 163 upper, 197 upper upper, 185 upper, 186 lower

White, Alastair, 1, 13

Wills, Russel, 164 lower, 165 upper

www.undiscoveredscotland.co.uk, 33 lower, 37 upper, 81 upper, 119 lower, 187 lower, 193 centre

Text credits

We would like to thank all contributors, in addition to those mentioned in the Preface, who have helped with the text either through research or by writing passages on special topics. We are also very grateful to the authors and their publishers who allowed us to include extracts and quotations from their work. It has not been possible to trace every author and copyright holder quoted, although every effort has been made through the Publishers' Association, British Library records and other sources. We trust that the holders of copyrights who have not been contacted will accept that we have used our best endeavours to trace them. They are identified in the list below by an asterisk.

Andrews, Jim, 198

Blake, George, Royal Northern & Clyde Yacht Club, 45

Bray*, Elizabeth, Collins, 181

Faux, Ronald, John Bartholomew & Sons, 12, 107

Hardie, Dr. Hamish, 40

Haswell-Smith, Hamish, Canongate Books, 136

Jamieson*, Isobel, William Blackwood & Sons, 61

Macdonald, Ian 53

Maxwell, Gavin, Campbell Thomson & McLaughlin Ltd on behalf of Gavin Maxwell Enterprises Ltd, 132

McLintock*, John, Blackie & Son, 119, 121, 173

Morgan, Adrian, *The Independent,* 13

Nicolson, Adam, Harper Collins, 194

Nicolson, Nigel, Weidenfeld and Nicolson, (an imprint of Orion Publishing Group, London), 189

O'Brien*, Conor, E. Arnold (republished by Rupert Hart Davis and Adlard Coles), 131

Purves, Libby, Grafton Books (republished by Hodder & Stoughton), 164

Routh, Jane, Gooseprint, 208

Rutherford*, Iain, Blackie & Son, 205

Shave, Paul, 127

Taggart, Sandy, 64

U. K. Hydrographic Office, 184

Ward, Dr. Robin, 13

Index